HALF THE

MANCHESTER
UNIVERSITY PRESS

HALF THE BATTLE

Civilian morale in Britain during the Second World War

ROBERT MACKAY

Manchester University Press

Manchester and New York

distributed exclusively in the USA by Palgrave

Published by Manchester University Press
Oxford Road, Manchester M13 9NR, UK
and Room 400, 175 Fifth Avenue, New York, NY 10010, USA
www.manchesteruniversitypress.co.uk

Distributed exclusively in the USA by
Palgrave, 175 Fifth Avenue, New York,
NY 10010, USA

Distributed exclusively in Canada by
UBC Press, University of British Columbia, 2029 West Mall,
Vancouver, BC, Canada V6T 1Z2

British Library Cataloguing-in-Publication Data
A catalogue record for this book is available from the British Library

Library of Congress Cataloging-in-Publication Data applied for
ISBN 0 7190 5893 7 *hardback*
     0 7190 5894 5 *paperback*

First published 2002

10 09 08 07 06 05 04 03 02   10 9 8 7 6 5 4 3 2 1

Typeset by Freelance Publishing Services, Brinscall, Lancs.
www.freelancepublishingservices.co.uk
Printed in Great Britain
by Bell & Bain Limited, Glasgow

CONTENTS

INTRODUCTION

What is 'morale' – and have I got any, or how much? And how much more could I call on in need, and where does it come from, and what is it composed of? Such a *lot* to wonder over.[1]

IN HISTORICAL WRITING the term 'civilian morale' is often used as freely as if its meaning were unproblematic, its definition unambiguous. In reality the term is susceptible to a range of meanings. Paul Addison described it as 'the woolliest concept of the war'.[2] Since it was in common use in the period under discussion, it seems appropriate to begin by asking what people at the time meant when they talked about civilian morale.

In the wartime Ministry of Information there was a section, the Home Intelligence Division, whose principal task was to monitor the state of public morale. While the Home Intelligence Division never set down a definition of what it was studying, it is evident from its reports and memoranda on the matter that it did have a rough notion of what the indicators of *low* morale might be: rumours, complaints and grumbles about official policies and about how the war was being experienced. For the first two years of the war Home Intelligence monitored these indicators in an almost obsessional way, taking the public's pulse by what it thought, felt and said. In rather the same way, the independent social research organization Mass-Observation – which, on commission for the Ministry of Information, made the charting of civilian morale one of its regular tasks – attached great importance to people's states of mind, measuring the fluctuations in cheerfulness, how much people were interested in the war news and whether they were optimistic about victory or the future more generally. Six months into the war Mass-Observation attempted a definition: 'Morale is the amount of interest people take in the war, how worthwhile they feel it is. If people are left bewildered, or if their leaders do not interest them (either in truthful or lying versions of the situation) then morale cannot be regarded as "good" and may easily become "bad".'[3] A year later, in the course of reporting on how people in Glasgow were coping with bombing, it offered a fuller definition:

By morale, we mean primarily not only determination to carry on, but also determination to carry on with the utmost energy, a determination based on a realization of the facts of life and with it a readiness for many minor and some major sacrifices, including, if necessary, the sacrifice of life itself. Good morale means hard and persistent work, means optimum production, maximum unity, reasonable awareness of the true situation, and absence of complacency and confidence which are not based on fact.[4]

While this definition still gives prominence to attitudes and feelings it has been noticeably enlarged to encompass behaviour. In October 1941 Home Intelligence showed signs that it, too, was updating its thinking along the same lines. Its director, Stephen Taylor, in a memorandum entitled 'Home Morale and Public Opinion', wrote that morale must be 'ultimately measured not by what a person thinks or says, but by what he does and how he does it'.[5] What the timing of these revisions suggests is that understanding was simply being informed by experience. In 1939 the watchers were proceeding from first principles; by 1941 they were living in the middle of a huge laboratory with field-test material on every hand.

Academic psychologists likewise needed the test of war itself to sort out their ideas on civilian morale. It was not until 1943, therefore, that J. T. MacCurdy wrote that although morale required 'a capacity to endure tribulation undismayed', this capacity was 'meaningless, or at least ineffective, unless it promotes action'.[6] Sanford and Conrad came to exactly the same conclusion: [morale] 'is of value only insofar as it facilitates or promotes favourable action'.[7]

By the third year of the war, then, there was agreement among contemporaries that morale was a composite of attitude and behaviour. If knowledge of the state of civilian morale was sought, therefore, it required more than getting people to respond to surveys and having agents report on what people were talking about in public houses. In this respect there is no great gap between what the morale watchers were looking at and what a historian today would want to examine. The historian approaching the official and semi-official record can do so with a definition of civilian morale that embraces both attitudes and behaviour and that might be set out as follows:

1 Feelings/attitudes
Low indicators: panic/hysteria; depression; apathy; pessimism; defeatism.
High indicators: calmness; cheerfulness; support for leaders; belief in ultimate victory; commitment to task in hand.

2 Behaviour
Low indicators: panic flight; refusal to leave shelters; grumbling; scapegoating; blaming of authorities; absenteeism; strikes; anti-social behaviour.
High indicators: calmness; cooperativeness and neighbourliness; high productivity; low absenteeism; volunteering.

For many years after 1945, a historiographical consensus about the morale of the British people in the Second World War existed undisturbed. The roots of this consensus went back to the war, notably to the year-long national crisis that began in June 1940. During this time, from a mixture of reality and propaganda, an image of the nation at war was created whose accuracy was later largely accepted by commentators. According to this picture, the people endured the dangers and burdens that total war imposed on them with fortitude, a capacity to adapt, and unwavering resolve. National solidarity, it was maintained, stayed firm under the strains of total war; indeed, it was reinforced by them. The shared experiences of evacuation, bombing, war service and austerity served only to demonstrate that the well-known differences relating to region, class and status were in the end less important than the sense of belonging to a national community. Of seminal influence in the formation of this picture of the home front was Richard Titmuss's *Problems of Social Policy*, written with free access to official records as one of the United Kingdom Civil Series of the official *History of the Second World War*, and published in 1950. Titmuss examined the strains of evacuation and air raids and concluded that pre-war fears of mass panic, mental breakdown and social disorder were wholly confounded; rather, the behaviour of the civilian population was consistent with mental resilience and a strong capacity to adjust to changed circumstances, even when these brought mortal danger, major disruption to living patterns and multiple daily stresses.[8] In confining his observations on civilian morale to the effects of evacuation and bombing, Titmuss encompassed two of its most significant factors; but this, it should be noted, ignored the role of other factors that might have had a bearing on morale. It is a problem of the historiography more generally, that much of what has been written also relates only to evacuation and air raids and is also often limited to the period September 1939–June 1941, thereby leaving relatively neglected the longer period to the end of the war. Titmuss's belief in the strengthening of social solidarity was echoed by Constantine Fitzgibbon, who wrote of the way the shared danger of the Blitz served to weaken rigid class prejudices and dissolve social reticence; and by David Thomson, who argued that once the road to survival was firmly indicated by Churchill's lead the British people 'set out resolutely and unitedly along it, with no delusions that it might be short or painless'.[9]

Titmuss's influence is to be discerned even upon the rather cynical A. J. P. Taylor. Writing in 1965, Taylor insisted that the bombing raids in the long term 'cemented national unity', and were 'a powerful solvent of class antagonism'; and that by showing they 'could take it' the people believed 'they were already on the way to winning the war'. Nearly twenty years later, Taylor had not altered his view: 'We were a united nation. Despite our fears we were convinced that we should win in the end. Strangers stopped me in the street and said: "Poor old Hitler. He's done for himself this time, now that he has taken us on".'[10] Taylor wrote of morale only in the context of the Emergency of 1940–41, seeming to take as read that it remained steady thereafter. But in the much-quoted final words of his *English History 1914–1945*, he chose to focus again on the ordinary people: 'This was a people's war. Not only were their needs considered. They themselves wanted to win ... they remained a peaceful and civilized people, tolerant, patient, and generous ... Few now sang "Land of Hope and Glory". Few even sang "England Arise". England had risen all the same.'[11] Arthur Marwick, writing in 1968, was in step with the prevailing tendency to treat the matter of civilian morale as uncontroversial, adding merely that although the 'Dunkirk spirit' was real enough, it was a temporary phenomenon, which, he implied, was superseded by something less proactive. He was equally content in 1976 to reaffirm this positive view, adding a reason for the resilience of the people: 'civilian morale was toughened by the direct involvement in the war'.[12] Marwick was impressed by the evidence of people keeping the war effort going despite being 'plunged ... into a front-line situation of incendiaries and high explosives', qualifying this only by noting that although 'passive morale' – carrying on – was good, high 'active morale' was less widespread, but 'can be clearly seen in police reports and censored letters, in the chirpy shop signs that were much photographed ... in the observations of middle-class commentators ... and in the smaller number of direct working-class records'.[13] Between these two books came Angus Calder's *The People's War* whose warts-and-all frankness about the behaviour of the British at war provided later historians (although not, it seems, Marwick) with material for challenging the received view. The book served to cast doubt on the veracity of this comfortable image of a nation united in the spirit of Dunkirk and the Blitz, cheerful, resourceful and unselfish. It drew attention to some discreditable features of the 'people's war' that had previously been ignored or neglected: panic and defeatism after big air raids; looting of bombed premises; crime and blackmarketeering; evasion of evacuation billeting obligations; class war and town versus country attitudes in the reception areas for evacuees; strikes, absenteeism and low productivity in industry; hostility towards refugees and ethnic minorities. The question was thus raised of whether these facets of wartime life were consistent with high civilian morale. If high morale meant 'behaving well', was there a case for arguing that the traditional picture of the civilian population during the war was inaccurate? Calder thought not, or at least, the picture was not so inaccurate as to require significant revision. He acknowledged that a degree of exaggeration of the virtues and ignoring of the vices had gone on, partly because this is what the official sources of information chose to do, in the belief that positive, optimistic attitudes needed to be promoted – a theme he resumed in his 1991 book *The Myth of the Blitz*. But beyond this he saw a people whose morale was threatened and from time to time shaken, but which in the end stood firm. The basis for this, he believed, was twofold: the capacity of people to adapt to the dangers and stresses of war; and the arousal of feelings of local pride – 'the feeling that if London could take it then Bristol or Plymouth should'. And although the evidence showed that some people lacked public spirit, it also showed that most did not.[14] In *Britain and the Second World War*, Henry Pelling, writing soon after Calder, in 1970, was content to confine his consideration of civilian morale to the context of the Blitz alone and to leave the general consensus undisturbed: 'What was important for Londoners', he concluded, 'was not the exceptional bravery of a few but rather the ordinary, persistent fortitude of the many – the capacity to carry on with their ordinary work under conditions of constant strain and loss of sleep and moderate but continuous danger.'[15] But if Calder had given many reason to think again about what had been previously unquestioned, it was Tom Harrisson in *Living Through the Blitz* (1976) who really set the revisionist ball rolling. Drawing heavily on the mainly unpublished records of Mass-Observation (see p. 10), of which he was a founder member, Harrisson catalogued the terrors and miseries of ordinary people under the bombs and the depressing failure of the authorities to rise to the (admittedly enormous) human problems that followed the raids. It was an angry book, full of recrimination towards officialdom. But its main burden and lasting impression was, as its title implied, that people did indeed, despite all, *live through* the Blitz: they adapted, they carried on, few of them succumbing to apathy or despair and many acting beyond the call of duty. As Harrisson put it: 'The Blitz was a terrible experience for millions, yes. But not terrible enough to disrupt the basic decency, loyalty (e.g. family ties), morality and optimism of the vast majority. It was supposed to destroy 'mass morale'. Whatever it did destroy, it failed over any period of more than days appreciably to diminish the human will, or at least the capacity to endure.' Verging on hyperbole, he concluded: 'Under all the varied circumstances the final achievement of so many Britons was enormous enough. Maybe monumental is not putting it too high. They did not let their soldiers or leaders down.'[16] It was thus rather against the overall thrust of Harrisson's book that others fed on his revelations to revise the received wisdom about human behaviour not only in the Blitz but in the home front war more generally. Edward Smithies concentrated on crime, the very existence of which, he implied, was an affront to the idea of wartime solidarity, its growth yet more so.[17] Like Smithies, Travis Crosby focused on just one aspect of the home front, the evacuation of children and other vulnerable people from the cities to safe areas in the country, seeing in it nothing to suggest social unity but only increased hostility between working class evacuees and middle-class hosts – many of whom, he emphasized, went to great lengths to avoid their obligations – and also between the urban working class and the rural working class.[18] John Macnicol was less concerned to emphasize class tensions, but he, too, presented a negative picture of the 1939 evacuation by concentrating almost entirely on the problems and difficulties of the operation.[19] In the most iconoclastic piece of revisionism yet produced, *1940: Myth and Reality*, Clive Ponting targeted what he took to be the least questioned period in Britain's war, the 'finest hour'. He concluded that the traditional version of these months was little more than lies, the work of assiduous Government propagandists and their mass media supporters. This conclusion was reached by a process of assembling every possible fragment of evidence that ran counter to the received view and the virtual exclusion of anything that confirmed it. Thus we read about the high living of the rich during the Emergency, the laziness of workers at the Vickers yard in Barrow and the rise in crime, but not about the surge of volunteering, the fall in the number of days lost to industrial disputes, or the huge response to calls for aluminium and the purchase of war bonds. Although he admitted that civilian morale did not crack, he found no virtue in this but dismissively explained it by saying that the people had no alternative other than to carry on.[20] Ponting's attraction towards the negative and blindness towards the positive was echoed by Harold Smith in *Britain in the Second World War: a Social History* (1996), a collection of contemporary documents, each preceded by a short commentary. These documents present a picture of wartime Britain so beset by class war, crime, low morale and declining health that the reader might wonder how it was at all possible for society to continue, let alone fight and win a war. The collection was introduced with a criticism of Titmuss, namely that he had 'paid insufficient attention to behaviour inconsistent with that idea [the emergence of the Dunkirk spirit]'; yet it was itself open to the same charge, for it contained not one document 'inconsistent with' the unremittingly negative picture created by the rest.[21] In similar vein, if less stridently, Steven Fielding's essay 'The Good War 1939–1945' emphasized social tension and bigotry. Thus the Evacuation 'did not necessarily promote egalitarianism: responses were mixed to say the least' (but he then illustrates with *only* the 'negative' responses); in the Blitz, the spirit of comradeship was more within class than between classes; some members of the middle classes resented measures improving the lives of manual workers (but no

evidence of this is offered); the upper classes remained hostile towards the lower classes and clung to the old social order – for this
the 'evidence' is Noel Coward's film *In Which We Serve* and Evelyn
Waugh's novel *Brideshead Revisited*. In a longer essay 'Popular attitudes in wartime', written a little earlier, he concluded: 'Taken
together ... this evidence qualifies the idea that the war straightfor-
wardly boosted social soldarity ... The image of a people standing
together in communal defiance of the German bombs seems to be,
in part, a myth.' The approach used to reach this verdict is more
balanced, but even here, the evidence for supporting the traditional
view is more cursorily examined than that for revising it.[22]

Revisionism has not carried all before it, however. Five recent
books have appeared that have served to buttress the traditional
standpoint. A short essay by Andrew Thorpe in *The Civilian in
War* reviewed the evidence of public opinion polls, the reports of
official 'morale watchers', the results of parliamentary by-elections,
the scale of volunteering and indicators of industrial performance,
concluding that 'Overall ... civilians supported the war effort, despite the hardships involved.'[23] Peter Hennessy concurred, writing
of the Blitz: 'what is remembered as the spirit of the Blitz could and
did prevail even in the most shattered circumstances', and, quoting
Tom Harrisson, 'they could and did carry on being people, *homo
sapiens*, albeit in varying degrees displaced'. His overall assessment
also matched Thorpe's: 'Wartime Britain ... was, certainly after May
1940, a more politically united nation than at any time in the twentieth century. It was better fed, more productive and less embittered
between its social gradations.'[24] John Ray, in *The Night Blitz 1940–
41*, was equally unmoved by the attempts to revise the accepted
view. Rejecting the suggestions of 'public fragility' in the 'finest
hour' and the claims that reports were suppressed by the Government, he contended that 'such arguments overlook the general feeling of the nation at the time' and are based 'on the thoughts and
writings of a small minority'.[25] Philip Ziegler, limiting his ambit to
London, accepted that there were blemishes in the 'performance' of
the capital's inhabitants, but that 'few ... behaved badly, many more
conspicuously well ... the population of London as a whole endured the blitz with dignity, courage, resolution and astonishing
good humour'. He went on to sum up their record in the war as a
whole: 'There is much that Londoners can look back on with pride,

remarkably little about which they need to feel ashamed.'[26] Finally, considering the year 1940 only, Malcolm Smith lent support to the traditional view, finding that such breakdowns in civilian morale as occurred were no more than local, temporary and 'passive'; of 'active' breakdowns there was no sign.[27]

This book was prompted by a sense that the revision being made to the traditional view was an over-correction, that there was a danger of a new received version taking root that was as overdrawn as that it sought to replace. I wondered how extensive the 'negative' features were, that is, to what extent they could be held to be typical of the people as a whole. I set out, therefore, to re-examine the totality of the civilian experience: the strains and stresses to which total war subjected the civilian population and the range and extent of its reactions to them. My ultimate purpose, however, was to explain as well as to describe. The second half of the book, therefore, is an attempt to identify and analyse the factors that shaped or influenced the morale of the people. It recognizes, as indeed those ministers and officials charged with devising policies to sustain morale recognized, that this is a moving target, that the constituents of civilian morale did not remain constant but rather evolved in response to the changing nature of war on the home front.

Among the mass of contemporary records that are able to throw light on this subject, two stand out as especially helpful: the reports of Home Intelligence and Mass-Observation. These reports have an essential feature in common: they are explicitly concerned with civilian morale, unlike the other sources, where this matter occurs incidentally or unwittingly. Their salience in my investigation demands an explanation of how these bodies were constituted and how they operated.

Home Intelligence was an integral part of the Ministry of Information from its creation at the outbreak of war; indeed, the importance of collecting information about the public's reactions to the war's events and to the Government's policies was acknowledged during the planning of the department from 1937.[28] The planners drew up a list of possible sources of information. These included the Ministry's own Regional Information Officers, Mass-Observation, the Federation of British Industry, trade unions and professional associations, school inspectors, Chambers of Commerce, Rotary

Clubs and the Workers' Educational Association. During the spring of 1940 other sources were added: police duty room reports collated and sent on by chief constables; the BBC, through its Listener Research unit, which collated the replies of its nationwide subject panels to questionnaires it sent out periodically; the British Institute of Public Opinion, which from 1937 under the name of the Gallup Polls produced soundings of public opinion on a variety of subjects, using modern social research techniques such as individual interviews and balanced samples of at least 1000 respondents; branch managers of W. H. Smith; managers of Granada cinemas; officials of political parties, voluntary societies, the London Passenger Transport Board and the Citizens' Advice Bureaux. In addition Postal Censorship, which examined up to 200,000 letters a week, made regular reports on public attitudes and morale; and Telephone censorship sent in reports based on its official eavesdropping. Finally, the Ministry set up a statistical survey unit, known as the Wartime Social Survey, and put it under the supervision of the London School of Economics. The material from all these sources was read by two Home Intelligence assessors, who summarized them in a report. This was the basis for a final version produced after discussion with the assessors, by the head of the division, Mary Adams. From 18 May until the end of September 1940 Home Intelligence produced daily reports on public opinion and mood, thereafter changing to weekly reports. Much of the raw data received at Home Intelligence was by its nature impressionistic rather than 'scientific' in a social research sense. Nevertheless, in quantity and range it was impressive, and the historian is bound to conclude that in its distilled form it was unlikely to be very far from the truth; among the jostling hubbub of individual testimonies its composite voice is indispensable.

Mass-Observation, too, qualifies for the label 'indispensable'. This privately-run social reporting organization was started in 1936 by the poet and journalist Charles Madge, the anthropologist Tom Harrisson and the documentary film maker Humphrey Jennings. It employed a nationwide panel of 1,500 voluntary observers, 150 diarists and smaller groups of trained full-timers to report on a wide range of individual and group habits and opinions, outlining its purpose as 'ascertaining the facts as accurately as possible; developing and improving the methods of ascertaining these facts;

disseminating the ascertained facts as widely as possible'. The basic method of the Mass-Observers was, as the designation suggests, to observe and listen rather than to conduct interviews. This anthropological approach was, as Tom Harrisson put it: 'derived partly from my own experience as a field ornithologist and member of four scientific expeditions where we had applied the methods which appeared (to me) equally applicable nearer home'.[29] In 1940 Mass-Observation accepted a commission from Home Intelligence to monitor civilian morale in different parts of the country, which meant producing reports that were for the eyes of Government officials only. This created some role conflict for the organization in respect of the last of its stated aims, but its financial health was not so good that it could refuse the work and, in any case, it was thereby able to expand its other investigations. Its general reports on morale were on a daily basis from mid-May to mid-July 1940, then weekly until October 1941 and monthly thereafter. In addition it did numerous special morale reports on bombed towns and reports on specific matters touching on morale, such as invasion fears, reactions to the introduction of rationing, industrial fatigue and absenteeism. As part of the arrangement with government departments the organization supplemented its 'observe and listen' method with formally conducted interviews, taking random samples of the population, correctly balanced according to the proportion of each age, sex and class in the community. In total, Mass-Observation's wartime files constitute a rich vein of raw material on how the people felt and acted at this time. Taken together, the reports of Home Intelligence and Mass-Observation are a resource that no one working on the period could feel able to ignore; in Paul Addison's words, they are 'a source for which there is no parallel or substitute in understanding wartime Britain'.[30] In this respect there is a fitting correspondence with the reception given to them by their first readers – Government ministers and civil servants. Before 1939 there was much official pessimism about how civilians would behave when total war was unleashed. Home Intelligence and Mass-Observation helped to show that pessimism to have been for the most part mistaken.

Pat Parker, who left her office job and, at the age of eighteen in 1942, became a 'lumberjill' in the Timber Corps of the Women's

Land Army and spent the rest of the war on the job in Herefordshire, recorded her view of those times half a century later: 'Our war was the best of times, and it was also the worst of times. I mean, people were being physically hurt, being hurt by losing some one, being hurt emotionally. Children were losing their parents and parents were losing their children. But the spirit of the country was terrific. I know people say it's jingoism, but we were going to win this war. We weren't going to let it get us down. I wish I could have bottled it so we could now say, 'Look, this is what it was like.'[31]

Recollections of this sort are common enough to be taken as typical among those who lived through the war years. For the most part, this book does not rely on such feats of memory, influenced as they inevitably are by the passage of time and all that the speaker has experienced since the events recalled. It rather places weight on testimony made at, or close to the time, which, for all its other inherent drawbacks, at least remains free of hindsight. Nevertheless, Pat's conviction that that is how it was – and, as we have seen, it is not so very far from the view of many scholars, too – will serve as a starting point, a question to be investigated.

Notes

1 Diary entry, April 1941, by Barrow housewife Nella Last. R. Broad and S. Fleming (eds), *Nella Last's War* (Falling Wall Press, 1981), p. 135.

2 P. Addison, *The Road to 1945: British Politics and the Second World War* (Pimlico, 1994), p. 121.

3 Mass-Observation Archive (M-O hereafter), File 27, February 1940.

4 M-O, File 606.

5 1 October 1941, INF 1/292.

6 J. T. MacCurdy, *The Structure of Morale* (Cambridge University Press, 1943), pp. 72, 141.

7 R. N. Sanford and H. S. Conrad, 'Some Personality Correlates of Morale', *Journal of Abnormal and Social Psychology*, vol. 38, 1943. It will be evident from the several definitions of morale cited here, that contemporary usage confusingly equated 'morale' with 'high morale', i.e. as if it were an absolute that did or did not exist. However, since the same sources, when seeking to illustrate the concept, invariably deploy the relatives 'high/good' or 'low/poor' morale, the usage will be treated here as a linguistic rather than semantic imprecision.

8 R. Titmuss, *Problems of Social Policy* (HMSO, 1950), pp. 340–4.

9 C. Fitzgibbon, *The Blitz* (Macdonald, 1957), p. 113; D. Thomson, *England in the Twentieth Century* (Penguin, 1965), p. 193.

10 A. J. P. Taylor, *English History 1914–1945* (Oxford University Press, 1965), pp. 502–3; *A Personal History* (Hamish Hamilton, 1983), p. 153.

11 Taylor, *English History 1914–1945*, p. 600.

12 A. Marwick, *Britain in the Century of Total War* (Penguin, 1970), p. 296; *The Home Front* (Thames & Hudson, 1976), p. 297.

13 A. Marwick, 'People's War and Top People's Peace? British Society and the Second World War', in A. Sked and C. Cook (eds), *Crisis and Controversy. Essays in Honour of A. J. P. Taylor* (Macmillan, 1976), pp. 148–64.

14 A. Calder, *The People's War: Britain 1939–45* (Jonathan Cape, 1969); *The Myth of the Blitz* (Jonathan Cape, 1991).

15 H. Pelling, *Britain and the Second World War* (Fontana, 1970), p. 100.

16 T. Harrisson, *Living Through the Blitz* (Collins, 1976), p. 280–1.

17 E. Smithies, *Crime in Wartime: A Social History of Crime in World War Two* (Allen & Unwin, 1982).

18 T. Crosby, *The Impact of Civilian Evacuation in the Second World War* (Croom Helm, 1986).

19 J. Macnicol, 'The evacuation of schoolchildren', in H. Smith (ed.), *War and Social Change: British Society in the Second World War* (Manchester University Press, 1986), pp. 3–31.

20 C. Ponting, *1940: Myth and Reality* (Hamish Hamilton, 1990).

21 H. Smith, *Britain in the Second World War: a Social History* (Manchester University Press, 1996), p. 2.

22 S. Fielding, 'The Good War 1939–1945', in N. Tiratsoo (ed.), *From Blitz to Blair* (Weidenfeld and Nicholson, 1997), pp. 25–52; S. Fielding, et al., *"England Arise": the Labour Party and Popular Politics in the 1940s* (Manchester University Press, 1995), pp. 19–45.

23 A. Thorpe, 'Britain', in J. Noakes (ed.), *The Civilian in War: The Home Front in Europe, Japan, and the USA in World War II* (Exeter University Press, 1992), p. 21.

24 P. Hennessy, *Never Again: Britain 1945–1951* (Jonathan Cape, 1992), pp. 34, 52.

25 J. Ray, *The Night Blitz 1940–41* (Arms and Armour, 1996), p. 12.

26 P. Ziegler, *London at War 1939–1945* (Alfred A. Knopf, 1995), pp. 163, 340.

27 M. Smith, *Britain and 1940: History, Myth and Poplar Memory* (Routledge, 2000).

28 For a comprehensive history of the Ministry of Information see I. McLaine, *Ministry of Morale* (Allen & Unwin, 1979).

29 Harrisson, *Living Through the Blitz* , p. 11.

30 P. Addison, 'Introduction', *The British People and World War II: Home Intelligence Reports on Opinion and Morale, 1940–1944* (University of Sussex, 1983), Reel 1, p. 8 (microfilm collection).

31 M. Nicholson (ed.), *What Did You Do in the War, Mummy? Women in World War II* (Pimlico, 1996), p. 49.

PART I

PROSPECT AND REALITY

I

War imagined

The prospect of total war – again

I T WAS WISH fulfilment rather than realism that drove the phrase 'a war to end wars' into the public consciousness during the unprecedented slaughter of 1914–18. When that nightmare was at last over, there was a natural human desire to believe its like could never again be contemplated, that it really had been 'a war to end war'. For a decade or more a traumatized mankind was in denial about its historic complacency towards the use of war as an instrument of policy. Pacifism became a mass movement of international dimensions. Millions of people, seasoned politicians among them, placed their trust in the newly formed League of Nations as their safeguard against the recurrence of the disaster of war. Nowhere was this more so than in Britain, where successive governments maintained the national role of stalwart of the League and where signed-up pacifism became a pervasive part of domestic political discourse. Its reality was manifest not just in the membership numbers of the peace associations and the official line of the Labour Party, but also in the winding-down of the defence establishment and the progressive reductions in defence spending. A country that ended military conscription as soon as the fighting had stopped and that reduced spending on the armed forces from £604m in 1919–20 to £102.7m in 1932–33 appeared to be signalling its belief that another world war was not only unimaginable but also altogether unlikely.

Within four years of that low point in defence spending the world looked a different place: economic recession had soured international relationships as governments everywhere acted unilaterally in the interest of their national economies; Japan had invaded the Chinese province of Manchuria and made it a Japanese protectorate, in defiance of the League of Nations; Adolf Hitler and the

National Socialists had come to power in Germany, with all that
portended for the peaceful conduct of international relations; the
Italian fascist leader Mussolini had launched an aggressive war
against a fellow member of the League of Nations, Abyssinia; a
civil war had broken out in Spain that threatened to escalate into
an international conflict. In these changed circumstances the British Government, like governments everywhere, was forced to contemplate the possibility of involvement in conflict leading to war.
For the remaining years of the 1930s the overriding questions of
the day were: Was war avoidable? If not, how soon might it come?
How best to prepare for the contingency?

To the last of these questions the obvious answer was rearmament. And indeed from 1936, alongside a diplomatic stance designed to prevent war by appeasing the revisionist dictator
governments, Britain's leaders threw economic orthodoxy to the
winds and began to spend much more on defence, focusing especially on the Royal Air Force.[1]

But weapons and fighting men, preponderant though they were,
were not the only considerations to engage the minds of politicians
and civil servants as they imagined the prospect of a Britain once
again engaged in war. For modern war meant total war, that is, a
war that engaged the energies of the whole nation, and not just
those of the armed forces; this was not the least of the lessons of the
First World War. In order to place and maintain in the field over
several years armies numbering millions, governments had discovered that nothing less than a complete reorganization of the national economy was needed. Without the cooperation of the civilian
population this enterprise was unrealizable. And so strenuous efforts were made to induce every citizen to contribute his energies to
that unprecedented phenomenon, the 'home front'. Thinking about
future war, therefore, meant envisaging and preparing for the active role of the civilian population in the pursuit of victory. The
crucial question was the willingness of the mass of the people to
share the leadership's commitment to winning the war and to bear
the burdens that this entailed over a period as long as or perhaps
longer than the First World War.

By 1939 this had come to be seen by the official mind as problematical. The conclusions of various committees, taking the earlier war
as a baseline, had cast doubt on the ability of any government

successfully to summon up a national effort like that of 1914–18 in the changed circumstances of the 1940s. In the first place, the history of the earlier conflict was as much a warning as a source of confidence. On the one hand, the people of Britain had responded to the sacrifice and effort demanded of them by the Government during 1914–18 with unselfish, patriotic ardour. On the other, the real possibility that things might easily have turned out otherwise was demonstrated by the social upheavals and collapse of the home fronts elsewhere – in Russia, Germany and Austria-Hungary in 1917–18. And even in Britain the signs of debilitating war-weariness were evident in the final eighteen months of the war. Secondly, in the years that followed the war, changes in the nature of warfare together with certain social and political developments, served to increase uncertainty about how the British people would behave in the event of another war.

Of the changes in the nature of warfare none was more significant in this regard than the emergence of the fighting air arm. In the First World War the role of airships and winged aircraft steadily grew in the four years of the conflict and in its final year constituted an important means of extending the battle zone from the fighting fronts to the home fronts. But the bombing of civilians in their workplaces and their homes, horrifying and unnerving though it was, had not been sufficiently extensive to make governments feel that civilian morale itself was seriously threatened. By 1939, however, the prospect was altogether more alarming. Aircraft design had evolved rapidly in the twenty years since the war. In every respect – speed, instrumentation and gunnery, but more significantly, in range and payloads – the machines of 1939 were greatly superior to those of 1918.[2] In a number of war theatres their devastating potential was demonstrated. The first, in 1932, involved Britain's own Royal Air Force Bomber Command: the bombing of recalcitrant Kurdish tribesmen in northern Iraq, a mission carried out at the request of King Faisal, the new ruler of this former British mandate territory. Then came the operations of the Italian air force, successfully subduing Abyssinian armies in 1935–36. Two years later German and Italian bombers were deployed in Spain on behalf of the rebel leader Franco; high profile daylight attacks on Barcelona, Madrid and Guernica were launched with impunity, to devastating effect on civilian life and property. Finally, in 1937 the

Japanese air force made a series of very destructive raids on China's coastal cities, including Shanghai, Nanking and Canton.

The record seemed to confirm that in future all wars would involve a significant role for the air forces of the combatants. It also suggested that not only would civilian populations become prime targets but that the targeting would be successful. Indeed, this had already by 1932 become received opinion in the ruling establishment, as was shown by the Prime Minister, Stanley Baldwin's gloomy words in a Commons debate, 'Let's face it, the bomber will always get through' – and this before the evidence of Guernica and the rest. With Germany identified – from 1935, at least – as Britain's most likely adversary in a future war, Government thinking was that Germany would attempt a knockout blow at once, even before actually declaring war, using its total air forces, and that heavy destruction and dislocation were to be expected. As Baldwin put it, 'tens of thousands of mangled people – men, women and children – before a single soldier or sailor suffered a scratch'.[3] It was assumed, moreover, that in addition to high explosives and incendiary bombs there would be bombs carrying poison gas and other lethal chemicals. This last forecast had entered public discourse at least as early as 1927, when, in fittingly alarmist language, the MP for Oldham, Alfred Duff Cooper, warned the House of Commons, 'Our cities will not merely be decimated but rendered uninhabitable by chemical bombs ... it is not war in the ordinary sense ... We are faced with the wiping out of civilisation.'[4] In like manner the former head of the Explosives Department in the First World War, Lord Halsbury, was predicting in 1933 that 'a single gas bomb, if dropped on Piccadilly Circus, would kill everybody in an area from Regent's Park to the Thames' – this area housed about one million people.[5] Official predictions about casualties were more modest, but shocking enough, none the less. The view of the Air Staff in 1924 was that 450 tons of bombs would be dropped on London in the first three days and that this would result in 3,800 dead and 7,500 wounded. By 1937 the Committee of Imperial Defence, taking the Air Staff's updated post-Barcelona rate of fifty casualties per ton of bombs as its guide, was forecasting 1,800,000 casualties in the first two months, one third of them killed. And in 1938 a Cabinet committee predicted that 3,500 tons of bombs would be dropped on London on the first day, 700 tons per day thereafter.

It can be fairly taken, then, that as war approached there was in official circles an accepted belief that its beginning would be marked by little less than a holocaust. What would happen next was the big question and on this there was less uniformity of view among the planners. An important influence was the experience of the First World War. Zeppelin raids on the Midlands in January 1916 had caused much public nervousness and the raids on the East End of London towards the end of 1917 had brought signs of panic among residents – 'trekking' out of the area and reluctance to leave the safety of the Underground railway. A report made by a Home Office sub-committee in 1924 reiterated the received wisdom of the time: 'It has been borne in on us that in the next war it may well be that the nation whose people can endure serial bombardment the longer and with greater stoicism will ultimately prove victorious.'[6] The first Marshall of the Royal Air Force, General Sir Hugh Trenchard, himself a believer in the omnipotence of the bomber, said in 1928, 'Once a raid has been experienced, false alarms are incessant and a state of panic remains in which work comes to a standstill.'[7] This was much in line with the thinking of the Italian strategist Giulio Douhet, who in 1930 attempted to popularize his views by writing a work of fiction, *La Guerra del 19 –* . In this he depicted a war between Germany and a Franco-Belgian alliance in which the Germans prevailed because they had perfected the use of the knockout blow from the air. 'By integrating the aerial arm with poison gas', he wrote, 'it is possible today to employ very effective action against the most vital and vulnerable spots of the enemy – that is, against his most important political, industrial, commercial and other centres – in order to create among his population a lowering of moral resistance so deep as to destroy the determination of the people to continue the war.'[8] Many public figures accepted the Douhet–Trenchard view. Winston Churchill, for example, predicted in the Commons in 1934 that the first raids would produce a panic flight from London of three to four million people; and the army would be too busy restoring order to do its job. 'This vast mass of human beings', he warned, 'without shelter and without food, without sanitation and without special provision for the maintenance of order, would confront the Government of the day with an administrative problem of the first magnitude.'[9] From another quarter came warning that alongside the problems of civilian deaths and injuries and the destruction of homes and services, would be large-scale hysteria and mental breakdown. A report produced by a committee of leading psychiatrists in the London teaching hospitals and presented to the Ministry of Health in October 1938 suggested that there would be three times as many mental casualties as physical casualties. This implied the swamping of the mental health services by between three and four million psychiatric cases.[10] The most pessimistic scenario was of mass panic leading to widespread clamour for peace on any terms and of a government, because of the paralysis of its military forces, forced to give way. All this pessimism about the power of bombing was mirrored in the official policy that in 1935 made the building of a deterrent bomber force the cornerstone of defence strategy; for only, it was believed, through having the means to wreck the morale of the civilians of a continental enemy through mass bombing could that enemy be deterred from unleashing its own bomber fleet upon the British people.

A more sceptical view of the decisive role of the bomber was expressed in 1938 by S. Possony, an academic theorist on the industrial implications of war, who argued that large cities were too dispersed to be destroyed by bombing and that, in any case, aircraft were vulnerable to defending artillery and fighters.[11] And not all public figures were gloomy about the moral fibre of the British people. Lord Woolton, for example, who in 1937 sat on a committee chaired by Lord Riverdale 'to inquire into the organization of the fire brigades of Great Britain', recalled: 'The brightest spot in it all was that we based our recommendations on the belief that the public of Britain, faced with unprecedented calamity, would be competent and resolute.'[12]

But in the main, the official view on the matter tended towards pessimism. In order to explain more fully why this was so, it is necessary to return to the interwar social and political developments already referred to.

A united nation?

Raw human terror before the prospect of mechanized destruction from the air was unavoidable but, as we shall see, it was a problem for which there were practical answers: things that the Government could do to mitigate, if not to solve. What was more worrying from the official standpoint was the basic patriotic loyalty of the civilian mass. Certainly, it had been tested and not found wanting in 1914–18, but it was not easy to be confident in 1939 that things had remained unchanged. On the contrary, there were good reasons for feeling doubtful about the matter. In the interwar years love of country had increasingly to compete with other loyalties – to peace, to class, to political ideology, to region. Although none of these necessarily excluded patriotic sentiment, they rendered that sentiment less certain, its strength an unknown quantity.

Pacifism had a long history in Britain. The Peace Society, the first in the world, was formed in London in 1816. Pacifists distinguished themselves during the nineteenth century by their support for international conventions on the conduct of war and for the building up of the general body of international law to reduce the resort to the violent solution of conflict. But the anti-war movement never became a mass movement in the nineteenth century. This was partly because pacifists were to some extent divided by their other affiliations – Christian, Marxist or Mazzinian – and partly because of the great and, in many ways, incompatible appeal of nationalism. For this was the age of nationalism, the time when many submerged nations claimed (and in some cases achieved) the status of nation state. Since war was often the only means to that end, pacifism did not seem to many to provide an answer to the problem of frustrated national feeling. It was also to pacifism's disadvantage that in the nineteenth century, wars were on the whole short and retained in the popular imagination many of the heroic features of wars of old. It was quite simply difficult to elicit mass support for the proposition that war was always a tragic, dirty affair that degraded man's humanity.

The First World War changed all this. Millions experienced the bloody reality of war at first hand. War as the natural expression of the heroic human spirit suffered a crippling blow; the apparently futile decimation of the populations of the combatant countries served to reclassify war as the ultimate human folly. Already, before it was over, men were writing books that said so; books that were to be the guiding texts of a nascent pacifist movement of mass proportions.[13] For it is no exaggeration to say that such was the transforming effect of the trauma of 1914–18. In the fifteen years that followed, the main impulse continued to be the Great War itself. In the universities of Aberystwyth and Oxford, chairs were established for the study of international relations with a view to promoting peace through knowledge of the causes of war. Learned institutions such as the David Davies Institute and the Royal Institute of International Affairs appeared with much the same aim. Some of the post mortem analyses of the causes of the First World War convinced many that sinister vested interests were implicated and that it had not been fought for worthy motives after all. The first peace group in the field was the Fellowship of Reconciliation, a Christian body established in 1919, followed by the mainly socialist No More War Movement in 1921. In terms of numbers of members the most successful was the League of Nations Union, which had over a million members by 1931. With the accession to power of Hitler and the Nazis, the threat to peace seemed much greater and the anti-war movement gained new adherents. In 1934 a popular radio preacher, Canon 'Dick' Sheppard founded the Peace Pledge Union. He hit upon the idea of demonstrating to the Government the strength of anti-war sentiment by getting people formally to pledge themselves not to fight in any future war; within two years 100,000 people had done so, sending their pledges on postcards to Sheppard. Even more telling was the 'Peace Ballot' organized by the League of Nations Union in 1935. Eleven and a half million people participated and nine out of ten voted in favour of multilateral disarmament and collective security through the League of Nations. This picture of a Britain humming with the anti-war message is completed by what was happening in the political mainstream. It was to be expected that the fading Liberal Party would adhere to the League of Nations ideal – and that is what happened. But more significant was its espousal by the Labour Party, one of the two main contenders for power in this period and in fact twice holding it in 1923–24 and 1929–31. During the period from 1931, when the Labour Party was in opposition, it showed its true colours by electing a confirmed pacifist, George Lansbury, as its leader. At its annual conference in 1933 delegates passed a resolution pledging the party to resist war, to take no part in it if it came, and to consider the possibility of using the weapon of a general strike, internationally organized, to prevent military mobilization. From this extreme pacifist position the party began to retreat in 1934, when it was becoming plain that their German partners in

this plan were disappearing under the Nazis' policy of 'coordination'. Meanwhile, the out and out pacifists of the Independent
Labour Party, once an important part of the Labour Party, but dis-
affiliated since 1932, continued under their leader James Maxton
to preach uncompromisng pacifism as the threat of war deepened.
The mainstream Labour Party placed its hopes instead in disarmament and the moral force of the League of Nations, still at that
time a credible institution. It probably helped that at this point the
Soviet Union decided to become a member of the League.

If pacifism as a mass movement had come to stay, what did this
mean for the behaviour of the masses in the event of war? This was
the biggest of the ruling National Government's worries in the 1930s,
when the prospects for peace looked increasingly gloomy. In the
earlier conflict about 16,000 young men had objected to military
service on grounds of conscience. That was at a time when pacifism
was yet the credo of a tiny minority regarded as eccentrics by the
rest. By 1939 this was clearly no longer the case. It would not be
unreasonable to infer – and this is just what the pessimists did –
that if war came, the refusal to fight would be on an altogether
much larger scale. It might also be assumed that no such problem
would present itself to the authoritarian dictatorships with whom
Britain was most likely to be at war. Britain's ability to exert its
power could therefore be fatally damaged simply by the numerical
inferiority of its armed forces; and there was similar uncertainty
about how much her main ally France might also be affected. Fur-
thermore, the weakness might be qualitative as well as quantita-
tive. This seemed to be the implication of the episode of the Oxford
University Union's debate in February 1933, when a resolution 'that
this House will in no circumstances fight for its king and country'
was passed by 275 votes to 153. Thus was the great recruiting call
of the First World War, 'Your King and Country Need You', mocked
by the young men of the middle classes – the officer class. In 1914
the middle classes had rallied to the call and they would be needed
once again to officer the mass army a new war would demand. The
numbers taking part in the Union debate were of course trifling,
but pessimists readily took them to represent what was happening
in the minds of educated young people throughout the nation.
Harold Nicolson recorded a summing-up of the average citizen's
position made by the philosopher Cyril Joad in December 1939:

'the ordinary person in England would be less unhappy after a Nazi victory than if he or she lost their sons, lovers or husbands'. Nicolson commented: 'He thinks only of the greatest happiness of the greatest number, and accuses me of national and spiritual pride.'[14]

The only comfort the nation's leaders could take from the situation was that by 1939 there was some evidence that pacifism had passed its peak. The failure of the League of Nations to deter the authoritarian governments from acts of aggression or effectively to punish them for their misdemeanours played a part in this. In a time of forceful *realpolitik* it was increasingly difficult to rebut the realist contention that force, or at least the threat of force, was the only language the dictators understood. Since the League had turned out to be no more than an advocate of restraint in international relations, the need for rearmament and the deterrent power of national forces seemed all the more apparent. The League of Nations Union could no longer claim the numbers of members that it had in 1931, its peak year. Signally, the Labour Party began to move away from its position of absolute faith in collective security at about the time of the League's failure to bring Mussolini to heel. It first replaced the pacifist leader Lansbury with the more realist Clement Attlee (and it was perhaps more than incidental that the Party encouraged the more mood-attuned usage *Major* Attlee); then, in 1937, it abandoned its opposition to rearmament. By October 1938, after the Munich crisis, Stafford Cripps was suggesting to his fellow frontbencher, Hugh Dalton, a common anti-appeasement front with the Eden–Churchill wing of the Conservative Party.[15]

Westminster gossip reasonably inferred Labour's belated conversion to political realism, even though its vote against the introduction of military service in April 1939 showed the conversion was not yet total. How much the rank and file of the party had accepted this shift was unknown; it was nevertheless held in Whitehall to be a reason for a little more optimism about the willingness of British manhood to stand up and be counted when war came.

Speculation about this, however, necessarily had to take account of the fact that in the 1930s, important though the Labour Party was in the political affiliations of the working class, it was not the sole contender for those affiliations. This was a time of growth for other ideologies, notably fascism, communism and Celtic nationalism. Any calculation of the strength of popular attachment to the existing political and constitutional order, therefore, properly needed to assess the pull of these rejectionist ideologies.

By the time the sides in the looming conflict had roughly formed themselves, the question of where to place Britain's fascists in the loyalty ratings was at least straightforward: they could be counted a clear liability, at best conscientious objectors, at worst fifth columnists if war with the fascist states ever came. But calm assessment of this situation would have shown little cause for alarm. The reality was that the amount of noise generated by the fascists in the politics of the 1930s was out of all proportion to their numbers. Oswald Mosley's British Union of Fascists could at its peak claim only about 20,000 members and it signally failed to work up sufficient support in by-elections or in the 1935 General Election to enable it to take a parliamentary seat. The high profile it achieved during the Spanish Civil war (1936–39) and through its carefully staged confrontations with the communists in the streets of the East End of London belied the fact that it was a fringe group, entirely marginal to the real politics of the country. It was naturally a little worrying to think that if Britain were at war there would be British nationals at large who were willing to assist the operations of the enemy. But realism suggested they were a manageable problem.

How Britain's communists rated was uncertain until the eleventh hour. For five years – from Stalin's injunction in 1934 to non-fascists everywhere to form a popular front against fascism – British communists could be counted on, or so it seemed, to rally to the national cause in the event of a war with the fascist states. Then, in August 1939, this calculation was falsified by the signing of the non-aggression pact between Nazi Germany and Soviet Russia. More war resisters? More defeatists? Again, calm appraisal should not have led to great alarm. Like the fascists, the communists were outside Britain's political mainstream; a noisy, vociferous presence, but in truth of little consequence. The Communist Party of Great Britain had a mere 17,000 members and in elections was only marginally more successful than Mosley's BUF, securing one parliamentary seat in 1935. Against this, the location of its influence was a cause for concern. Communists were disproportionately numerous among trade union officials and activists, men who had the power to influence the attitudes of the industrial workforce. In the hardship years of the Depression it was not difficult to persuade men

that capitalism was exploitative and heartless and to encourage
them to feel that it represented an order not worth fighting for. This
was particularly so in Scotland and Wales. In 1939 one quarter of
the insured population of Wales was employed in coal. The Miners
Federation represented 135,000 miners and sponsored thirteen
Labour MPs; but its leader, Arthur Horner, was a communist and
communists were well established in its Executive Council. Similarly in Scotland, the West Fife area, a mining constituency, elected
the communist Willie Gallagher to Parliament in 1935. It was a
matter of record that much of the industrial strife in the war industries during the First World War was associated with the activities
of militant Marxist shop stewards; Gallagher had himself been
deeply involved in the industrial militancy that gave Clydeside its
'Red' reputation. If, as then, victory turned on the ability of the war
industries to meet the demands of the armed forces, then the communist presence in the mines, yards and factories could turn out to
be a source of national weakness.

The Depression was notoriously variable in the way it affected
the different parts of the country. In the south east and in the Midlands unemployment had never been as bad as in the north, the
West Country, Wales and Scotland, where iron, steel, coal, shipbuilding and textiles were the chief livelihoods of the population.
In Scotland and Wales the hardship was compounded by a sense of
being part of a Celtic margin neglected by the English ruling establishment. Towards the end of the 1930s, when some degree of pros-
perity had returned to the favoured regions, Wales and Scotland
failed to benefit. This was fertile soil, then, for the growth of sepa-
ratist feeling and in both regions there was such a growth. In Wales
Plaid Cymru was founded in 1925. It was radical, Nonconformist
and pacifist in outlook, best described as a cultural pressure group
passionate about saving the declining Welsh language. In the 1930s
it was committed to winning home rule as a dominion, like New
Zealand or Canada, and to gaining for Wales a seat at the League
of Nations. At the same time some of its adherents became militant
and began making symbols of English domination their targets. In
1936 three of its members including Saunders Lewis the leader were
tried for burning down an RAF bombing school at Pen-y-Berth in
Caernarvonshire. The Government decided that a Welsh court would
be biased and removed the trial to the Old Bailey. This brought

vociferous protests and a guarantee of national news coverage. When the three, who refused to give evidence in English, were sentenced to nine months' imprisonment they became Welsh martyrs in the eyes of many, and later returned to Wales national heroes. But it turned out a short-lived triumph and it did not translate into a significant rise in Plaid Cymru's membership. Although the party tried to widen its support by following the respectable route of securing a voice at Westminster and representation in local government, it made scant impression on voters. Its best result was in the contest for the Caernarvonshire seat in 1935 when it took only 5.7 per cent of the vote and lost its deposit. Evidently, the guardians of the United Kingdom had little to fear from Welsh nationalism, in the short term at least. Plaid Cymru's counterpart, the Scottish National Party came into being in 1934 as a result of a merger between the National Party of Scotland, founded in 1928, and the more recently formed Scottish Party. Like the Welsh, the Scots aimed at home rule and like them, too, tried to get a political voice by establishing a presence at Westminster. They did rather better at the polls than the Welsh. In the 1935 General Election, for example, they contested eight seats and although they failed to win one they took a respectable 16 per cent of the vote. In terms of membership, too, they outdid Plaid Cymru's 2,000 with 10,000 members in 1934. From the start the party had been pacifist in outlook. The chairman, and financial backer, Roland Muirhead and the secretary John MacCormick were staunch pacifists and together they ensured that the Party was committed to oppose military conscription.

In terms of their influence on the mass of the people in Wales and Scotland in the event of war the record of the nationalists suggested that there was no cause for real anxiety. They were a salient part of political discourse in those regions but they had clearly failed to become mass movements. Such concern as they did engender in government circles was more the product of the accumulation of negative indicators in Wales and Scotland than of any threat from the national parties alone. These regions, as has been observed, happened also to be those where the Depression had left a bitter legacy and where pacifism and communism had both done relatively well. Whether these indices of possible disaffection would together amount to anything very significant was the nagging question, to which only the test of war itself would provide the answer.

A footnote, as it were, to this question was the special case of Northern Ireland. The neutrality of the Republic of Ireland and uncertain
loyalty of the Roman Catholic minority in the six counties were seen
as problematical in London. A new campaign of violence by the IRA
had begun in January 1939; explosions damaged telephone exchanges,
power stations and factories in Manchester, Birmingham and London, and by August there had been 127 such explosions in England.
To avoid antagonising further the Irish government and boosting the
strength of the Irish Republican Army, the decision was made to
exempt Northern Ireland from the provisions of the Military Training Act of May 1939, which introduced conscription for twenty and
twenty-one year olds. The fierce loyalty of the Protestant/Unionist
majority could find its outlet in voluntary enlistment.[16]

Any attempt to weigh up the mood of the British people was
bound to begin with the explicitly articulated allegiances just described. But the honest enquirer would know that there was beyond these an inchoate entity that was as potentially debilitating as
any of them. Britain in the 1930s was a divided society. The faultline
lay between those who were victims of the Depression and those
who were spared its ravages; those whose living standards fell and
those who came out relatively better off. Such was the reality that
lay behind figures showing a rise in average real incomes and a rise
in average living standards. Whereas unemployment levels might
be in single figures in the south east part of the country, where new
consumer goods and service industries were growing, in the areas
that relied on the old staple industries as many as 35 per cent of the
insured population might be jobless. The partial economic recovery and the rearmament programme still left one and a third million people registered as unemployed in 1939, that is, 12 per cent of
the insured population. Mass unemployment meant that millions
suffered from poverty, bad housing, ill health and poor nutrition.
These were the losers in British society, people who had little cause to
feel they had a stake in it. Would they fight for it? The desperation
that underlay the hunger marches and demonstrations of the National Unemployed Workers' Movement was an unpromising culture medium for regrowing the national spirit. From the standpoint
of our imaginary assessor the Depression's victims must surely be
counted a poor resource in the mobilization of the nation for total
war.

Taken together, the various elements of potential disaffection and dissidence constituted a significant, if intrinsically unquantifiable, cause for official concern in the peace-threatening years from 1935 to the actual outbreak of war in 1939. Only time would tell whether Britain was still capable of generating the national spirit that underpinned the victory of 1918.

Preparing for the storm

In the meantime, there were practical steps that the Government could take to mitigate the baleful amalgam of fear, apathy and dissidence that had apparently taken root among the people. And so, with apprehension and less-than-absolute conviction of its value, hoping all the while that diplomacy would in any case make it redundant, the governments of Baldwin and Chamberlain embarked on a programme of measures to make it possible to fight and win a people's war.

In the first place it was recognized that, even accepting that enemy bombers would 'always get through', it made sense to try to limit the damage they might do to popular morale. However puny they might seem, measures of physical protection were judged worth making. The concept of Air Raid Precautions (ARP) was not new: an ARP sub-committee was appointed in 1924 under the chairmanship of the Permanent Under Secretary of State for the Home Department and this committee remained in being until 1935 when an ARP Department of the Home Office was set up. The work of this department was reviewed by a sub-committee of the Committee of Imperial Defence, formed in 1937, under Warren Fisher's chairmanship, to report on existing provision and make recommendations for its improvement. This committee defined the aims of the ARP services, firstly to maintain the morale of the people; secondly to ensure continued functioning of the activities vital to the effective prosecution of the war and the life of the community; and thirdly to reduce to a minimum the destruction of life and property likely to be produced by air raids.[17] In accepting its recommendations, therefore, the Government endorsed its view of civilian morale as the first priority of air raid precautions. During the progress of the Air Raid Precautions Bill through Parliament the Home Secretary put the matter even more plainly: the Bill's primary job, he said, 'was to ensure the country against panic'.[18]

A key recommendation of the Warren Fisher Committee was the making of a plan to evacuate from the presumed danger areas all those people, i.e. infants and their mothers, schoolchildren, the sick and elderly, who could make no contribution to the war effort, and to settle them in safe districts scheduled as 'reception areas'. In the case of London this amounted to about two million people, a quarter of them schoolchildren. It was not just that these were *bouches inutiles*: the thinking behind the plan recognized that the bombing of civilian areas would be deliberately undertaken by the enemy in order to damage the morale of the armed forces, men away from home worried about the safety of their families. Evacuation of those families from the danger areas was therefore a way of alleviating worries and at the same time of countering the enemy's tactic.[19] It was also calculated to preserve the peace of mind of those able-bodied adults who would need to stay in the cities to maintain the home front war effort. Parents working in vital war industries whose children were of school age, for example, would, it was believed, be more productive in the war economy if those children were safe in the country. The committee's thinking was in part influenced by information and press cuttings collected by civil servants on the bombing of a school at Getalfe, Madrid, in October 1936, when seventy-six children were killed. There was a further objective in the committee's recommendation. It was expected that the onset of war would in any case cause a mass exodus from the capital and probably other cities, too. Taking at least a part of this movement into an orderly evacuation plan would prevent it from becoming a panic flight. In this way it was hoped to neutralize something which could itself lower civilian morale. If, as was claimed by Tom Harrisson, Britain's pre-war preparations for the eventuality of bombing were 'widely based on the "chaos" concept', then officials were at least seeing this in less-than-absolute terms and making a serious attempt to grapple with and mitigate the chaos.[20]

Detailed plans were slow to take shape, however. They were far from complete when the Munich crisis erupted in October 1938, but fortunately the hastily put together partial schemes were cancelled at the last moment when diplomatic breakthrough was achieved. The alarm of the Munich crisis demonstrated the urgent need to press on with detailed arrangements. For the belief that a mass flight would occur on the outbreak of war was confirmed by the clogging of roads and railways out of the capital during the crisis. In what remained of peacetime, plans were brought to completion. After much wrangling about who was to pay for the operation, it was agreed that, while the Government would defray the costs of transport and billeting, the organization of the whole would fall to the local authorities, working within centrally framed guidelines.

Another sort of evacuation was considered as part of official preparations for the contingency of war: that of the seat of government. There were obvious advantages to having the active war-making departments in safe places, but against these was the damaging effect an official exodus from the capital might have on the morale of the civilian population that remained. The first ARP Committee came to the conclusion that the cost to morale outweighed the administrative gain.[21] And so, from this very early point in pre-war preparations, the principle was established that the government would share the dangers of war with the people: a clear indication of the seriousness with which Government and civil servants took the claim that in modern war the morale of the people was the key to victory. By 1939, however, episodes like Guernica had sufficiently changed the official perspective on bombing to prompt second thoughts, and contingent plans were made for the evacuation of the civil service from Whitehall ('Yellow Move') and for the evacuation of the government itself ('Black Move).[22] Evidently, morale dictated that leaders were more use alive than dead.

Since it was essential that many millions not be evacuated but remain in the cities to man the factories supplying the forces, it was the aim of ARP to minimize the threat to their safety and to their spirits that living with air raids would inevitably bring. Of the practical measures taken to achieve this end none was more important than the provision of shelters. If the likelihood of being killed or injured by bombs could be made no more than a remote risk then, it was calculated, people might bear the destruction of property and the other dislocations that raids would bring without significant loss of morale.

Such were the developments in high explosives since the First World War that the civil servants working on the plans to provide bomb shelters quickly came to the conclusion that there was no type of surface shelter that offered more than protection from blast;

for proof against direct hits nothing less than very deep shelters would do. Deep shelters would be expensive to build and would take a long time to construct in sufficient numbers to provide mass protection.[23] They also ran counter to a principle that was established in official thinking about ARP as early as 1917 and reaffirmed through the following two decades: the principle of dispersal. Under this it was taken as axiomatic that casualties would be fewer if large assemblies of people were avoided. It followed that protection would have to be mainly through the erection of domestic shelters and the strengthening of houses that had basements. But underlying the aim to reduce casualties was another motive: the absolute protection afforded by deep shelters would, it was believed, lead to large numbers of people 'going to earth', and remaining there. The mere existence of deep shelters would encourage a retreatist mentality and create a nation of 'troglodytes', when what was needed was committed activity on the war production front. That this view was deeply rooted in official thinking is plain from the report of the Hailey Conference, a body set up in February 1939 under the chairmanship of Lord Hailey to survey the question of deep shelter provision. In recommending against building deep shelters the Conference was strongly influenced (at least, according to him) by the voice of one of its members, Lord Woolton. He recalled his experience in a large shelter in the First World War, when the assembling and confining of large numbers produced a 'hysterical and emotional atmosphere'.[24] When it became public in April 1939 that no deep shelters were to be built, the campaign for them that had begun the year before was intensified. Since the leading voice in this campaign was that of the Communist Party, the Government saw it as an attempt to undermine public confidence in ARP. And when in August the Nazi–Soviet pact was made and the communists became even more vociferous in the deep shelter campaign, this seemed confirmation of the thesis that a collapse of civilian morale was indeed the first object of enemy strategy.

The Hailey Conference was not entirely negative in its observations about shelters and morale. It thought that the most important consideration in this regard was equality of provision: an equal standard of protection in areas exposed to equal danger. With Hailey's recommendations as a guide, the Government pressed ahead with the enormous task of providing the physical protection that was believed necessary to sustain civilian morale. Working through the local authorities, public shelters were improvised by the reinforcement of the basements of existing steelframed buildings, domestic shelters were devised for erection in people's own gardens, and brick and concrete street shelters were designed for people living in blocks of flats or in houses without gardens. Notwithstanding the priority given to the programme, on the outbreak of war much remained to be done. About one and a half million domestic shelters had been delivered but this represented only two-thirds of the planned issue and most were yet to be installed; the street shelters built were too few to protect their designated population; and only a start had been made on the strengthening of large buildings for use as public shelters. There was, then, a gap between intention and fulfilment. The Home Secretary, Sir John Anderson, was unable to announce the completion of the shelter programme until June 1940; he was fortunate to have been given the unexpected nine-month respite of the Phoney War, when mercifully no bombs fell.[25]

The shelter story was by no means over, as the Blitz of 1940–41 was to show. In the meantime arrangements were in place that exactly reflected official thinking about the morale implications of mass bombing. On the one hand, basic shelter protection was essential to maintaining the morale of the civilian body; on the other, the over-protection represented by deep shelters risked undermining it. As in so much of its contingency planning the Government could only speculate as to the real consequences of heavy bombing on densely populated areas. Decisions on the various forms of shelter were made before the data were established about high explosive attack. What mattered in 1939, however, was that some provision was made and was seen by an apprehensive populace to have been made.

Providing for the contingency of poison gas attack was thought psychologically as necessary as making sure people had shelter from high explosives, for there was certainly widespread fear of this form of attack. In the popular imagination gas was a more horrifying prospect than explosives and incendiary bombs. It had been successfully used by the Italians against the Abyssinians in 1936, confirming, it seemed, the projection of future war in the film *Things to Come*, which had appeared in 1936. (This film is discussed on page 40.) From the official standpoint, the state of civilian morale might depend on how successfully the fear of gas could be allayed by official action. Fortunately this was an altogether more manageable problem than the provision of shelters. Respirators, as the authorities called them (everyone else called them gas masks), could be cheaply mass-produced. The Government decided in October 1935 that stocks of gas masks should be accumulated in sufficient numbers to supply free of charge in an emergency to all people in the parts of the country liable to attack (an estimated twenty million). In February 1936 it was decided to supply the entire civilian population, including infants, for whom a device described as an 'anti-gas helmet' was being designed. Distribution was to be held back until the last moment partly to avoid alarming the public prematurely about the imminence of war, partly because it was thought that once out of their containers, the masks – especially their rubber component – would start to deteriorate. The Munich crisis provided the signal for distribution (incidentally confirming the extent of official anxiety about the likelihood of war at that time) and within days most people had their gas masks. There was an outcry about the gaps in the provision – there was as yet no mask for small children and the gas helmets for babies were not ready. Both these omissions were made good before the outbreak of war, but in this episode the Government was given a glimpse of public feeling about gas that confirmed its own suppositions and reassured it that the decision to offer protection to the entire population was correct.

Air defence was not seriously considered before 1938. Until then the basic defence strategy was one of deterrence: the retaliating power of the RAF would be so great as to deter a would-be aggressor from initiating an airborne attack on Britain. It was only when it became clear that the bomber-building programme had begun too late to have this influence that a switch of resources to air defence was made.[26] Although the need to do this came mainly from the failure of diplomacy to buy the necessary time, the decision makers were also mindful of the gain in civilian morale to be made from the building up of the visible (and audible) means of striking back at enemy raiders, represented by fighter planes and anti-aircraft batteries, along with their apparatus of barrage balloons and searchlights. The great expansion of anti-aircraft capacity had begun in January 1936, when the first AA division of the Territorial Army was formed. By June 1937 there were two divisions, numbering 45,000 men overall. At this point the Government decided to create five divisions, totalling 100,000 men. In October 1938 the Territorial Army Reserve was formed. Men were recruited from key factories; if war came they would switch from workbench to AA guns to defend their factory from attack.[27]

It was recognized that the actual effect on attackers bent on dropping bombs on cities was likely to be puny. The rationale was simply that if no visible defence was offered against the raiders, people 'might feel abandoned and helpless'.[28] Shelters, gas masks and AA batteries were the most visible evidence for people that the Government was moving strongly to ensure their safety. They had the additional merit, in theory at least, of fulfilling that function should war come. But there were also numerous other measures dedicated to this end that were less visible. The ARP programme involved the setting up of an elaborate system of emergency services to meet every foreseeable contingency. About one and a half million people, some three-quarters of them voluntary part-timers, were recruited to staff these services: wardens, firemen, rescue men, ambulance drivers, medical staff, telephonists and messengers. Each of the 250 local authorities appointed an ARP controller who, working to Home Office guidelines and acting in conjunction with the chief medical officer, the local authority surveyor, the chief warden, and the local heads of the police and fire brigade, set up the practical arrangements for limiting the effects of air attack. Some were more diligent than others, but Whitehall was at the outbreak of war happy that a system was in place that would both minister to physical needs and serve the morale maintenance function of ARP. To be doubly sure, it established a layer of organization at regional level, designating twelve regions, each with a Regional Commissioner, whose wartime task would be to coordinate in his area the actions of government departments with civil defence functions. Significantly, the instructions to the Regional Commissioners emphasized the arrangements for police reinforcements within and between regions and for the use of troops 'to sustain public morale'.[29] At the same time the instructions made by the Army Council to General Officers Commanding-in-Chief gave the sustaining of popular morale as the first task of the troops. 'The public should be aware', they stated, 'that there are available formed and disciplined bodies of troops ready to assist in minimising the effect of air raids.'[30]

In two other areas of pre-war planning – rationing and information – official concern for morale is discernible behind the osten-
sible purposes of seeing that people were fed and told what to do.
The rationing of certain foods had been necessary in the previous
war and since the conditions that required it then would recur if
war came again it was clearly wise to plan for it. Looming large in
the official mind was the clear message from that earlier conflict
that failure to ensure an adequate food supply could lead to a weak-
ening of popular resolve and even to the collapse of morale. The
demand for improvements to the supply of food was as important
as any other single issue in the street demonstrations that preceded
the revolution in St Petersburg in February 1917; and food figured
importantly in the war-weariness that set in that same year in both
Austria-Hungary and Germany. It was, moreover, high food prices
and consequent industrial unrest in Britain in December 1916 that
had led to the appointment of the first Food Controller. The contribution of the first Ministry of Food's rationing scheme to the winning of the war was widely recognized. Taking this precedent to
heart, therefore, the Government set officials to prepare in advance
of need a fully comprehensive scheme for the rationing of essential
foods. By the outbreak of war all was ready. Ration books had
been printed, to be issued at the point when the Government judged
shortages were sufficiently bad to stoke unwanted inflation and
cause discontent among the less well off.

The creation of a Ministry of Information first came under consideration in 1935 and its formation was completed shortly before
the outbreak of war. In its set up there was no division dedicated
exclusively to maintaining civilian morale. Almost by default this
fell to the Publicity Division, which was set eight objectives, the
fifth and sixth of which were, 'To prevent panics, to allay appre-
hensions and to remove misconceptions', and 'Generally to keep
the public in good heart.'[31] In this there seems to be an early iden-
tification of a need to use mass communication to sustain civilian
morale. Home propaganda 'must rank at least equal in status to all
measures of offence and defence', was how it was put by Stephen
King-Hall, who was co-opted to help in the planning.[32] The Ministry of Information itself was, however, accorded low status and
little attention by the Cabinet. Planners chosen by the Home Office
to set up the new department were not even released to do it full-

time, but had to fit it in alongside their work in their own departments.[33] And yet it was to have supervision of the BBC and the
cinema industry. Perhaps Cabinet ministers were not among the
nineteen million people who bought a cinema ticket every week
and perhaps the Chamberlain household was not included in the
nine million that had a radio receiver. For the reality was that by
1939 the cinema and radio were truly media of mass communication, firmly established in the everyday lives of most people. The
potential they had for influencing the public mood was evident to
all – except, it would seem, the nation's leaders. Chamberlain even
spoke of closing the BBC down altogether, as a needless waste of
resources. This blind spot in the Prime Minister's knowledge of the
world stands in sharp contrast to the great importance attached in
Germany to the manipulation of popular feelings through mass
communication.[34] While the creation of the MoI was an essential
administrative preliminary, therefore, to the use of propaganda as
a means of sustaining civilian morale, this was one of the least well-
developed aspects of the Government's pre-war preparations.

The view from below

There can be no doubt that in 1939 the people, in contrast to their
predecessors in 1914, had a fairly clear idea of what a major war
would be like. The main source of their enlightenment was the cinema. Between the wars cinema became truly 'modern', that is, films
had sound, colour and the verisimilitude of twenty-four frames per
second. Since a large majority of the population had acquired the
habit of going to the cinema at least once a week, the newsreels
they saw there were a source of their knowledge of the world to
rival that of newspapers. When images were shown of the aerial
destruction of modern cities like Barcelona, Guernica or Shanghai,
it was not difficult for the millions who saw them to imagine comparable havoc in, say, Birmingham or Glasgow. The impression
conveyed was that nowhere was safe from the worst that modern
war could bring. Margery Allingham, writing in 1941, expressed it
thus: 'we had heard about Spain and seen horrifying newsreels from
China and we had no illusions whatever about the value of the
aeroplane as an offensive weapon'.[35] But newsreels were not the only
film source of understandings about modern war. As if newsreels

left too much to the imagination, film producers took to making feature films that depicted future war as Armageddon. The first of these, Maurice Elvey's *High Treason* (1929) has war beginning with a surprise air attack on London in 1940. Exactly the same scenario was used in the film version of H. G. Wells's 1933 novel *The Shape of Things to Come,* made under the title *Things to Come,* by Alexander Korda and William Cameron Menzies in 1936. In its opening sequence, 'motorcyclists surge across the screen, the roar of planes is heard overhead, and though we never see the planes their bombs bring destruction to the busy streets as searchlights vainly probe the sky. The panic and devastation ends with a slow and eloquent track into the body of a child buried in the rubble.'[36]

Wells's novel was merely the best known of a large body of popular books about future war that appeared in the 1930s. Some of the titles indicate the content and tone: *The Air War of 1936, The Gas War of 1940, The Poison War, War upon Women, Menace, Air Reprisal, Four Days' War.* The first of these was written in 1932 by a German writer, Robert Knauss, but significantly it was immediately translated into French and English and sold well in francophone and anglophone countries. In this tale Paris is the scene of destruction and the attacker is Britain. The RAF is described launching a daylight raid on the French capital, unloading with pinpoint accuracy 700 tons of HE, 3,000 incendiary bombs, and ten tons of mustard gas. The Eiffel Tower crashes across the Seine, the Gare du Nord is obliterated, all services stop – water, electricity, gas, telephones, Métro – and all public buildings are left in ruins. The defences are ineffectual and the raiders return intact to their bases. In similar vein, the 1931 novel *The Gas War of 1940* by Stephen Miles depicted the effects of a massive attack on London:

> And then, in a moment, the lights of London vanished, as if blotted out by a gigantic extinguisher. And in the dark streets the burned and wounded, bewildered and panic-stricken, fought and struggled like beasts, scrambling over the dead and dying alike, until they fell and were in turn trodden underfoot by the ever-increasing multitudes about them.[37]

That the lurid depictions of film and print took hold in the popular imagination is amply borne out in contemporary testimony and subsequent recollection. Edward Blishen recalled his own vision of future war:

... the vision we all had then. It was a vision built up from reality partly – from Guernica – but also from the film of H. G. Wells's *Shape of Things to Come*. We all knew what war would be, the moment it was declared: the fleets, the endless fleets of bombers throbbing into our skies, the cities exploding, the instant anarchy. Life would become an instant horror film. They wouldn't know how to bury the dead.[38]

Margery Allingham, admitting to imaginative excess, set down a similar vision at the time: 'We expected London to be razed in a week, and I know my own private fear was the idiotic notion that a terrorised city population would spread out like rings in a puddle all over the Home Counties, bringing fear and quarrels and chaos with it.'[39] Writing a little shamefacedly at the end of the day war broke out, writer George Beardmore recorded in his diary:

It would be impossible to convey the sense of utter panic with which we heard the first Air Raid warning, ten minutes after the outbreak of war. We had all taken *The Shape of Things to Come* too much to heart, also the dire prophecies of scientists, journalists, and even politicians of the devastation and disease that would follow the first air raid. We pictured St. Paul's in ruins and a hole in the ground where the Houses of Parliament had stood.[40]

Harold Macmillan was one of the politicians to whom Beardmore and other informed and intelligent people like him listened. Macmillan recalled the apocalyptic vision that characterized the thinking of people in his circle: 'We thought of air warfare in 1938 rather as people think of nuclear war today.'[41] This was the sort of sentiment that drove a former First World War general, F. P. Crozier, to become a pacifist, convinced that defence had become useless and that German bombers could reduce England to chaos and starvation in a few weeks.[42]

Mass-Observation monitored public expectations of war in the last two years of peace. It found that despite the rumours of war, the recurrent international crises and the visible evidence of ARP, there was only low expectation that war would come soon, or ever, and widespread cynicism about government information. People had a fairly good idea of what a future war would be like, as depicted in books and films, but their attitude towards the prospect was not so much fearful as resigned, or as Mass-Observation summed up, 'a mixture of fatalism and apathy', characterized by remarks like, 'If your number's on it', and 'What can *I* do?'[43] These findings were rather at variance with official worries about mass hysteria; they suggest, perhaps, that the Government and the chattering classes were over-reacting and that the wider public was more phlegmatic. They nevertheless gave no cause for optimism about public morale. Apathy and fatalism might not be the stuff from which mass panic was made, but their very opposites would be needed for the successful pursuit of victory.

When the imagining came to an end and Neville Chamberlain reluctantly took his country into war there remained many uncertainties about what lay ahead. Much had been accomplished to prepare for the worst contingencies; but the preparations had come late and were rushed, and whether they would be enough to prevent the collapse of civilian morale was debatable. Above all, until the test of war itself was experienced there could be no knowing whether the various forces that made the British look a less unanimous people than in the earlier conflict, would nullify the preparations and bring inertia, implosion and defeat.

Notes

1 In 1932–33 defence expenditure was £103m, representing 12.9 per cent of the budget; the corresponding figures for 1936–37 were £86.7m and 33.4 per cent. By 1939 the annual estimates were for a total of £942m of which £250m was for defence (plus £380m to be found by borrowing). See W. A. Morton, *British Finance 1930–1940* (University of Wisconsin Press,1943), p. 286.

2 In 1930 bombers had a range of about 800 miles and a maximum payload of 5,000 lbs. Britain's most advanced bomber in 1939, the Wellington, had a range of 2,200 miles and a payload of 29,000 lbs. D. Richards, *The Hardest Victory: RAF Bomber Command in the Second World War* (Hodder & Stoughton, 1994), p. 14.

3 T. H. O'Brien, *Civil Defence* (HMSO, 1955), p. 282. The official belief that war would begin with a massed air assault on London is also reflected in the plans made for radio transmissions, whereby the enemy would be denied the possibility of using them as guide beams for bombers.

4 Hansard, 11 July 1927, vol. 208, col. 1813.

5 Cited in T. Cook, 'Perception of Gas Warfare, 1915–1939', *War and Society*, vol. 18, 1, 2000.

6 O'Brien, *Civil Defence*, p. 39.

7 Memorandum, 1928. Cited in T. Harrisson, *Living Through the Blitz* (Collins, 1976), pp. 20–1.

8 See I. F. Clarke, *Voices Prophesying War: Future Wars 1763–3749* (Oxford University Press, 1992) p. 155.

9 Hansard, 28 September 1934, vol. 295, col. 859.

10 R. Titmuss, *Problems of Social Policy* (HMSO, 1950), p. 20.

11 S. Possony, *Tomorrow's War – its Planning, Management and Cost* (1938). See M. Pearton, *The Knowledgeable State: Diplomacy, War and Technology Since 1830* (Burnett Books, 1982), pp. 200–4.

12 Lord Woolton, *Memoirs* (Cassell 1959), pp. 143–4.

13 For example, Henri Barbusse, *Under Fire* (1916). These were to be followed in the post-war years by numerous other anti-war books, e.g. Erich Maria Remarque, *All Quiet on the Western Front* (1929), Ernest Hemingway, *A Farewell to Arms* (1929), R. C. Sherriff, *Journey's End* (1929), Siegfried Sassoon, *The Complete Memoirs of George Sherston* (1937), Robert Graves, *Goodbye to All That* (1929), Philip Noel-Baker, *Hawkers of Death* (1934), C. S. Forester, *The General* (1936).

14 Harold Nicolson, *Diaries and Letters 1939–45* (Collins,1967), p. 52.

15 Hugh Dalton, *The Fateful Years* (Frederick Muller, 1957), p. 200.

16 See J. Bardon, *A History of Ulster* (The Blackstaff Press, 1992), pp. 552–5.

17 O'Brien, *Civil Defence*, pp. 95–6.

18 Hansard, 15 November 1937, vol. 329, col. 42.

19 Report of the Committee on Evacuation, Cmd. 5837, p. 3.

20 Harrisson, *Living Through the Blitz*, p. 22–3.

21 O'Brien, *Civil Defence*, p. 25.

22 *Ibid.*, pp. 362–3.

23 Herbert Morrison, Home Secretary in Churchill's Government, defended the cautious nature of pre-war provision: 'if everything had been done before the war broke out, any government would have been accused of waste had war not come'. H. Morrison, *An Autobiography* (Odhams, 1960), p. 185.

24 Woolton, *Memoirs* , pp. 143–4.

25 Strictly speaking, it was not a completely bomb-free time: there was a bombing raid on cruisers in the Firth of Forth and people living in Dunfermline and Edinburgh experienced shrapnel falls.

26 See D. C. Watt, *Too Serious a Business* (Temple Smith, 1975), p. 73.

27 R. J. Minney, *The Private Papers of Hore-Belisha* (Collins, 1960), pp. 152–4.

28 Harrisson, *Living Through the Blitz*, p. 31.

29 O'Brien, *Civil Defence*, p. 155.

30 Titmuss, *Problems of Social Policy*, p. 19.

31 Report of Home Publicity Sub-Committee, 27 September 1938, INF 1/20.

32 Memorandum by Stephen King-Hall, September 1938, INF 1/713.

33 I. McLaine, *Ministry of Morale: Home Front Morale and the Ministry of Information in World War II* (Allen & Unwin, 1979), p. 14.

34 The lack of urgency shown by the Government in organizing information services fits uneasily with the claim that is sometimes made that it had already in the 1930s naively accepted the assumptions of some sociologists about the susceptibility of the attitudes and behaviour of the masses in modern society to manipulation by the mass communications media. See, for example, J. Curran, 'Broadcasting and the Blitz', in J. Curran and J. Seaton, *Power Without Responsibility: the Press and Broadcasting in Britain* (Routledge, 1985), pp. 149–50.

35 M. Allingham, *The Oaken Heart: the Story of an English Village at War* (Michael Joseph, 1941), p. 42.

36 J. Richards, *The Age of the Dream Palace* (Routledge, 1984), pp. 281–2.

37 Clarke, *Voices Prophesying War*, p. 159.

38 E. Blishen, *A Cackhanded War* (Thames & Hudson, 1972), p. 11.

39 Allingham, *The Oaken Heart*, p. 51.

40 G. Beardmore, *Civilians at War: Journals 1938–46* (Oxford University Press, 1986), p. 34.

41 H. Macmillan, *Winds of Change* (Macmillan, 1956), p. 522.

42 G. Orwell, Review of Crozier's *The Men I Have Killed*, *New Statesman and Nation*, 28 August 1937.

43 Harrisson, *Living Through the Blitz*, pp. 26–7.

2

War experienced:
September 1939–May 1941

THE HOLOCAUST did not happen. Although air raid sirens sounded in London within minutes of the expiry of Britain's ultimatum to Germany, it proved a false alarm. And the falseness of the alarm persisted. For a full eight months, until the Anglo-French expedition to Norway, apart from isolated engagements at sea, both sides held their fire. No massed flights of German bombers appeared above Britain's cities to batter the citizens into submission. The 'Phoney War', as it was called, was a big anti-climax, an absolute confounding of everyone's expectations. If there was a problem of public morale it was nothing like that anticipated and prepared for. The Phoney War turned out to be but the first of four phases in the evolution of the problem, each phase having its distinct characteristics. After the eight months of relative inactivity there came a period of momentous events: the evacuation of the British Expeditionary Force at Dunkirk, the collapse of France, the threat of invasion, the Battle of Britain. This was followed by a period from September 1940 to May 1941 when London and several provincial cities were subjected to heavy bombing and the threat of invasion persisted. Finally there was the period from mid-1941 to the end of the war in which the threat of invasion receded, the bombing became more patchy and intermittent and the war took on the character of a long haul to victory. In each of these phases the nature of the pressures on civilian morale was substantially different. This meant that there was a mismatch between much of what was prepared and the needs revealed by the actuality of war. And this in turn produced an evolution of official perceptions of the nature of the problem of morale, and of the best ways of addressing it.

The Phoney War

Since the starting gun was in effect fired by Britain it was possible
to ensure that the first phase of morale management went more or
less according to plan: the evacuation between 1–3 September of
one and a half million *bouches inutiles* from the danger areas to the
reception areas. Although this number was far fewer than the Government had hoped for, the idea of making the scheme compulsory
was discounted as likely to be counter-productive for civilian morale. It was at least carried out in an orderly, organized way, without any suggestion of a panic rush. None the less, in various ways
the evacuation did turn out to be a source of pressure on civilian
morale. Official propaganda was naturally positive about the whole
operation. Short documentary films made for general release showed
the evacuees settling down happily among welcoming hosts in the
countryside, enjoying the change of scene and at the same time
gaining an educationally enriching experience. The attempt to reassure was not, however, sufficient to allay the emotional strains
experienced at both ends of the operation. Three groups of people
were involved: the evacuees themselves – schoolchildren with their
teachers and infants with their mothers; close relatives of the evacuees who remained in the cities or were in the forces; and the country dwellers on whom the evacuees were billeted.

Much has been written on the evacuation from the standpoint
of those who went, the greater part of it emphasizing the traumatic
aspects of the experience. Pregnant women and mothers with small
children typically felt at first that separation from home and spouse
was a small price to pay for the safety they had gained. But fitting
in with life in the country was often difficult. Apart from the problems of sharing domestic facilities – problems that would have arisen
anywhere – the country presented special difficulties for the
townsperson. To those used to the town's readily available markets
and shops and the opportunities for leisure pursuits such as cinemas, dance halls and dog tracks, the country could appear an empty,
lonely and essentially boring place. Its social life could seem strange
and inaccessible and the inhabitants equally so. Had the bombing
of the cities actually occurred these refugees from the slaughter would
doubtless have counted their blessings. As it was, the military inactivity of the Phoney War made their continued residence in the so-

called 'safe areas' – everywhere was safe now – seem futile and the hardship of separation from home and family more difficult to accept.

City schoolchildren were no less subject to the problems of coping with the separation from home and family and of fitting into a strange and in many ways unfriendly environment. While it is true that they were typically in the company of the familiar classmates and teachers of their city school and were thereby spared an absolute rupture of their previous situation, there were cases where siblings were billeted in different houses and in some cases in different villages. And children's well-known ability to adapt to change should not lead us to accept at face value the official perception that the evacuees had survived the move without emotional trauma. The evacuation scheme was put together by civil servants who typically came from that section of society that chose as a matter of course to send its own children away to boarding schools from the age of six or seven and for whom, therefore, the notion of homesickness was merely a rite of passage of no lasting importance. There were in some instances good reasons why a minority of evacuee children continued to feel miserable. In some places the billeting process was managed by the local authority in a crude and insensitive manner. Tales were heard of hosts ranging the assembled children and choosing according to their need for unpaid help on the farm or in the house. A relationship that began in the atmosphere of the cattle market was unlikely to prove warm and loving. It was also one of the ways in which separation of siblings was sure to occur. If exploitation was the lot of some unlucky children, there was worse in store for yet others. In testimony only recently given it has become clear that perhaps as many as 10 per cent of child evacuees were physically or sexually abused by their hosts.[1]

Numerous other testimonies confirm that for the large majority of evacuees the experience was a happy one, and one that they could look back on without real regret. Even for these, however, it was a testing time, a time when their emotional life was subject to strain. That in itself was a consideration in the morale of the nation as a whole. More specifically, though, it had significance for the state of mind of those on whom the war effort more obviously depended. For all the peace of mind that came to war workers and service personnel from putting their children far from the dangers of air raids, sending them away was often a hard decision to make and to live with afterwards. Richard Brown, an Ipswich draughtsman, had resisted the Government's injunction to evacuate in September 1939 but by the following May he was agonizing over the pros and cons: 'It's a fearful predicament ... On the whole it might be best for them to go but I shall miss them terribly ... We'll both feel pretty sick if the kids get hurt but there are so many drawbacks to them going.'[2] Mothers, especially, suffered from the physical separation from their children. In an age when most women with school-age children did not take paid work outside the home, the departure of the children robbed many of their sense of purpose in life. There was, too, the fear that the separation would cause the children to become alienated from them. For millions of people the war brought loneliness; for women whose children were old enough to be evacuated and whose husbands were young enough to be called up there was a doubly deep well of loneliness, compounding the anxiety they already had about the wellbeing of the absentees.[3] Serving husbands, for their part, could feel that the peace of mind that came from knowing the children were safe was offset to some extent by their wives' loneliness and sense of abandonment. Since participation in the evacuation was entirely voluntary, it was open to those who could not bear its stresses to reunite mother, home and children. But it was not an easy solution. As Richard Brown recorded, the price of keeping the family together was exposure to life-threatening danger; it was part of the stress of war that there were often no easy solutions to the problems it presented.

So far examination of the stresses of evacuation has concentrated on the evacuees and their families. As strong a case can be made for arguing that it was equally stressful for the people who found themselves accommodating the escaping thousands in their homes in the reception areas. For the visitors were frequently difficult to provide for. Hosts who were expecting to act as parent substitutes to one or two children aged between five and ten might find themselves landed with a pair of strapping, streetwise teenagers, or even with a young mother, infants in tow and requiring a share of the kitchen facilities. Sometimes there were difficulties arising out of differences in social mores. It was inevitable that many of the evacuees were from the poorest section of the population, coming as they did mainly from the inner parts of the large industrial cities. Equally inevitable was the fact that in the reception areas the houses that were most

likely to have spare rooms belonged to the middle classes. The social mismatching that occurred, therefore, was mainly that of poor
city children and affluent rural hosts. Newspapers were soon full of
horror stories about the intolerable experiences of country hosts
trying to cope with dirty and foul-mouthed slum children unused
to parental control, or with complaining, slatternly young mothers
who did not take the toilet training of their infant children seriously. It is no surprise, then, that in the rural areas the evacuation
proved to be a potent source of resentment that was at odds with
the official campaign to promote social solidarity as the engine of
the war effort. An intrinsic element in this resentment was the compulsory nature of the burden placed on the reception areas. Once
its area was so designated, a Local Authority was under an obligation to identify the houses which had 'unoccupied' space, and billeting officers had the powers to insist that unwilling owners take
in evacuees. There was also a perception that the billeting system
was not fair. A Mass-Observation diarist in Yorkshire cited the case
of a Baildon widow from the previous war who was fined for refusing evacuees because she needed to supplement her meagre pension
by taking in boarders, whereas wealthy people with large houses in
the district had no evacuees billeted on them.[4] But while it is true
that in places people used influence with the billeting officer to
avoid their obligation, most spare accommodation was in fact req-
uisitioned for the refugees, and the rural householders had to endure the consequences. It is perhaps inevitable that the
uncooperativeness of some has bulked larger in the record than the
selfless generosity of others: a five-bedroom house without evacuees is conspicuous and it would take few such cases in a district to
create a misleading impression of the extent of evasion. This has
led some commentators to claim that the evacuation, far from presenting a people united in a common purpose, revealed a society
riven by class antagonism deep enough to override patriotic duty.[5]
A less harsh judgement would take account of the mitigating factors: the very real lifestyle adaptations that the evacuation often
involved, the numerous practical problems that had not been fore-
seen and, above all, the fact that it took place at a time when the
absence of bombing made the whole exercise seem unnecessary.
And there were aspects of the evacuation that can be counted as
positive morale factors. One such was the role of the women's

organizations. In the reception areas members of the Women's Institute, the Townswomen's Guild, the Women's Voluntary Services
and others were active in dealing with the practical problems thrown
up by the evacuation. Their response to the call was both an indicator of the high morale of a significant number of women and,
through example, itself a source of good morale in others. A Barrow in Furness housewife, Nella Last, who kept a diary for Mass-
Observation, recorded on 5 September 1939: 'I went to the WVS
Centre today and was amazed at the huge crowd ... every table
was crowded with eager workers.'[6] This in turn had an invigorat-
ing effect on the organizations and brought them numerous other
wartime roles that made them a continuing valuable resource at a
time of labour scarcity.[7]

Some of the negative effects of the evacuation on civilian morale
were softened by the partial reversal of the exodus from the cities
that began when the expected bombing failed to occur. Families
were reunited and reluctant hosts were relieved of their troublesome visitors. The drift back to the cities was never total, however,
and further waves of evacuation took place when the air raids finally came in the autumn of 1940, lasting with varying intensity
and location until early 1945. Evacuation, therefore, remained a
facet of the war, an ever-present element in the bundle of stresses
that marked life on the home front.

Large though it bulked in the lives of those participating, the evacuation was the experience of only a minority of the civilian population, a minority even of those 'eligible'. For everyone else the Phoney
War brought the least expected of problems: boredom. The nation
was at 'action stations', but the action refused to start. Instead,
while the guns stayed silent an avalanche of official regulations
descended on the nation, bringing with them restrictions and inconveniences that would have been more tolerable had there been a
real sense that the country faced a crisis. As Harold Nicolson, an
MP with a post in the Ministry of Information, recorded in his
diary: 'We have all the apparatus of war without war conditions.
The result is general disillusion and grumbling, from which soil
defeatism may grow.'[8] He wrote thus because he knew that the
fighting war would eventually come and he worried about what in
the meanwhile was happening to the nation's mental readiness for

it. But for all Nicolson's pessimism, a Gallup poll in late September seemed to show a public mood that was determined enough: 89 per cent gave an unequivocal 'Yes' to the question 'Should we continue to fight till Hitler goes?' and 84 per cent were confident that Britain would win.[9]

Of all the restrictions on the daily life of the citizen none was more irksome than those imposed by the blackout: Mass-Observation's observer panel found in November 1939 that the blackout was felt by the public to be by far the most inconvenient aspect of the war; many more grumbles were recorded about the blackout than about anything else. Harold Nicolson wrote in February: 'When I ask my constituents what they really mind most about the war it is always the blackout which comes first in their list of evils.'[10] The attempt to deny a would-be raider any guide to his target entailed a more or less total absence of lighting in public places and the concealment from outside view of all interior lights. Traffic lights were reduced to small coloured crosses, vehicle lights to pinpoints, with adverse effects on road safety. Every householder was caught up in the nightly routine of ensuring that his house was fully 'blacked out'; failure to do so was more than likely to draw on him the anger of the air raid warden and the neighbours, and persistent offending to result in a summons to the magistrates court. The blackout's effect on social life was significant, especially once the winter closed in. Activities that involved travelling fell off and people's leisure was more confined to home-based pursuits; for the darkness not only made accidents on the roads and footways more likely – Gallup found that 18 per cent of adults suffered some injury in the course of the first winter of the war – it tended to make people feel vulnerable to attack by thieves taking advantage of the improved cover. Certain activities and traditions had to be suspended altogether: fireworks and bonfires on Guy Fawkes Night, fairground lights, Christmas illuminations, evening services in churches whose windows could not be satisfactorily blacked out. In the continued absence of bombing the whole blackout system seemed increasingly pointless. It was partly in response to a sense of public exasperation, therefore, that the Government ordered a relaxation of the regulations. From the end of the year 'glimmer' lighting was permitted at crossroads and junctions, and vehicles were allowed to use masked headlights. Low level lighting – not enough to read by – was restored to train carriages and pedestrians were permitted to carry dimmed hand torches. Shops, until this point denied lighted display windows, henceforth could show their wares under a faint, bluish lighting. Most of these concessions were conditional on there being no air raid; the minute an alert was sounded they were to be suspended. Considering how matters might have turned out after war was declared, the blackout should have been a bearable burden. But people seem quickly to have taken the lack of raids for granted; paradoxically, morale was impaired not by a fear of bombing but by the very apparatus set up to allay such fear. Resentment against the blackout extended to its enforcers, the air raid wardens, and to civil defence workers more generally. At the start of the war, there were one and a half million men and women in the civil defence services. Only a quarter of these were paid full-timers but this did not spare the three-quarters who were unpaid volunteers from the resentment shown towards their paid colleagues. Doubtless there were a proportion among them of self-important individuals officiously revelling in the chance to order their fellow citizens about, but the real problem was the apparent redundancy of the whole civil defence set up. As long as the real war held off, a gap yawned between what had been prepared for and what was happening. With civil defence workers being openly jeered at and some newspapers suggesting that the service was a refuge for people trying to escape conscription, the Government judiciously cut back the numbers of paid workers.[11] It was worried about doing so, nevertheless. The Home Secretary, Sir John Anderson, thought the cutbacks might be interpreted as an admission that the civil defence programme had overestimated the risks. 'At the present moment', he warned the Cabinet, 'public opinion is only too ready to discount the risks of large scale air attack, merely because no such attack has yet been delivered; and unless active steps are taken to counter this spirit of false optimism we may well find that, by the time the blow falls, we shall have dissipated the resources and broken the morale which we have built up to resist it.'[12]

Government action or inaction was behind other sources of public discontent in these early months. Mass-Observation discovered that the matters that people most complained about (after the blackout) were prices, food and transport, in that order of importance.[13] An excess of demand over supply quickly appeared for a wide range of

goods, more as a consequence of customer hoarding and commercial opportunism than a reordering of production and import priorities (since the Chamberlain Government was slow to make a
start on the latter). Price inflation naturally followed, as did shortages and queuing. As has been shown in Chapter 1, preparations –
notably plans for rationing – had been made before the war to
prevent this happening. However, the Government hesitated. The
ration books were issued to everyone in September 1939 but no
starting date for the scheme was set; petrol alone was subjected to
rationing. In late October the Cabinet discussed the possibility of
introducing limited food rationing. Some members were for it but
those against prevailed, among them the First Lord of the Admiralty, Winston Churchill, who argued that it could damage morale.
There were signs in the press of all political shades, he observed,
that public opinion was becoming increasingly critical of governmental control and interference with the liberty of the individual. It
was open to doubt whether the governmental machine could operate the rationing arrangements without creating resentment and
unrest more serious even than if there were no rationing.[14] But a
Gallup poll in November showed that 60 per cent of the public
were in favour of food rationing. It was only after four months of
free-for-all that the Government got wind of public discontent
(which, incidentally, the newspapers failed properly to report) and
reluctantly tiptoed away from laissez-faire by introducing rationing on bacon, butter and sugar.

Rationing also lay at the heart of the transport problem. For
those with cars (about 10 per cent) the allowance of enough petrol
for only two hundred miles per month was a tiresome constraint on
social activity. Since this minority came mainly from the articulate
middle classes, who had greater access to the media, its views tended
to be heard more at the time and to survive disproportionately in
the record. But when most people travelled it was by public transport. Here the effect of the war was simply to reduce the number of
buses and trains available. Conscription reduced the workforce of
busdrivers, conductors and maintenance workers; the conversion
of the motor industry to the production of military vehicles and
armaments virtually ended the manufacture of new buses and spare
parts; rubber and petrol became scarce commodities – for the civilian sector, at least. As a result, city services were reduced by the

removal of some routes and the ending of late-evening buses; in central London alone eight hundred buses had been withdrawn by December 1939. In the rural areas some services were withdrawn altogether. On the railways it was much the same story: the Government took into its control the four main railway companies and the London Passenger Transport Board even before war was declared, signalling the important strategic role it envisaged for the network. From the start trains were to have as their priority the servicing of the needs of the military and the war economy. Civilian passengers had to make do with what was left after those needs had been met. The knock-on effect of all this in terms of queuing, overcrowding and curtailment of social life constituted one of the more depressing features of wartime life as it was experienced by most people.

Some compensation ought to have been found in greater availability of work for the unemployed, since by normal reckoning war put labour at a premium. But so slow was the process of reshaping the economy for war that unemployment actually rose in the early months as workers were laid off in trades like tourism and building, which were immediately affected by the state of war. Work traditionally done by women was particularly badly affected by this contraction. The total of unemployed did not begin to fall until March 1940 and was still above a million in April. In addition, therefore, to all its other effects the Phoney War brought financial anxiety to thousands of families. And to make this harder to bear, the forces of nature conspired to deliver the severest winter since 1895.

It was one of the paradoxes of the Phoney War that its very unexciting, inactive character itself became a threat to popular morale. When relief and gratitude at being spared the forecast horrors ought reasonably to have been the prevailing sentiment, instead there was a perverse sense of irritation at the continued disruption and constraints. To a large degree the Government itself was to blame for this souring of the public mood. Although it appeared to recognize the importance of persuading the people of the necessity for its wartime policies and getting them to participate actively in the war effort, in practice it was incompetent at both. The citizen's role in the Emergency was set out in the numerous public information leaflets that went to every household and the

BBC broadcast a steady stream of public announcements. But news about what was happening in the war was hard to come by and no attempt was made to set out Britain's war aims in a comprehensible way. The censorship reduced the BBC and the press to repackaging the frustratingly uninformative releases of the Ministry of Information and the service ministries. To the ordinary citizen the impression was given that one was regarded as a pawn in policies conceived by remote people who did not feel the need to explain them; one was simply expected to comply with a lot of inconvenient regulations and ask no questions. *Picture Post* expressed this 'you' and 'us' impression in a mocked-up photograph of a estate signboard carrying the words: 'Keep Out! This is a private war. The War Office, the Admiralty, the Air Ministry and the Ministry of Information are engaged in a war against the Nazis. They are on no account to be disturbed. Nothing is to be photographed. No one is to come near.'[15] The danger was that the official posture could erode any sense the public might have that it was 'their' war, that there was a national unity of purpose in the enterprise. Mass-Observation's Tom Harrisson thought that people's morale might easily deteriorate if their natural interest in the war was frustrated by official secrecy and obfuscation.[16] None the less, at this point Gallup found that 60 per cent of their respondents were satisfied with the Government's conduct of the war and only 18 per cent were dissatisfied. Chamberlain's support, 50 per cent before the outbreak of war, was at 68 per cent in November and 64 per cent in December. Four months later Mass-Observation was linking what it judged to be low public morale to the reluctance of the authorities to take the public into its confidence. People felt that the facts of the war were being held back from them and so they did not understand what was going on or what would happen in the short or long term about invasion, security, prices, jobs, and so on.[17]

In one department of government, at least, there were individuals who acknowledged the problem. A Ministry of Information adviser Professor Ifor Evans, who resigned from his position in October, warned in his last memorandum: 'If there is no major action on the Western Front and the war of what may be called the "mental blackout" proceeds, the enemy will attempt to destroy our morale at home in many ways.'[18] The Minister himself, Sir John Reith, worried that the British public had become a receptive culture

medium for the growth of rumours such as those planted by the
enemy's radio propagandist William Joyce ('Lord Haw-Haw'). He
believed there was much apathy and boredom among 'the less informed classes' and that there was a general feeling that individuals
did not count in the conduct of the war and that getting on with
normal life was the best thing to do.[19] Who better to inform the
'less-informed', it might be asked, than the Ministry of Information? The problem was that in this phase of the war the Ministry
was a troubled department. In order to carry out its brief of maintaining public morale it needed to be able to tell it what was happening. However, the true guardians of the news were the service
departments, and they took the view that the least the public knew
the better. The Ministry of Information was therefore as dependent
as anyone else on the miserly rations of hard news released by other
departments. Its misfortune was that it was blamed for the virtual
news blackout and so was sarcastically referred to in the Press as
the 'Ministry of Disinformation'.

By February, according to Mass-Observation, people were depressed, pessimistic and apathetic about the war and showed it by
leaving their gas masks at home (those still carrying them had declined to 5 or 6 per cent in London) and failing to observe the
blackout regulations strictly. 'War has settled into absolute dull-
ness, increasing pointlessness for the mass of people', it reported,
detecting that 'a new restlessness is setting in, a desire for something to happen, however unpleasant.'[20] As it happened something
unpleasant was indeed about to happen. Events in Europe brought
the eery suspense of the Phoney War to an end and, ironically,
brought simultaneous relief to the frustrated officials of the Ministry of Information.

The disruptions and inconveniences of the home front had not
brought out the best in the British people. But apathy did not mean
defeatism. While it is true that by January 1940 one in six adults
was listening regularly to Radio Hamburg, which put out propaganda in English, the broadcasts seemed to be having no discernible effect on their views or behaviour.[21] Nor were the various
anti-war groups such as the Communist Party, the British Union of
Fascists and the Independent Labour Party able to claim that they
had won new adherents in the eight months following the declaration of war, despite the increased level of their propaganda. In by-

elections in the period up to May 1941 none of the fifteen candidates from these parties were successful – most, indeed lost their deposits. Even in the first eight months of this period, when low morale theoretically gave opposition to the war its best chance, the anti-war platform failed to attract votes. The banning of the BUF and internment of its members in May 1940, moreover, had overwhelming public support.[22] As for the nationalist parties in Wales and Scotland, some progress was made in attracting votes in by-elections, culminating late in the war with the election of the Secretary of the SNP, Robert McIntyre, in Motherwell. It must be borne in mind, however, that wartime elections were peculiarly artificial affairs. The Conservative, Labour and Liberal parties had made an 'electoral truce' by which they agreed not to contest by-elections against the candidate of the party that held the seat at the start of the war. This left the way open for fringe parties to make a bigger impression on the electors than in peacetime. If the leaders of the SNP and Plaid Cymru were encouraged by the electoral progress they appeared to be making, therefore, it was to some extent illusory. In any event, there were no other indications among the Celts of sentiment that posed a potential threat to the war effort or any reason for the Government to judge that the patriotic commitment of the people in those regions was any different from that in the rest of the United Kingdom. It is true that the 'aggressively neutral' stance of the Soviet Union until June 1941 made the relatively stronger presence of the Communist Party in the industrial parts of Scotland and Wales a matter of anxious official observation. Home Intelligence received reports in 1940 that some industrial unrest was occurring in Scotland and that the communists were behind it. But after Clydeside was heavily bombed in March 1941, the reports concluded that industrial relations had actually improved. And once the Soviet Union had been attacked by Germany and was fighting for its very existence, there were no keener toilers for victory than the communists, wherever in the United Kingdom they lived. The vulnerability of Northern Ireland to enemy subversion was increased with the fall of France. In consequence four divisions of troops were stationed in the province to deter an incursion via the Republic. Anti-war 'incidents' began in the first days of the war and attacks by the IRA on the police continued on and off well into 1942. But the capture and internment of IRA activists by the Royal Ulster

Constabulary and the cooperation of the Irish government south of the border in doing likewise effectively suppressed IRA activity. Anxiety about the attitude of the civilian population towards the war subsided when it became clear that the IRA was not succeeding in exploiting the situation to increase its support. If anything, the shared experience of air raids in Belfast served to produce an unusual degree of communal harmony. Meanwhile, the war economy slowly began to make inroads into the high unemployment in the province, especially through new orders for the shipyards, aircraft factories and munitions makers; and 60,000 workers crossed over to Britain to take advantage of high wages in the war factories.[23] Like the other parts of the Celtic fringe, Northern Ireland, too, was a dog that did not bark.

If huge numbers of men had pleaded conscientious objection to military service, this might have been judged indicative of a generally poor spirit. But in the first age group to be called up only 2.2 per cent registered as conscientious objectors. And as the registrations continued, the proportion of objectors fell: 1.6 per cent in March, 0.6 per cent in June.[24] Nella Last noted the contrast in Barrow in Furness between the start of this war and the point in the previous one when conscription was introduced, when there was a 'mad stampede of boys and men to rush to the Shipyard and get under the "Vickers Umbrella", making them indispensable on munitions so they wouldn't be called up'.[25] While the soundings of public sentiment do record boredom and a degree of apathy, this had not translated into behaviour of a kind to cause real concern in official quarters that civilian morale was dangerously low. At no time in these months, moreover, was there any check to public confidence that the war would (eventually) be won. Looking back from the vantage point of May 1940, Mass-Observation judged that at the outset there had been overconfidence and strong belief in Chamberlain.[26] The failure of the Norway expedition in April–May dented these sentiments. It was the first real engagement with the enemy and it had been accompanied by both a sense of relief that the action was at last starting and a high expectation that it would be a triumph for British arms. Anglo-French forces were despatched too late: the Germans got wind of the plan and moved first, carrying out an air and sea operation that eluded Allied intelligence and ended in their occupation of Norway and Denmark. In the following three weeks, although landings were made in Norway and about half of the German fleet was destroyed or damaged, the Allies failed to dislodge the occupiers and the campaign had to be abandoned. This reverse was a shock to the nation, the more so because official reports on the campaign were optimistic almost to the end. 'The general feeling about this new phase of the war is optimistic', wrote journalist Mollie Panter-Downes for the transatlantic readers of the *New Yorker* on 21 April. 'People are delighted that Hitler has finally come out into the open, and say that if this is really the overture to his much heralded *Blitzkrieg*, so much the better.'[27] But the public were first buoyed up then let down. Hopes were deflated and doubts about Britain's strength were created. Moreover, the realization that they had been given misleading reports during the campaign undermined the people's confidence in official information and in the Press and the BBC.[28] As a Mass-Observation diarist lamented, 'The whole show is disheartening. You just have to forget it and be happy doing and talking about other things.'[29]

The Emergency – May–September 1940

The Norway setback heralded the start of a phase of momentous developments in the war that presented the utmost challenge to the national spirit. First, on 10 May, Hitler began his western offensive with an attack on the Low Countries. Then, following a confidence vote in the Commons – which he won, but not well enough – Chamberlain resigned and a coalition government was formed under Winston Churchill. In the next few days the Germans overran the Netherlands and most of Belgium and, soon after, the main western offensive on France was launched. Within six weeks German forces had again triumphed. France capitulated as the British Expeditionary Force first retreated and then, humiliatingly, pulled out altogether, leaving all its heavy equipment behind. The disaster cost 11,000 killed, 1,400 wounded and 41,000 missing or taken prisoner. Now without allies – apart from the Dominions of Australia, New Zealand, Canada and South Africa – Britain was threatened with invasion and defeat. The USA was sympathetic but unwilling to depart from its neutral stance. Soviet Russia was meanwhile expanding its control over the Baltic states, and Italy had joined the war on the German side. For their part, the Germans were more menacing than ever: not only had the superiority of their armed forces been convincingly demonstrated; their successes had brought them great gains in war booty, notably the entire military and economic resources of Britain's erstwhile ally France.

Throughout July and August the threat of invasion seemed very real. Government measures against the contingency in any case forced the matter onto public attention. A second wave of evacuation was effected; defences in the coastal areas were reinforced; road signs and railway station names were removed; pillboxes and gun mountings were erected on likely invasion routes; obstructions were placed on possible landing grounds such as sports fields and lowland pastures. A call went out to men aged between sixteen and sixty-five, who were not already in the armed forces, to volunteer for a new local defence force, to be called the Local Defence Volunteers. To every household a leaflet was sent telling people what to do in the event of an invasion. Meanwhile, stories of fifth columnists helping the German invaders in Denmark, Norway and the Netherlands led to the rounding up and internment of all enemy aliens living in Britain. The tension produced by this situation was relieved only in mid-September when the battle for control of the air space above the invasion route was fought and resolved in Britain's favour.

This period, bounded by the retreat in Norway and the Battle of Britain, ought by any calculation to have been a time of low civilian morale. Until the check of the Battle of Britain almost everything went Germany's way. In June, notwithstanding the loss through RAF bombing of the French fleet at Oran, the odds favoured Germany. Assuming Germany would attempt invasion, no objective observer either then, or for the following three months, could have expected Britain to survive. And yet, the evidence is that the people were in good heart during these months. Churchill's approval-rating was an unprecedented 88 per cent, according to a Gallup poll taken in July. There were some fluctuations in the public mood, but the overall picture is of a nation apparently undismayed by setback and committed to resistance in a spirit of optimism about ultimate victory.

Norway should have prepared public opinion for the events in the Low Countries. Even so, the ease with which the Germans overcame the defenders was shocking. 'It must be remembered', Home Intelligence reported, 'that the defence of the Low Countries had been continually built up in the press ... Not one person in a thousand could visualise the Germans breaking through into France.'[30] But Mollie Panter-Downes reported that the popular mood in London during the week of the invasion of the Low Countries was calm and cheerful and in the following weeks, as the unremittingly depressing war news came in, she reiterated her impression.[31] Writer Frances Partridge's diary entry for 10 May, at the start of the western Blitzkrieg, confirmed the almost bracing effect of the news: 'Now it's going to start in real earnest – and it's almost a relief, as if one had lain for ages on the operating table and at last the surgeon was going to begin.'[32] A very concrete indication of the public's state of mind was the remarkable response to the appeal for recruits for the Local Defence Volunteers, made by the Secretary of State for War, Anthony Eden, on 14 May, the day that the Dutch army capitulated. Within a day over 250,000 men had offered their services. By the end of June the LDV was 500,000 strong, all of them unpaid volunteers. A week later the Minister of Supply, Herbert Morrison, added his own appeal. He asked workers to 'Go to it', and they went to it with a will. Many factories went over to seven-day working. Shifts of ten or twelve hours became routine in whole sectors of war industry. And, it should be noted, all this was achieved without the Government needing to resort to coercive measures. In harmony with this mood, there was a big decline in time lost through industrial disputes, showing a restraint among workers that extended even to the miners; 1940 turned out to be the year in which fewer days were lost to industrial disputes since records began in 1893.[33] Mass-Observation recorded that 'everywhere people were eagerly waiting for directions. They were itching for something to do.' As a young woman told them: 'There is no denying that there is a great fount of energy in this country, seething and boiling to get on with things. I do hope that Churchill is today going to announce a *real* mobilisation of our resources. People are dying for it.'[34] In the face of these behavioural indications of a rallying public spirit, the Ministry of Information, on the contrary, appeared to be worried about civilian morale. On 18 May Home Intelligence reported that 'public morale is at a low ebb'; a week later it expressed concern about the apparent spread of rumours that the royal family was about to leave for Canada and that the Government planned to move there, too, as soon as the enemy started to invade. 'Rumour during the last few days has tended to emphasize some aspect of our own feebleness and futility', it noted, concluding that 'This kind of rumour is clearly unhealthy, for it is an unconscious reflection of privately held opinion.'[35] And yet, at the same time demands were coming in from many quarters for the restriction of racing and other sports, because they used resources like petrol and food.[36] In the same spirit was the overwhelmingly positive response, a month or so later, to the appeal of the Minister of Aircraft Production, Lord Beaverbrook, for the donation of aluminium cooking pots, which he said could be melted down to help build war-winning fighter planes for the RAF, at that time engaging in the first rounds of the Battle of Britain. Beaverbrook was also the skilful exploiter, if not the originator, of the Spitfire Funds, another manifestation of the desire of ordinary people to make an active contribution to national defence. Everyone understood that Britain's survival depended on the building of more planes. The Spitfire Funds enabled people to, as it were, build their own. All over the country the price of a Spitfire (£5,000) was set as a target by individual communities such as a town or a profession and in this way thousands of Spitfires were 'built'. Smaller units of people such as a school or a factory set themselves to raise on their own the price of a Spitfire wing, body, or smaller part. By April 1941 more than £13m had been donated. Here was an answer to the pessimists who thought the war was all but over. As Mollie Panter-Downes noted: 'Belatedly, this country appears to be asking for and getting the self-sacrificing gestures of everyday life which the totalitarian governments have enforced on their people for years.'[37]

A Gallup poll taken at the end of May found that only 3 per cent of the British people thought Britain might lose the war. Writing in his diary during the week of the fall of France, Richard Brown was grim but optimistic: 'We are in for a rough time but we shall weather it.'[38] Mass-Observation, charting the fluctuations in public optimism in May and early June, noted that the German successes did have a depressing effect by raising fears of bombing, invasion and even defeat.[39] Conversations overheard in Bolton in mid-June included some despairing and defeatist remarks: 'It looks black, doesn't it?', 'We don't seem to have a chance', 'It won't be long now. We are in a bad way', 'I don't see what can be done ... it's no use throwing away a lot of lives when there is no hope', 'I bet the King and Queen are packing to go if they've not gone already ... I bet the Government's ready to fly, too', 'There's no doubt we shall be exterminated'.[40] By the end of June the ratio of pessimists to optimists was 2.33:1. A 25-year-old architect told a Mass-Observer as France surrendered: 'Someone said to me a month ago – the trouble with the English people is they never learn when they are beaten. I'm afraid that virtue is going to cost us everything. We won't give up till England is destroyed and to what end? In the long run I think it would be wiser to absorb Hitlerism and convert it.'[41]

But the dips in optimism were typically short-lived, and by mid-July, when there was a lull in the flow of bad news, the ratio was 0.26:1.[42] And even among the pessimists there were those whose stance was pugnacious, like the fishfrier who told a Mass-Observer: 'Myself, I passionately want us to go on fighting. Of course, I have not been under a bombing attack or been in a war area. That might alter my tune. But I cannot conceive of us laying down our arms.'[43] Most people did not even entertain the idea of seeking terms with Germany; approval of the idea of discussing peace terms had in fact peaked at 29 per cent in February. Even as Mass-Observation picked up pessimistic resonances in Bolton they were coming across other citizens – about 50 per cent, it was estimated – who contemplated fighting on alone with confidence: 'There won't be any COs now', 'I tell you it's alright ... we shall hold him.'[44] Nella Last, who had frequently recorded her dread of what the war held in store, admitted, after reading the accounts of the Dunkirk evacuation: 'The story made me feel part of something that was undying and never old ... somehow I felt everything to be worthwhile, and I felt glad I was of the same race as the rescuers and the rescued.'[45] More impressive still was the demeanour of people who really were under attack. In the first week of June Dover came within range of German shellfire from Boulogne. Bombardments took place daily. Charles Ritchie, a Canadian diplomat recorded his impressions of a visit to the town:

> the life of the town is going on just the same. We could see the groups of old ladies coming out of church after eleven o'clock service and standing for a minute to chat in the sun ... Two little girls were shrilly calling to each other from their bicycles as they rode in and out of the small

gardens in front of a row of houses at the foot of the great bluff of cliff behind the docks.[46]

Evidence of high morale in the early summer of 1940 is not hard to come by. The examples offered here might be multiplied many-fold from the contemporary record. Some features of the period, however, jarr with the general picture – enough to lead some commentators to suggest that behind the steadfast equanimity of the people at this time of crisis there was an undertow of 'fear and paranoia bordering on panic'.[47] The evidence relates to the internment of enemy aliens, the spread of rumour, and the scare about spies and a 'Fifth Column'.

There were about 80,000 German or Austrian nationals living in Britain of whom 600 or so were thought dangerous and were therefore interned at the beginning of the war. A further 9,000 were subjected to movement restrictions. The remainder, considered harmless, remained free and unrestricted. In June, as France fell and the number of enemy aliens was augmented by Italy's entry into the war, these arrangements were swept aside and the authorities rounded up all aliens and interned them in hastily improvised 'camps'. This action certainly had all the appearance of panic. But whose panic? The impetus for the round up came not from the public but from the Army, a handful of MPs and the Press. The *Daily Express* and the *Sunday Dispatch* had led the anti-alien campaign from early in the year. They seized on the words of Britain's ambassador to the Netherlands, Sir Neville Bland, who returned to Britain with a tale of alien and Fifth Column treachery assisting the German conquest, and a warning that the same thing could happen in Britain if enemy aliens living here were allowed to remain free. On 14 April the *Dispatch* insisted that Germany had a Fifth Column in Britain 'made up of Fascists, Communists, peace fanatics and alien refugees in league with Berlin and Moscow'. The *Daily Mail* screamed 'INTERN THE LOT!' It was in this overheated atmosphere that the military authorities succeeded in persuading the Home Secretary, Sir John Anderson, to authorize the round-up.[48] The general public seem to have been more resistant to the scaremongers. Mass-Observation sounded out opinion at the height of the press campaign and found that there was no ready support for interning all aliens indiscriminately and little understanding of the idea of a Fifth Column, let alone a belief that it existed. A Gallup poll taken in July showed that while 43 per cent wanted all aliens interned, 48 per cent thought this unnecessary. Another indication that the public were in a calmer state of mind than their leaders and opinion-formers was their continued attachment to humane and liberal values. Signally, Francis Lafitte's Penguin Special, *The Internment of Enemy Aliens,* a blistering attack on the police state methods used in the internment operation, found nearly 50,000 purchasers when it appeared in November. It is certainly true that there was no outcry at the internment of Sir Oswald Mosley and as many members of the British Union of Fascists as the police could catch, but after all, these were people who had made no secret of their pro-Nazi sympathies. No reasonable person could argue that they were not a risk to national security, therefore.

Churchill believed that the spreading of rumours could be harmful to morale and so in July he ordered the Ministry of Information to set up a campaign to counter it. On the basis of rather flimsy evidence from Mass-Observation and the MoI's own Home Intelligence department, the word was that the country was awash with alarming rumours about spies, saboteurs, agents provocateurs and hilltop signallers to enemy planes. Many of these rumours supposedly originated in William Joyce's broadcasts on Radio Hamburg. The MoI duly mounted its 'Silent Column' campaign on posters, in the press and on the BBC. Rumourmongers were personified in the characters of 'Mr Knowall', 'Miss Leaky Mouth' and 'Mr Glumpot'; the advice to the public was to 'TELL THESE PEOPLE TO JOIN BRITAIN'S SILENT COLUMN' and to report persistent offenders to the police. The campaign appears to have backfired. Letters to the newspapers and Mass-Observers' soundings suggest that the ordinary citizen was insulted or at least irritated by the implication that he or she knew no better than idly to spread alarm and despondency. He was suspicious, moreover, that the campaign was indirectly aimed at free speech. Angus Calder offered the view that the public reaction to the Silent Column campaign, apparently heartening evidence for 'the predominance at this time of British tolerance and phlegm', may in reality have been a way of showing 'revulsion against the earlier, very widespread, fifth column mania'.[49] Perhaps, but this begs the question of *whose* mania; Calder offered little more to show that it reached beyond Fleet Street, Westminster and the War Office. As the evidence stands, the alarm was more a product of the establishment mentality that gave birth to the Silent Column campaign than a reflection of the state of mind of ordinary civilians in the summer of 1940.

The Silent Column campaign probably did more to damage morale than to sustain it. Much the same might be said of another government initiative: the Wartime Social Survey. This was an attempt by the Minister of Information, Duff Cooper, to discover the exact state of popular morale by the use of modern social survey methods. Although the complete anonymity of the respondent householders was preserved, the newspapers took against the operation, the *Daily Herald* christening the survey team 'Cooper's Snoopers'. They were charged with needlessly prying into people's lives and causing resentment by so doing. *The Times* declared that the public was 'exasperated by the manifestation of the Ministry as self-appointed custodian of its morale'.[50] Some MPs joined the attack, Sir Archibald Southby declaring the survey to be an unnecessary invasion of privacy. Since the people's morale was perfectly sound why take action that would only result in lowering it?[51] Scandalized newspaper editors and MPs did not speak for the man in the street, however. The proportion of those approached who refused to respond was as low as 0.4 per cent. And when it looked into the matter at the height of the press campaign Mass-Observation found very little public objection to the survey and next to no interest in the press's campaign against it.[52] The war had brought plenty of things to grumble about but this was not one of them. Far from being an indicator of low morale, the affair turned out to be, in Cooper's own words: 'nothing more than a press stunt'.[53]

From the end of June light air raids and air raid alerts were experienced in many parts of the country and in the following two months their frequency increased. Despite this sign that the war that had already been experienced across the Channel was ineluctably approaching Britain and contrary to the gloomy predictions of the pre-war pessimists, there is scant evidence that people were more fearful or were expecting defeat. The reports of Home Intelligence give little space to fear of air raids. When they do, they show that in towns that had been bombed morale seemed rather to have improved: 'confidence is increased, opinion is stiffer and there is a feeling of growing exhilaration. The spirit of the people in raided areas is excellent.'[54] The fact that people were grumbling about the late sounding of warning sirens and about the official policy of withholding casualty figures and names of towns bombed, was not cause for alarm, it was thought, but merely a reflection of the public's reasonable desire to know more about the business in which they were willy-nilly involved. Home Intelligence also noted increasing public scepticism about the imminence or even the likelihood of invasion.[55]

Up to 10 August there had been only about three hundred casualties. From this point until the start of the London Blitz on 7 September there was a steady intensification of attack. Harold Nicolson confided his anxiety to his diary. He wondered how Britain could possibly win. The prospect was bleak, he thought: Britain and her Empire were about to be assailed on all sides by Hitler and his allies.

> Then will come the heavy bombing here and great peace propaganda both here and in the United States ... And then gradually the Fifth Column here will get to work. There will be the extreme left taking its orders from Moscow. There will be the extreme right ... feeling that anything is better than the triumph of the Reds. There will be the lower middle-classes who will be frightened of the bombs, and will say 'Anything better than this. What does Aden or Malta matter to us?' And then there will be the pacifists and the Oxford Group people who will say that material defeat means nothing and that we can find in moral rearmament that strength that is greater than the riches of this world.[56]

But Nicolson's doom scenario said more about him than about his compatriots. From his position at the Ministry of Information he ought to have known better (to his credit, he later admitted this). The fact was that the general war outlook and the intensification of the bombing seemed paradoxically to be having the effect of arousing people's determination to meet the challenge. Mollie Panter-Downes was entirely typical in finding about her a new sense of vitality and purpose, a mood she speculatively put down to Britain being alone and not having to trust to others – relief in the 'simplification of things'. As the story of the Battle of Britain unfolded through the weeks of August and into September the feeling of 'better alone' was reinforced. Mass-Observation, noting the positive effect of the battle on people's feelings, recorded one respondent thus: 'If we go on like this, we shall beat them alright'. This was despite the increase in air raids, which Mass-Observation found were having the effect of 'making people feel part of the war'.[57] It noted that

while the increase had created some nervousness in densely populated areas – the East End of London, especially – many people
ignored the warning sirens (less than one fifth leaving cinemas when
the siren sounded) and a majority went about without their gas
masks. People were still spending time and money enjoying themselves. There were 13,000 spectators for cricket at Lords on one
Saturday; Fulham pubs were getting increasing numbers of customers; dances at Richmond were so popular that an extra evening
a week was arranged to meet the demand.[58] After a big raid on
Croydon on 16 August a young South Londoner, Colin Perry, cycled
over to take a look. He recorded his surprise at what he saw in his
diary: 'the people were absolutely normal; no evidence of alarm or
tension, but just a perfect day, and everyone was happy ... [we
were] staggered that everyone for all the world took it as normal
event'.[59]

The Big Blitz

The next phase of the war was, for those caught up in it, rather
more difficult to take as a normal event. On the night of 7 September a devastating raid was carried out on the dockland area of London. For seventy-six consecutive nights after this (2 November
excepted) fleets of over 200 German bombers unloaded their cargo
of firebombs and high explosives onto the capital, killing nearly
10,000 people and injuring and dehousing many thousands more.
In November the attack was extended to provincial cities, beginning with Coventry on 14 November and then in the following
months to nearly all the main industrial centres. Of inland cities,
Birmingham and Manchester were hardest hit but the really big
blitzes, those that carried on for several nights, were on the ports –
Southampton, Plymouth, Bristol, Clydeside, Merseyside and Hull.
The attack on London continued with fluctuating intensity, culminating in May 1941 with a heavy series that destroyed the Cham-
ber of the House of Commons and brought all but one of the main
railway stations to a halt. This brought to an end the 'Big Blitz', at
which point about 43,000 people had been killed by bombs.

For the civilian, the whole previous year of war had produced
nothing to compare with living through the Blitz. Beside it, the strains
of coping with the blackout, the rationing and the queuing were

trifling. As Lilian Borthwick a young war worker in Liverpool put it: 'We didn't really understand what it meant to be at war until the bombs started dropping, and even then we didn't understand why it was happening to us. Our world was suddenly turned upside down.'[60] Daily life under the bombs was a frontline life, the pre-war vision of total war made real. Bombing was to continue to be part of the civilian experience of the war for another four years, but rarely was it felt with the intensity of the eight-month Blitz of 1940–41. And always in the background of the bombing was the fear that it was the prelude to invasion. This period defines itself as distinct, with strains particular to it, and therefore worthy of special attention.

Above all, people in the Blitz became familiar with sudden, violent death. If they did not actually witness it they unavoidably came close to it through the steady toll among family, friends, neighbours and colleagues. Few were spared the experience of a 'near miss'; everyone, it seemed, had his tale to tell on this score. Many more people were injured by bombs than killed by them. This, too, became a firsthand or secondhand matter for millions of people. To live through an experience in which, all around, others were being killed or injured, was to carry a burden of fear that one's own survival was uncertain. Fear of violent death, then, was the lot of all those civilians – the majority – who remained in the target areas to carry on the activities the war effort required of them. The occasional lull or bomb-free night might reduce the pressure from time to time, but the reality was that the sense of living under a more or less continual threat was the worst of the multiple strains of life in the Blitz.

Next to killing and maiming, bombing applied the cruel torture of sleep deprivation. At the very least, an air raid alert, as the sirens sounded, aroused sleepers and sentenced them to a period of waiting, often in some form of shelter, until the skies were judged free of the enemy. The amount of disturbance caused by alerts was out of all proportion to the actual danger, since it was bound to be that the entire area under the flight path of the raiders was alerted even though the target might be a distant one; thus did the writer Frances Partridge, deep in rural Wiltshire, report disturbance from bomber fleets heading for Bristol and Swindon. In the target cities the sleep-wrecking sirens were more relevant to actual danger but even there false alarms were unavoidably frequent.

The noise of the sirens was, of course, merely the prelude to the much more disturbing noise of exploding bombs and equally noisy anti-aircraft fire that followed when the warning turned out to be real. To those whose loss of sleep was, so to speak, incidental, we must add those whose duties virtually ensured it. Alongside the 6,000 regular full-time firemen and the 60,000 full-time auxiliary firemen were hundreds of thousands of part-time auxiliaries, that is, men who had day-time jobs as well. Their choice of voluntary work guaranteed them broken nights whenever air raids occurred. As it did, indeed, for the part-time volunteers who undertook other duties that involved night work. Of the one and a half million civilians who made up the 'fourth arm' of wardens, firemen, rescue men, ambulance drivers, medical staff, telephonists and messengers, four-fifths were part-time volunteers. In addition, after the very destructive incendiary raid on the City of London on 29 September, the Home Secretary, Herbert Morrison, introduced nationwide compulsory firewatching; all men between the ages of sixteen and sixty were thereafter required to do forty-eight hours a month firewatching, and soon the order was extended to women.

For everyone, those in ARP and those who were not, the worst form of bombing-induced strain was that which went with serial air raids. For even if it meant no more than spending nights in the discomfort of a shelter, there was little chance of getting a normal amount of sleep. The London Blitz was the prototype and the worst case, but wherever it occurred, as for example the five spaced nights in late April in Plymouth or the eight successive nights on Liverpool and Birkenhead in early May, the citizens were tested to near exhaustion.[61] Compared to death or injury, loss of sleep might seem a trivial matter, but the people who suffered it for more than a week or so came to understand just how great a menace it could be to the will to carry on. On 16 September Mass-Observation carried out a survey into how people had slept the night before and how they were adjusting to loss of sleep. It found that eight days of disturbance were beginning to have their effect: 'Sleep! You couldn't sleep! We can't go on like this, can we?' 'Can't sleep well. I feel a bit of a wreck myself. A few more nights of this would put the tin lid on it.' 'It's tragic to see people with children pouring out of the shelters, tired, cramped, and aching from six hours sitting on hard benches.'[62]

But total breakdown rarely occurred. Most people, miraculously, did adjust to the disturbance – apparently getting better at it with practice.

Air raid shelters, whether communal shelters, street shelters or domestic shelters all suffered from the same basic defect: they were designed to provide short-term cover in daytime. Most of the strains associated with shelters arose from the fact that the pattern of air raids required them to be used for long periods, usually at night. The garden shelter, known as the Anderson, afforded proof against bomb blast at the price of great discomfort. It could just about accommodate six adults sitting but could take only two lying down. Because it was set half into the ground it was inevitably damp – waterlogged in many locations and conditions – and it had no services to hand. For millions of suburb dwellers (27 per cent of all shelterers) the Blitz routinely meant cold, damp nights in the cramped discomfort of the family Anderson. In the city centres, where gardens were uncommon, the residents had to depend on non-domestic cover. The first street shelters were unheated and poorly ventilated and were without water, electricity and lavatories. Even part of a night in one of these was a test of endurance for adults, let alone the many children who, despite the evacuation still lived in the cities and whose nearest cover was a street shelter. Within a few days of the start of the Blitz it became clear that in addition to their other inadequacies, many of the street shelters were unsafe. They were not designed to withstand a direct hit, but it emerged that they were not proof against blast either. Collapsing street shelters drove people to the alternatives: the large communal shelters in the basements of strong buildings and any subterranean space such as, in the case of London, the Underground railway system; in Bristol some old tunnels under the city; and in Liverpool and Birkenhead, the Mersey Tunnel. A shelter census made in November showed that 9 per cent of Londoners were spending the nights in communal shelters and 4 per cent in the Underground.[63] In these large refuges people felt, and generally were, safer than above ground. But the conditions of their safety were, especially at the start of the Blitz, desperately primitive. These places were usually overcrowded and noisy, privacy was impossible, the atmosphere was foetid and sleep was difficult on the hard floor. A Mass-Observer reported from Liverpool: 'Improvised arrangements ... have created conditions for many citizens which abolish most of the improvements in sanitation, cleanliness and health made during the last century. The squalor revealed in some of the shelters visited was almost Hogarthian.'[64] In time the authorities adjusted to the needs that experience revealed by installing facilities such as bunk beds, lavatories and refreshment providers. But shelter life remained something to be endured; fear alone made people endure it. There was an alternative, an extreme one at that: trekking. In the first week of the London Blitz some thousands of East Enders sought to escape the nightly air raids by journeying to the outskirts – Epping Forest was the choice of many – sleeping out and returning to homes and jobs in the day. This was a pattern that was replicated in Coventry, Southampton, Plymouth and elsewhere, as the attack moved out from the capital. As a solution it was clearly a desperate one, for it was little better than the life of the tramp. That it was chosen at all was because it permitted people to stay in their jobs, thereby maintaining income, and also because it allowed them to keep an eye on their half-abandoned homes and possessions, if only in the form of a flying visit before or after work or in the meal break. Few kept up sleeping rough for long; those who could afford to found rural billets from which they continued to trek.

One of the consequences of the bombing – indeed, one of its intended consequences – was the dehousing of thousands of city dwellers. Hundreds of thousands of houses were destroyed or so damaged as to be uninhabitable. For the victims there was first the shock of losing their home and possessions, followed by the often miserable experience of a stay in a rest centre and then on to some sort of temporary place to live, at best with relatives, but often in billets found by the local authority. Forty years later a Liverpool woman recalled: 'My mother never really got over the house being bombed ... All she had to show was in that house ... and it had taken years to get the furniture and stuff together ... She was never the same again ... Starting from scratch.'[65] The experience could rarely be got through without major disruption to work and family life. Housewife Kathleen Benn recalled being bombed out several times in Dover:

> The whole of our street had been completely flattened during a very heavy shelling raid. The government gave me £9 to buy furniture, curtains, carpets and clothes. When we went to town shopping, if the siren

sounded, everyone had to take shelter ... Often we spent hours – sometimes up to six or seven hours – in the basements of shops ... We managed to find another house, 5 Bulwark Street, and there were just seven
months when we were bombed out again. We were given another £9 to
replace our belongings once more. By then we had had so much of it we
used to sleep in the caves, cut out of the White Cliffs ... After we lost
our second home, we stayed in the caves a lot, until we got another
house, quite near the caves. I then gave birth to another son, Raymond.
When he was only two hours old, the vibration from the guns on the
cliffs shattered my windows, with the glass flying all over the bed.[66]

Mrs Benn's matter of fact retelling of her traumatic experience does
not mention the additional misery of temporary dependence on the
post-raid services provided by the local authorities. The detailed
reports that Mass-Observation made in a dozen provincial cities
following air raids reveal the inadequacies of the provision in almost every case. All had got as far as designating particular buildings as rest centres for the 'bombed-out' – typically church halls.
However, these were rarely well-supplied with the things that their
'customers' needed: hot food, bedding, washing and cooking facilities. Since people might need to spend days in one of these centres
while more permanent accommodation was found for them, the
experience served to compound the upset and wretchedness of losing their home.

Civilians caught up in the provincial blitzes were spared the
months-long attack that was unique to London. But because of its
size London's capacity for coping with the bombing was greater;
on any one night's attack some parts would be hit while others
were unscathed. This enabled the emergency and post-raid services
of the spared districts to be diverted to the needs of their unfortu-
nate neighbours. In a provincial city, a heavy raid might attract the
support of neighbouring firefighting services but for rescue, clear-
up, communal feeding, rehousing – the post-raid services – it was
effectively on its own. In this situation the civilians were often less
well served than their counterparts in the capital. Mass-Observation investigated post-raid Southampton and found a situation there
that later surveys elsewhere confirmed as typical. The devastated
centre was without water, gas and electricity, the food shops had
run out of supplies and public transport had virtually stopped. People
living there discovered that the local authority had underestimated
the need for rest centres and communal feeding, was slow to organize

orderly evacuation to the city's hinterland, and had devised no efficient way of informing the public about how and where to get access to post-raid services. Although voluntary services moved in,
there was never enough help to fill the gap left by the Council. The
inadequacy of official provision and the apparent inability of city
councils to learn from the experience of other previously bombed
cities, certainly made the citizens' experience of bombing worse
than it need have been.

Most people were not bombed out. But even for this fortunate
majority, trying to carry on as usual in an environment that had
been disrupted by bombing, was a severe strain. For many people
the night was, in any case, a time of voluntary work that was as
much a robber of sleep as the bombs. A middle-aged worker in
Portsmouth said: 'Take last weekend. I was at work all day. I did
'Ome Guard till four in the morning. Then I had to start work
again at six!' A night of broken sleep would often be followed by a
breakfast made without gas or electricity and a journey to work
prolonged by delays and rerouting of bus or train. Work itself might
have to be undertaken in impaired conditions – dust and broken
glass, power cuts, frequent air raid alerts and the frustrating delays
and improvisations arising from the absence of colleagues and interruptions to supplies. The pressure to maintain or increase output
did not slacken, however, and it was reflected in the length of the
working day. A dockyard worker in Portsmouth admitted to suffering from fatigue: 'You have to work long hours nowadays and its
that that makes you tired as much as anything, rather than pressure
or slackness of work.' And the working day would end with a re-
peat of the travelling hazards of the morning. Those trying to keep
the home going were equally beset with difficulties. When asked by
Mass-Observation to name these difficulties, housewives in four
streets in Portsmouth in June 1941 listed, in order, health and general strain ('nerves', etc.), money worries, food supplies and rationing, shelters, fuel and cooking, broken window and other minor
house repairs.[67] Thus did bombing distort the daily lives of whole
communities, placing, as it was intended to place, a constant, nagging strain upon morale.

It will be recalled that the worst pre-war imaginings had the people
giving way to hysteria, panic and despair, as they were plunged into

the holocaust. A fair assessment of the reality of 1940–41 would first have to acknowledge that, intense though they were while they lasted, the air assaults on London, Coventry and the rest, fell short of the predicted cataclysm. The behaviour that contemporary observers recorded was therefore a reaction to something that might have been incomparably worse and inherently less bearable. That said, the picture they give is of a high degree of popular resilience, endurance and resolution during this most severe of all the stresses of total war. Mollie Panter-Downes noted that the start of the Big Blitz in September failed to produce the hysterical, panic-driven exodus from London that was forecast. The roads were not clogged with exiting traffic. Some departed, but most stayed. The US military attaché, General Raymond E. Lee, was impressed by what he found as the bombing began. He got all the US consuls in Britain to report on the state of morale in their districts: 'The answers came in today and what was striking was that the spirit among the workers in the industrial districts which have been frequently bombed was the best of all. It was high everywhere and no consul but thought the people would see the thing through ... By every test and measure I am able to apply, these people are staunch to the bone and won't quit'. At the end of a month of the London Blitz, he wrote in his diary: 'the British are stronger and in a better position than they were at its beginning'.[68] His soundings tallied with the more scientific findings of Gallup: in October 80 per cent of the public felt it was impossible for Germany to win the war solely by air attacks and 89 per cent said they were behind Churchill's leadership. Lee's colleague General George Strong, Chief of Army War Plans Division, was equally impressed, and so, too, was the US ambassador, John G. Winant, noting especially 'the effort made to maintain the appearance of normal life in the face of danger (and) the patient acceptance of hardships and hazards by ordinary people'.[69] Returning to the USA after a month's staff talks in London, he reported: 'The bombings have been rather severe in London since September 7, but they have not affected the morale of the British people.'[70] Lee visited Coventry on 1 December and noted that the factories that had not been damaged were working at full blast and, moreover, that 'There was no evidence whatever that anyone was shaken in his determination to keep on with the war.' And after visiting Liverpool he reflected on Hitler's misjudgement in

'assailing the social life of the workers and knocking it to pieces ...
He does not understand the dogged determination of the British
people and how angry this has made them.'[71]

Encomiums of this sort are common in the abundant evidence
about how the British people behaved under bombardment. They
are the archetype of the consensus that held for a generation after
the war. A number of recent studies, however, have drawn attention to certain negative features in the behaviour of civilians during
the Big Blitz: displays of fear, hysteria and mental disorder; apathy,
defeatism and anti-war feeling; the spread of rumours; 'trekking'
and 'shelter mentality'; blaming of the authorities and the seeking
of scapegoats; looting (see pp. 6–8). Attitudes and behaviour such
as these do not fit comfortably into the cherished picture. They
imply not that the earlier picture was false, but that it was overdrawn, unduly influenced, perhaps, by contemporary official
mythmaking about the sturdy and selfless response of the British
people at this time. But how extensive were they and how significant are they for any conclusion about wartime civilian morale?

According to Mass-Observation reports, fear, panic and hysteria were present among civilians subjected to bombing. Its first reports on the London Blitz showed people in a state of shock: 'We
never thought we'd see it like in the cinema.' In the shelters there
was screaming and quarrelling. When raids were over and people
came out of the shelters, 'there are screams of horror at the sight of
the damage ... smashed windows and roofs everywhere ... People
push and scramble out of the shelter doorway, and there is a wild
clamour of shouting, weeping and calling for absent relatives'. As a
multiple funeral moves towards Stepney cemetery on 10 September
a woman sobs; 'It might be anyone, It might be anyone ... It's not
fair we should have to suffer like this! We never thought it coming.
It's coming to all of us.'[72] Whole streets of people daily abandon
their homes for shelter in what they believe to be safer parts of
London – the West End or the semi-rural outskirts of Epping Forest. The anti-aircraft barrage, initially so comforting, soon ceased
to sustain confidence: 'He comes when he wants. There's no stop-
ping him.'[73] When Mass-Observation came to report people's reactions to bombing in provincial cities, they again found signs of panic.
In Coventry they were especially struck by the impact of the enormous attack of 14 November:

There were more open signs of hysteria, terror, neurosis, observed than during the whole of the previous two months together in all areas. Women were seen to cry, scream, to tremble all over, to faint in the street, to attack a fireman, and so on. The overwhelmingly dominant feeling on Friday (the raid was on Thursday) was the feeling of utter helplessness. The tremendous impact of the previous night had left people practically speechless in many cases. And it made them feel impotent ... On Friday evening there were several signs of suppressed panic as darkness approached. In two cases people were fighting to get into cars, which they thought would take them into the country.[74]

This bleak picture was confirmed by Home Intelligence in its own report of 19 November: 'there was great depression, a widespread feeling of impotence and many open signs of hysteria. "This is the end of Coventry" expressed the general feeling'.[75] In Liverpool, as in Coventry, Mass-Observation formed a very different impression from General Lee. Observers noted for the first time people arguing for immediate surrender, and the city rife with rumours, such as that there had been a peace demonstration in London and the Government had been petitioned to sue for peace. A woman who had been a child in Liverpool at this time recalled that her mother was so frightened that she had developed irrational behaviour such as insisting the family had their evening meal in the shelter even when there was no alert and unplugging the radio 'in case a German plane was passing overhead and homed in on it'.[76] The defeatism that Mass-Observation detected in Liverpool was also evident in Bristol. Here in December, Home Intelligence agents overheard 'much talk of having been let down by the Government, and of the possibility of a negotiated peace'.[77]

However, what is striking about the evidence of hysteria, panic and defeatism is its paucity. Home Intelligence reports contain only three references to defeatism – in London, Coventry and Southampton – and it is surely significant that already by October Home Intelligence had switched from daily to weekly reports on morale: by this time it was clear that here was no immediate danger that morale would collapse. In fact, even in its very first report on Coventry, Home Intelligence had noted that 'a fine morning changed the atmosphere for the better', and that 'There was very little grumbling ... little recrimination or blame.'[78] More typically its reports, even when the general tone was gloomy, recognized resilience in the population of bombed cities. In Portsmouth, for instance, it reported: 'The morale of the city may be summed up in a sentence often repeated, "The spirit of the people is unbroken, but their nerve has gone". That is to say, though they have been badly shaken by their experiences and are afraid, they do not want to give in.'[79] Mass-Observation seems to have been axe-grinding here. Its reports repeatedly caution against complacency, so that when its Observers are confronted with people remaining calm and 'carrying on' they often present this as a fragile and unstable state. It has been argued that since Mass-Observation had a vested interest in retaining its commissions from the Ministry of Information to report on public morale, it was too ready to dismiss the evidence that there was little for the Government to worry about and rather to present morale as more a complex matter than was suggested by appearances.[80]

Others have suggested that the relative pessimism of Mass-Observation's reports reflected the assumption on which the organization was founded – that there was in Britain an inherent gap between the governors and the governed.[81] In the end, however, the organization's commitment to scientific objectivity prevailed. When it became clear that outbursts of panic or hysteria were not only rather rare but were invariably ephemeral episodes, Mass-Observation faithfully reported the fact. From as early as 12 September, after a bad week of raids on London, it was noting that people were more cheerful and that they were getting into a routine of living with the fact of bombing.[82] The steady acclimatization continued. In early October a marked decrease was recorded in the numbers of people who wished to stop the war at once and an increase in those 'who wanted to fight on to the bitter end regardless of the consequences'.[83] By the first week of December, when the worst of the London bombing was over, Mass-Observers found people admitting to *enjoying* the odd raid. In a small area where two high explosive bombs and twenty incendiaries had been dropped one resident said: 'Of course I wouldn't want the same thing to happen every night, but last night was different. I don't think I'm exaggerating when I say most people enjoyed it.' Another agreed: 'I wouldn't mind having an evening like it, say, once a week. It relieves the monotony.' In the same report Mass-Observers say that they found shelter queues were cheerful, sociable gatherings, the women enjoying the break from housework.[84] Exactly the same pattern of adaptation and adjustment was disclosed when post-raid surveys were made in provincial towns, even those like Liverpool and Coventry, where first impressions of the state of morale had been so gloomy. A crucial factor here may have been the exact nature of the damage a town suffered. In a comparison of Liverpool, Manchester and Hull, B. Beaven and D. Thoms showed that the resilience of the people of Liverpool, compared with those of Manchester and Hull, corresponded with the fact that in Liverpool the community infrastructure of the city centre – public houses, cinemas, public utilities and transport system – was left virtually unscathed by the raids, whereas in the other two cities it was seriously damaged. They argued that rather than the special 'Liverpool spirit' that Mass-Observers thought inherent in the city, it was the survival of Liverpool's recreational institutions, public utilities and city landmarks, permitting the maintenance of its normal life, that helped to sustain the morale of its citizens; and that conversely, the virtual destruction of this infrastructure in Manchester and Hull impeded the recovery of morale.[85]

More generally, it is probable that part of the explanation for recovery and adaptation was that the minority who really were in a state of panic did not stay, so that those who remained were the inherently more adaptable. This seemed to be in Constantine Fitzgibbon's mind when he offered an explanation of the disproportionately large number of rumours of panic and despair in east London following the first two nights of the Blitz on 7–8 September: they were started by the very first people who fled after the first bombs. They had not stayed to witness the fortitude of those who had. And he cited two contemporary accounts that, in refutation of the rumours, 'tell of bitterness, anger, perhaps despair, but not of panic'.[86] As for the official concern that allowing the Underground to be used as shelter would encourage a retreatist, 'troglodyte' mentality, in the event, shelterers left when told and obeyed the porters without police intervention. Even when a few large stations were left open to all-day stayers, few took up the opportunity. In any case, a preference for staying in the Underground at night did not necessarily signify retreatism. As Richard Titmuss pointed out, the prospect of bedding down in close proximity to others was scarcely daunting for large families used to sleeping in rows in tiny rooms in the East End; and it at least promised a more restful night than above ground.[87] By the end of September young Londoners had resumed going out at nights for entertainment, rejecting their parents' urgings to come into the shelters straight after supper.[88] A Civil Defence report to the War Cabinet by the Minister of Home Security in October noted, 'Morale continues to be good', and a memorandum on the air raids over the September to November period, written by Anderson's successor at the end of the year, was equally positive: 'The effects of the raids can be considered as the transient and the durable. The transient effects were those on morale and general disorganisation. London lost much sleep and suffered anxiety and discomfort, but there was no breakdown, no panic and no mass evacuation, except the small, heavily-bombed areas.'[89] Meanwhile, censorship reports on letters leaving the country confirmed the general picture: 'Morale is highest in London, but the provinces run a good second, and only a few letters from Liverpool, mostly from Irish writers, show any signs of panic'.[90] At the start of the Blitz the Government secretly put the 4th Battalion Grenadier Guards at Wanstead on stand-by to help police keep order in the East End. In April they were stood down, never having been called on for this task.[91]

Another measure of the mental state of people under bombing, besides their own statements, is the rate of admission to hospital of psychiatric cases. The Government evidently expected a flood of patients: as the bombing began a network of clinics near London was made ready to deal with them. Six months later the situation was reviewed. A Home Intelligence report for 12–19 February 1941 included the findings of the Ministry of Health on the matter. It was found that people suffering from nervous shock formed only 5 per cent of all air raid casualties, and most of these recovered within two weeks. By December 1940 the number of 'civilian neuroses' due to air raids admitted to special psychiatric hospitals was twenty-five in London and three in the whole of the rest of England. In January the number had gone down. Cases not admitted but seen in outpatient clinics were fewer in 1940 than in 1939. And, as if in deliberate contradiction of Mass-Observation's and Home Intelligence's alarmist reports on Coventry, the Ministry of Health tersely noted that after the big raid on that town, 'the number of neurotic outpatients was the same as usual'.[92] The special psychiatric clinics were closed. In May 1941, after nine months of raids, Dr

Felix Brown of Guy's Hospital reported from the 'front line'. In an article in *The Lancet* he wrote: 'The incidence of genuine psychiatric air raid casualties has been much lower than expected; the average previously healthy citizen has proved remarkably adjustable.'[93] In short, the story of mental health in the Blitz was the complete refutation of pre-war expert opinion; by any measure the people were as healthy in mind as before the bombing, if not more so.

As a response to air raids, 'trekking' occurred almost everywhere, especially when it seemed to people that their city was in for a series of attacks. Clearly, some people felt too afraid to pass the nights in their homes and were not convinced of the power of the authorities to protect them from the danger, even when the provision of shelters was adequate. It was the provincial counterpart of the action of thousands of East Enders, who defied officialdom and took to spending the nights in the deepest stations of the Underground. But was trekking a sign of poor morale? The Ministry of Information thought so. Reviewing the situation in April 1941 it offered a condescending picture of the trekkers:

> It is known that there is a section of the population, estimated at a maximum of one-tenth, who are of a weaker constitutional mental make-up than the rest. These people react to different situations in two ways – either by a cowardly retreat, or by a neurotic mental breakdown ... The potentially neurotic section of the population takes to the roads each evening and seeks safety in dispersal.[94]

This assumption – that trekkers were neurotic people behaving in a characteristically irrational way – begs the question of whether wanting to avoid being killed or maimed by bombs was irrational. From an alternative standpoint, moreover, such as the desire to stay alive in order to continue to work for victory, or simply to make sure of getting a good night's sleep, the behaviour looks not only sensible but positively public-spirited. Sir Solly Zukermann, investigating the effects of bombing on civilians in Hull and Birmingham, found no anti-social behaviour and no effect on general health and described trekking in Hull – 'much publicised as a sign of breaking morale' – as rather to be taken as 'a considered response to the situation'.[95] When it is considered that in very many instances, trekking was merely the result of the failure or inability of the local authority to meet its bombed-out citizens' need of somewhere to sleep, then the whole idea of using trekking as a bell-wether of civilian morale looks absurd. In any case, as the Ministry of Health analysis itself observed, the 'neurotics' constituted only 10 per cent of the population: hardly grounds for attaching great importance to their behaviour.

Linked to trekking was the equally widespread phenomenon of people feeling resentment towards the authorities for failing to do enough to protect them from death or injury. Harold Nicolson saw this as a bad sign, leading him in the third week of the Blitz to wonder if London would be able to stand the continuation of the bombing: 'Already the Communists are getting people in shelters to sign a peace petition to Churchill. One cannot expect the population of a great city to sit up all night in shelters week after week without losing their spirit.'[96] Both Home Intelligence and Mass-Observation monitored the nature and amount of grumbles, complaints and accusations about the public authorities. They found plenty to work on. Some of it had to be taken seriously, notably the gathering storm of complaint culminating in the People's Convention, which assembled in London in January 1941. The Convention ostensibly drew together various groups and individuals who wanted Britain's war aims to be clarified in terms of the sort of society that, through social reform, would be born out of the war. In reality it was a communist front organization whose covert objective was to advance the electoral chances of the Communist Party. A short-term expedient for this project was campaigning for the improvement of ARP (more and better shelters, in particular), improvements in servicemen's conditions, an end to war profiteering and the restoration of living standards eroded by price rises. The Government was not deceived as to the political purpose of these campaigns – and the link between a party that was insisting the war was an 'imperialist war' in which the people were victims, and the issue that was probably more critical to morale than any other on the home front, was worrying, to say the least. But it was more concerned about the potentially damaging effect upon civilian morale this sort of high profile agitation might have. The Ministry of Information was (via Mass-Observation) at least able to take comfort from the knowledge that there appeared to be no mass support behind the campaigners. Twelve out of twenty people, when asked, were willing to sign a petition for action on poor quality shelters, but that was about as far as it went.[97] The Government took

seriously public disquiet about the sort of practical issues raised by
the Convention and took positive steps to address them.[98] But when
other indicators suggested no link between the intensity of grumbling and low morale, it justifiably felt that official alarm was misplaced. Grumbling about the authorities, it concluded, was within
certain limits 'normal' behaviour, a British tradition even, and the
wartime regime inevitably gave people plenty of things to grumble
about. As such it was something to be lived with.[99]

Casting around for someone to blame also took the form of an
increase in anti-Semitic feeling. Mass-Observation noted this as early
as 10 September 1940 in the East End and reported it spreading in
a huge circle around London covering the area into which East
Enders had evacuated. Jews were accused of hogging the shelters
or, alternatively, of grabbing the best billets in the country around
the capital.[100] Margaret Crompton, who lived in East London, recorded in her diary an outburst of anti-Semitic graffiti in her
neighbourhood.[101] Anti-Semitism was not limited to London, however. Mass-Observation found that in Bedford and Leicester there
was some expressed resentment towards refugees from the Blitz
and that the terms 'evacuees' and 'Jews' were used interchangeably.
In Oxford, which had taken in many East End refugees, the tension
was not so much between the visitors and the local people but among
the refugees themselves.[102] A Home Intelligence report for early
July referred to grumbling about Jews in Liverpool, where, after
the May raids, they were supposed to have shirked firewatching
and to have got themselves the safest billets in the hinterland.[103]
George Orwell recorded in November hearing 'murmurings about
the number of Jews' in rural Baldock, where he was then living.[104]
The evidence seems clear enough: there does seem to have been an
increase in the amount of anti-Semitism, particularly during and
immediately after air raids. In assessing the significance of the phenomenon for the state of civilian morale more generally, it should
first be noted that mild anti-Semitism was present at all levels in
pre-war society, along with a general prejudice against foreigners,
into which category Jews were perceived to belong. Explaining the
rise in feeling against Jews in the East End in the first days of the
Blitz, Mass-Observation pointed out that the raids forced Jews and
Cockneys into proximity, especially in the communal shelters. In
these trying conditions, underlying antagonisms were fanned into

flame. But it also noted that the tensions typically abated once people had begun to adjust to the Blitz routine. Already by early October it was reporting that anti-Semitism, although still well up on pre-war levels, was in discernible decline.[105] The seeking of scapegoats for one's troubles is never an admirable aspect of human behaviour, and in this instance it certainly detracts from the image of social solidarity at a time of national crisis – internecine discord was, beyond a certain point, scarcely compatible with good morale. But unpleasant though it was, it was never on such a scale as to be taken as characteristic. And in that alarm-sensitive organization, the Ministry of Information, no alarm bells rang on this account.

The ugly phenomenon of looting became a national scandal when the press splashed the story of the bombing of the Café de Paris on 8 March 1941. It was said that robbers quickly exploited the chaos following the blast to strip the dead and wounded of their money and jewellery and even to rifle the handbags of helpers.[106] Reports of looting after raids were not uncommon wherever they occurred. In Portsmouth the local authority took them seriously enough to request troops to stand guard through the town to deter looters. Following stories in the press that workers in demolition gangs were guilty of abusing their position to help themselves to undamaged objects in buildings they were making safe, Mass-Observation decided to investigate, placing one of its Observers undercover in a demolition squad. He reported that looting did occur in his gang and that conversations he had with his fellow workers led him to understand it was rife throughout the service. He learned that sometimes gangers were involved, working in cooperation with drivers and selected workers and that some men were known to do the work for looting alone. The cover for the operation was salvaging, which, he observed, could in any case easily turn into looting.[107] How much looting was really taking place is difficult to say with certainty. It was an aspect of life on the home front that was intrinsically rumour-prone. Who had not heard of a case in his own neighbourhood where looters had supposedly been at work? Looting provided good gossip material and good copy for newspapers. That it existed became part of the received wisdom of the time, even finding its way into the rather more enduring record of literary fiction. In a 1942 Rose Macaulay story the Blitz catches up with the heroine, Miss Anstruther, wrecking her apartment and leaving her lamenting the fate of her possessions: 'Perhaps ... in the safekeeping of the police, more likely in the wholly unsafe keeping of some rescue-squad man or private looter.' Later, 'Miss Anstruther continued to haunt her ruins, where now the demolition men were at work, 'digging and sorting and pocketing as they worked'.[108] Suspicions that in London looting was organized by professional criminals rather than opportunists have some credibility, given the length of the Blitz and the consequent scope it afforded for working out a system.[109] If looting was as widespread and as common as rumour had it the implications for the state of civilian morale were clear: communal feeling was lacking and the whole project of victory through national solidarity was dubious. It is perhaps significant that the decision of Portsmouth Council to have soldiers brought in was received with anger and outrage by residents, who bitterly resented the implied aspersion cast upon their characters. This reaction was surely a sign of a still proud sense of community. The anger seems to have been justified, moreover, for the army units reported seeing no sign of looting at all.[110] As for the extent of the problem of looting in the country as a whole, the authorities never were in the position of being able to quantify it. And in a general context that provided ample evidence of the strength of community spirit they could, while publicly condemning looting, afford to regard it as a regrettable blemish on society rather than a symptom of its rottenness. As a postscript on the subject it is noteworthy that when, a generation later, a historian came to research crime during the war he found sufficient evidence on looting for a mere nine lines in the book that resulted.[111]

Fear of invasion had the potential for sapping morale during this time. Newspapers continued to speculate about when, where and how it would take place. The writer Mollie Panter-Downes found it still a topic of anxious discussion in her circle in February and Richard Brown in his as late as June.[112] A Gallup poll taken in January and reported in the *News Chronicle* was probably the stimulus for such talk, for no less than 62 per cent of respondents thought that Germany would attempt an invasion during the year. Mass-Observation had decided in June 1940 to monitor popular anxiety about invasion; it was well-placed, therefore, to record how it was affected by the Blitz. Its survey, conducted in London in January 1941, contradicted Gallup's. It found that only a quarter of those questioned thought there would be an invasion and even among these there was often the qualifying 'might' or 'may'. Just over half thought that there would definitely not be an attempted invasion. Many thought invasion talk was designed by the Government to keep people working hard. Most said they'd be glad if invasion came and were confident about the outcome. No sign, then, according to this survey, taken while the bombing was still severe, that people were dispirited because they feared the enemy was coming.[113] By February those expecting invasion had risen to 44 per cent, moving closer to Gallup's findings and lending support to Panter-Downes's impressions, but in May this figure had fallen back to only 19 per cent.[114] The surveys show that although the figures fluctuate, there is always (Gallup's January poll apart) a majority confident that the enemy would not invade. At the height of the Blitz, moreover, 77 per cent of people, when asked, rejected the idea of making overtures of peace with Germany and 82 per cent still thought that ultimately, Britain would win the war.[115] This suggests that invasion fears did not play a critical part in the nation's state of mind during the Blitz period. Nevertheless, the people's responses to inquirers' questions about their fears must be treated with caution. Mass-Observers occasionally noted their impression that respondents were reluctant to admit being afraid and even thought to do so was 'letting the side down'. Naomi Mitchison sensed this, too: 'There is not fear, but acute apprehension. In face of that one must be ashamed to do anything or think anything outside it; one cannot break the solidarity.'[116] The positive side of this was that it conduced to 'carrying on', thereby frustrating the enemy's presumed aim of smoothing the path to invasion by battering the people into a state of hopelessness. And once the model of how to 'carry on' was established by the news media's representation of Londoners' 'performance', citizens of other cities seem to have felt under challenge to follow that model and at least match that performance – as, indeed, did Londoners themselves during later spells of air raids on the capital.

On 22 June 1941 Hitler launched his invasion of the Soviet Union. The news came when the worst of the bombing seemed to have passed. Whatever lay ahead, the crisis that began twelve months before seemed at least to have passed its peak. At this point, though bruised, battered and still under great strain, the people of Britain were, on the evidence discussed here, in generally good heart. The worst fears about the capacity of civilians to bear the strains of total war had not been realized. Rather, the people had risen to the challenge and astonished their leaders by their resilience and public-spiritedness. People had been afraid and there had been moments of panic and defeatism; but, as has been shown, the psychiatric hospitals remained underoccupied. People had grumbled, spread rumours and sought to blame others; but meanwhile they worked longer hours and volunteered their spare time. Many had 'trekked' nightly to escape the bombs; but they returned every morning and continued to do their jobs as before. In short, in terms of how they behaved at the most testing time, the people demonstrated that their morale was sound. Like all propaganda, the official image of the British people heroically battling through this national crisis contained some exaggeration, but it was not a great departure from the truth. As for the future, everyone, leaders and led alike, could take comfort from the knowledge that Britain was no longer alone against the power of Germany. Russia's involvement meant that victory was not quite so difficult to imagine. Morale would be easier from now on.

Notes

1 In 1999 BBC Radio 4 produced a series of programmes on the evacuation. In response to a question asking 500 former evacuees if they believed they had suffered physical or sexual abuse 12 per cent considered that they had.

2 H. Millgate (ed.), *Mr Brown's War: a Diary of the Second World War* (Sutton, 1998), p. 41.

3 See R. Padley & M. Cole, *Evacuation Survey* (Routledge, 1940), p. 191–2.

4 Mass-Observation (hereafter M-O), Volunteer worker's diary, 20 October 1941. Diarist No. 5423.

5 See especially T. Crosby, *The Impact of Civilian Evacuation in the Second World War* (Croom Helm, 1986).

6 R. Broad and S. Fleming (eds), *Nella Last's War* (Falling Wall Press, 1981), p. 12.

7 See D. Sheridan, *Wartime Women* (Heinemann, 1990), pp. 73–8.

8 H. Nicolson, *Diaries and Letters 1939–45* (Collins, 1967), p. 36.

9 R. Wybrow, *Britain Speaks Out: 1935–1987* (Macmillan, 1989), p. 8.

10 M-O, File Report 15A; *The Spectator*, 4 February 1940.

11 Constantine Fitzgibbon, *The Blitz* (Macdonald, 1957), p. 31.

12 Memorandum by the Home Secretary, 20 December 1939, CAB 67/3.

13 M-O, File Report 15A.

14 Cabinet Minutes, 28 October 1939.

15 *Picture Post*, 4 November 1939. Evelyn Waugh in his 1943 novel *Put Out More Flags* had the same idea. The hero, Basil Seal, having failed to get the Ministry of Information to give him a job, complains: 'No imagination. They won't take suggestions from outsiders. You know Sonia this war is developing into a kind of club enclosure on a racecourse. If you aren't wearing the right badge they won't let you in.' Evelyn Waugh, *Put Out More Flags* (Penguin, 1943), p. 72.

16 M-O, File Report 27, February 1940.

17 M-O, File Report 89, April 1940.

18 Ifor Evans to the Director General, 9 November 1939, INF 1/47.

19 Memorandum, from the Minister of Information, February 1940, INF 1/867.

20 M-O, File Report 27.

21 BBC Listener Research report, 8 March 1940, INF 1/61.

22 M-O, File Report 135.

23 See J. Bardon, *A History of Ulster* (The Blackstaff Press, 1992), pp. 581–6.

24 H. M. D, Parker, *Manpower* (HMSO, 1957), pp. 188–90.

25 Broad and Fleming (eds), *Nella Last's War*, p. 12.

26 M-O, May 1940, File Report 127. A Gallup poll confirmed Mass-Observation's findings on Chamberlain and showed that he was maintaining his popularity: in the third week of January 56 per cent approved of his leadership. See *News Chronicle*, 20 January 1940.

27 Mollie Panter-Downes, *London War Notes 1939–1945* (Longman, 1972), p. 53.

28 See M-O reports on morale in April and May, File Reports 73 and 98.

29 M-O, Diary No. 5324, 6 May 1940.

30 H. I. Daily Report, 18 May 1940, INF 1/264.

31 Panter-Downes, *London War Notes*, pp. 56–7, 65–6, 71.

32 Frances Partridge, *A Pacifist's War* (Phoenix, 1996), pp. 38–9.

33 W. H. B. Court, *Coal* (HMSO, 1951), p. 124; H. Pelling, *A History of British Trade Unionism* (Penguin, 1976), p. 295.

34 M-O, File Report 2130, June 1940.

35 INF 1/264 Daily Reports, 18 and 25 May 1940.

36 T. H. O'Brien, *Civil Defence* (HMSO, 1955), 365–6.

37 Panter-Downes, *London War Notes*, p. 79.

38 Millgate (ed.), *Mr Brown's War*, p. 48.

39 M-O, File Reports 105, 107, 109, 111, 124.

40 M-O, File Report 181, 17 June 1940.

41 M-O, File Report 2130.

42 M-O, File Report 282.

43 *Ibid.*

44 Wybrow, *Britain Speaks Out*, p. 11. M-O, File Report 282.

45 Broad and Fleming (eds), *Nella Last's War*, p. 62.

46 C. Ritchie, *The Siren Years* (Macmillan, 1974), pp. 74–5.

47 A. Calder, *The Myth of the Blitz* (Jonathan Cape, 1991), p. 125.

48 M-O, File Report 107.

49 Calder, *Myth of the Blitz*, p. 126.

50 *The Times*, 2 August 1940.

51 Hansard, 1 August 1940, vol. 363, cols 1548–55.

52 M-O, File Reports 325, 334, 336.

53 Hansard, 1 August 1940, vol. 363, cols 1513–19.

54 H. I. Report, 17 August 1940, INF 1/264.

55 H. I. Reports, 23 July, 16 August 1940, INF 1/264.

56 Nicolson, *Diaries*, pp. 105–6.

57 M-O, File Report 356.

58 M-O, File Report 365, 370, 381.

59 Colin Perry, *Boy in the Blitz* (Colin A. Perry Ltd., 1972), pp. 66–7.

60 Lilian Borthwick, in C. and E. Townsend, *War Wives: a Second World War Anthology* (Grafton Books, 1989), p. 289.

61 M-O, File Report 683 on Plymouth, 4 May 1941.

62 M-O, File Report 408, 'Human Adjustments in Air-raids'.

63 O'Brien, *Civil Defence*, p. 392.

64 M-O, File Report 538.

65 Cited in P. Ayers, *Women at War* (Liver Press, 1988), p. 12.

66 C. and E. Townsend, *War Wives*, pp. 90–1.

67 M-O, File Report 850 (fatigued workers); T. Harrisson, *Living Through the Blitz* (Collins, 1976), p. 194 (housewives).

68 J. Leutze (ed.), *The London Observer. The Journal of General Raymond E. Lee 1940–41* (Hutchinson, 1972), pp. 25, 59.

69 J. G. Winant, *Letter from Grosvenor Square* (Hodder & Stoughton, 1947), p. 44.

70 *Ibid.*, p. 65.

71 J. Leutze (ed.), *The London Observer*, pp. 152, 175.

72 Harrisson, *Living Through the Blitz*, pp. 61, 64.

73 M-O, File Report 449.

74 M-O, 'The Effects of Bombing in Coventry', File 495.

75 H. I., 'Special report on Coventry', 19 November 1940, INF 1/292.

76 Oral report, quoted in Ayers, *Women at War*, p. 11.

77 H. I., Weekly Report, 4–11 December 1940, INF 1/292.

78 H. I., 'Special report on Coventry', INF 1/292.

79 H. I., 'Special Report on Portsmouth, 19–24 May 1941, INF 1/292.

80 Calder, *Myth of the Blitz*, pp. 150–1.

81 See for example M. Smith, *Britain and 1940: History, Myth and Popular Memory* (Routledge, 2000).

82 M-O, File Report 395.

83 M-O, File 439. In all its many surveys on this question, Mass-Observation never recorded a figure higher than one in twelve wanting a negotiated peace or other immediate end to the war.

84 M-O, File Report 521.

85 B. Beaven and D. Thoms, 'The Blitz and Civilian Morale in Three Northern Cities, 1940–1942', *Northern History,* vol. 32, 1996, pp. 195–203.

86 Fitzgibbon, *The Blitz*, pp. 66–78. The accounts referred to are E. Doreen Idle's *War Over West Ham* and Ritchie Calder's *The Lesson of London*.

87 R. Titmuss, *Problems of Social Policy* (HMSO, 1950), p. 342.

88 Harrisson, *Living Through the Blitz*, pp. 75, 112–13.

89 CAB 68/7/WP(R) (40) 196; CAB 67/9 (41) 44.

90 CAB 66/12 WP(40) 407.
91 P. Ziegler, *London at War 1939–1945*, (Alfred A. Knopf, 1995), p. 170.
92 H. I. Report, 12–19 February 1941, INF 1/292.
93 F. Brown, 'Civilian Psychiatric Air-Raid Casualties', *The Lancet*, 31 May 1941.
94 H. I. Report, 23–30 April 1941, NF 1/292.
95 S. Zukermann, *From Apes to Warlords* (Hamish Hamilton, 1978), pp. 137–46.
96 Nicolson, *Diaries,* pp. 115–16.
97 M-O, File Report 291.
98 See Chapter 5, pp. 186–95.
99 A Home Office study of towns that had suffered badly from bombing con-
     firmed the 'normality' of complaints about post-raid services and the local
     authority's role, and the absence of any link between complaints and low
     morale. See C. W. Emmens, 'The Assessment of Air-Raid Morale from the
     Local Press, Home Intelligence, Social Survey and Damage Reports in Brit-
     ain', 24 June 1943, HO 199/456.
100 M-O, File Reports 392, 449, 502.
101 M. Crompton, Diary, Imperial War Museum.
102 M-O, File Reports 418, 439.
103 H. I. Weekly Report, 2–9 July 1941, INF 1/292.
104 S. Orwell and I. Angus (eds), *The Collected Essays, Journalism and Letters of
     George Orwell, vol. 2* (Penguin, 1970), p. 427.
105 M-O, File Reports 392, 439.
106 *Daily Mirror*, 10 March 1941.
107 M-O, File Report 768, July 1941.
108 Rose Macaulay, 'Miss Anstruther's Letters', in Storm Jameson (ed.), *London
     Calling* (Harper, 1942), pp. 67–8.
109 See Fitzgibbon, *The Blitz*, pp. 259–60.
110 M-O, File Report 590.
111 E. Smithies, *Crime in Wartime: a Social History of Crime in World War Two*
     (Allen & Unwin, 1982), p. 49.
112 Panter-Downes, *London War Notes*, p. 135; Millgate (ed.), *Mr Brown's War*,
     p. 100.
113 M-O, File Report 544.
114 M-O, File Report 729.
115 Wybrow, *Britain Speaks Out*, p. 13.
116 D. Sheridan (ed.), *Among You Taking Notes: the Wartime Diary of Naomi
     Mitchison 1939–1945* (Oxford University Press, 1986), p. 114.

3

War experienced: 1941–45

A different sort of war

WITH THE ENDING of the Big Blitz in May 1941 the war as experienced on the home front changed and with it the nature of the challenge to civilian morale. Instead of living with the pervasive threat of invasion and the daily experience of violent assault from the air, the country entered a period of improved outlook abroad and relative quiet at home. The bombing slackened off and return to a semblance of normality was possible. Britain was no longer alone in her fight: first the Soviet Union and then the USA became allies. The fear that the war would soon come to a disastrous conclusion was replaced by a sense that it would eventually be won, albeit only after a protracted struggle. And so it turned out to be. In time, defeats and setbacks gave way to victories and advances on all fronts and the steady progress to victory was established. So radical a change to both the physical and psychological environment inevitably altered the nature of the pressure on the mentality of the people and the way they responded to it.

The figures for civilian deaths from bombing chart a key element in the change. In 1940, 23,767 were killed; in 1941, 19,918; in 1942, 3,236. Thus did the threat of sudden, violent death from enemy action – real enough in 1940–41 – become a remote possibility before the war had started its third year. This is not to make light of the raids on English cathedral cities in April–May 1942, the 'Little Blitz' on London, Bristol, South Wales and Hull from February to April 1944, nor the flying-bomb attacks (pilotless aircraft and rockets) on the south east corner of Britain between June 1944 and March 1945. Indeed, the last accounted for 14.5 per cent of all British civilians killed in the war. But the general absence of bombing – for months on end in most places – lent a quite different quality to wartime life. ARP routines were maintained and alerts continued to be heard in many places, but raw fear largely disappeared as part of everyone's experience. Also, when the threat of being bombed became remote people found it easier to get used to living with the possibility of it happening. Frances Partridge reflected on this in February 1943 when she heard that nearby Newbury had been bombed in daylight and children in school had been killed: 'If this had happened earlier in the war people would have stopped sending their children in to school in Newbury. Now, it's as if being bombed by the Germans was one of the hazards of life, like being run over by a motor car, and there was no use trying to avoid it.' Mollie Panter-Downes, too, noticed how the perception of reduced risk led thousands of evacuees to return to London in August 1941 a development that Mass-Observation warningly described as 'signs of a return to complacency'.[1] Politicians began to pick up the theme. Brendan Bracken, the Minister of Information, identified complacency as 'public enemy number two', and at the TUC conference Clement Attlee and the TUC secretary Walter Citrine both delivered speeches deploring any tendency towards complacency.

Part of the terror of the Blitz had been the fear that it was merely the prelude to invasion. Accordingly, as the bombing petered out so, too, did the dread subside of the arrival by sea and air of the triumphant *Wehrmacht*. Mass-Observation had found in February 1941 that 44 per cent of those asked still expected invasion to be attempted. By June, exactly matching Gallup's poll in the same month, this figure had fallen to 39 per cent. Among these was Richard Brown in Ipswich, thrown once again into worry about whether to send his wife and children away: 'It is all so unsettling – they tell us to "Stay put" if invasion comes and then say "Well, you are special. Please evacuate." And now they speak of compulsion.'[2] Rumours of imminent invasion recurred from time to time; as late as May 1942, George Orwell, writing in his war diary, recorded hearing a rumour that invasion was set for the 25th.[3] But the fear of invasion inevitably lessened as events in the war caused the threat to retreat. As it happened, within three days of Richard Brown's anxious diary entry, one such event occurred: the German attack on Russia. At once, the feeling of being alone – alone in Europe at least – was gone. In one important sense, the strain of war was from this point more tolerable for most people: at least invasion and defeat no longer seemed likely. Even among the minority who thought the Germans still intended to invade Britain, 80 per cent thought they would be defeated if they did. Support for proposals of peace with Germany had fallen away to almost nothing.[4] An indirect but revealing indicator of confidence in victory was the readiness of people to back Britain financially. The patriotic giving of the Spitfire Funds has already been mentioned in Chapter 1, but complementing this was the spectacular public response to the Government's campaign to get people to invest their spare money in National Savings and Defence Bonds. In 1939 small savings amounted to £62m, public issues to £10m. By 1940 savings were at £466m and public issues at £567m. This evidence of people's belief that they were not throwing their money away continued to be shown in subsequent years. Small savings were £602m in 1941 and peaked at £719m in 1943; public issues came to £1,031m in 1941 and reached their highest at £1,176m in 1945.[5]

When the excitement of Russia's entry into the war began to wear off, and the news of her defeats and retreats accumulated, optimism about an early end to the war or even about victory itself receded. Mass-Observation recorded a marked increase in depression at, for example, the news in October that Odessa and Kharkov had fallen to the Germans.[6] This instance illustrates a facet of this phase of the war: for a long time good news about the war was far outweighed by bad. Even the USA's entry into the war in December, heartening though it was, did nothing to stem the stream of news about defeats, retreats and losses. Russia's survival, it seemed, continued to hang by a thread. British possessions in the Far East successively fell to the Japanese: Hong Kong, Malaya, Burma, Singapore. In Cyrenaica, an Axis army under General Rommel captured Tobruk, along with 33,000 prisoners, and the British and Commonwealth forces were driven back into Egypt. In the Battle of the Atlantic the improved position on shipping losses during the last quarter of 1941 was not sustained: 4,500,000 tons of Allied shipping were sunk in the first half of 1942. As the morale watchers recorded, the effect on civilian morale of this catalogue of disaster was predictably negative. For what it implied was that victory, if it was even possible, would be a long time coming. The mental burden of the war no longer included acute fear of invasion but it remained onerous, none the less. To the extent that the other strains of war were tolerable as long as the end was in view, this long drawn-out road to ultimate victory was a severe test. Elizabeth Bowen captured this time exactly in her post-war novel, *The Heat of the Day*: 'Reverses, losses, deadlocks now almost unnoticed bred one another; every day the news hammered one more nail into a consciousness that no longer resounded. Everywhere hung the heaviness of the even worse you could not be told and could not desire to hear. This was the lightless middle of the tunnel.'[7] Even the constitutionally cheerful and resilient Richard Brown admitted to allowing the lack of good news to get him down: 'News in general is very disturbing. I have an idea that when we look back some time hence, this period will be regarded as a sort of transition or waiting period. I suppose I ought to take a long view but there is a tendency to see only that which is before one's nose and candidly I feel a bit depressed.'[8] Mass-Observation found a correlation between bad news from the war and a drop in Winston Churchill's popularity; thus his normal rating of 80 per cent dropped to 74 per cent during Hitler's drive into Russia, 77 per cent after Japan's initial successes, 73 per cent on the fall of Singapore and 66 per cent on the fall of Rangoon.[9] And following the fall of Tobruk in June 1942 only 35 per cent declared themselves satisfied with the Government's conduct of the war – the lowest rating in the whole war. None of this, however, shook the support of the majority for carrying on the struggle: 84 per cent in a Gallup poll in November 1941 rejected any idea of negotiation with Germany.[10]

Negotiation was not, in any case, on anyone's agenda. People did not need to be told that the enemy was ruthless and barbaric. Once the Blitz had happened, Hitler was believed capable of any brutality. That he was considered beyond the pale was demonstrated not only by the official dismissal of his 'peace offer' of 19 July 1941, but also by the mocking and contemptuous way in which ordinary people treated copies of his speech *A Last Appeal to Reason*, which the German air force had dropped in August: in places they were auctioned to raise funds for local Spitfire and Red Cross Funds.[11] The 1942 'Baedeker' raids and the reports of German mistreatment of civilians in occupied Europe merely confirmed the general view that there could be no compromise, that the policy of demanding 'unconditional surrender' by Germany was right. A Home Intelligence report of February 1943 noted: 'Hatred of

Germany – "enemy No. 1" – is expressed ... as well as a hope that
the Russians get to Germany before we do, "as they're more ruthless".[12] As Ian McLaine explains, the Ministry of Information did
not put out German atrocity propaganda because the public needed
no encouragement to think the worst of the Germans, citing the
example of its report on the 'extreme annoyance' elicited by the
photograph appearing in the newspapers in November 1942 of General Montgomery hosting a meal for General von Thoma, one of
the commanders of the defeated *Afrika Korps*, 'treating him as if he
were the captain of an opposing cricket team'.[13]

Naturally, good news, when it finally came, also had an effect
on morale. In November 1942, for example, Mass-Observation
reported the dramatic impact at home of the victory at El Alamein,
the advances in Libya and the Allied landings in Morocco and Al-
geria: much more interest in the news, increased optimism, the disappearance of war- weariness and a surge in production in the war
factories.[14] Brendan Bracken wrote of the barely suppressed public
excitement at the long awaited good news: 'they are now as suspicious as the ancient Greeks of any exultation that seems to challenge fate'.[15] On 15 November the ringing of church bells, silent
since the start of the war, when they had been reserved as an invasion signal, was a conscious symbol of the rise in popular morale.
About this time Mollie Panter-Downes noticed a subtle change in
popular speech, an increase in the use of the phrase 'after the war'.
'People talk about the end of the war', she observed, 'as though it
were a perfectly matter-of-fact objective on the horizon and not
just a nice pipe dream'.[16] In December, satisfaction with Churchill's
leadership reached 93 per cent in Gallup's poll.

There lay ahead many more events like El Alamein to celebrate:
Stalingrad, Sicily, the D-Day landings. By March 1944 the
Government's conduct of the war was approved by 75 per cent in a
Gallup poll and in June, following the successful landings in
Normandy, it rose to 80 per cent.[17] 'It really looks as if it might be
over in months if not weeks', wrote Frances Partridge, when the
Normandy campaign was successful. Correspondence between the
state of civilian morale and the big news events of the war is con-
firmed in a chart compiled by the MoI from its weekly reports from
March 1941 to December 1944. The low points match those identified in Mass-Observation's surveys: the withdrawal from Crete, the

fall of Singapore, the fall of Tobruk, the 'Little Blitz' of early 1944; and the high points predictably come after successes like El Alamein, the German defeat at Stalingrad and the Normandy landings.[18]

But even after the turning of the tide, when advances were being made on every front, the fact remained that the war was dragging on. 'We all sit, like people in the waiting room of a hospital while a life or death operation goes on', commented Frances Partridge.[19] Hopes for an ending of the war in 1942 were deferred to 1943, then to 1944 and finally to 1945, blunting the morale boosting effect of the victories won along the way. Hope, moreover, was an awkward customer to carry about with one, and made life 'more agitating and restless than despair or fatalistic resignation'[20]. Many people, as Mollie Panter-Downes observed, found Christmas 1944 almost unbearably depressing because they had come to believe it would be celebrated in peacetime; instead the Battle of the Bulge promised a continuing hard slog before victory was attained.[21]

As we have seen in Chapter 2, the year-long emergency of 1940–41 disclosed remarkable reserves of spirited resilience among a majority of the population. The years that followed required of them different but no less demanding qualities. Instead of sinew-straining effort from everyone – intrinsically unsustainable, any-way – what was needed was a patient and steady persistence, a willingness to accept deferment of life plans and to endure the cramp-ing narrowness and dispiriting routine of wartime life without the prospect of it soon coming to an end. 'What they [the ordinary people] have been through in the last six months', wrote Mollie Panter-Downes in July 1942, 'has been less noisy, perhaps, but no less wearing to the spirit and nerves than were the bad times of 1940, when the bombs were falling.'[22] Edward Blishen, a young conscientious objector stuck in the tedious round of agricultural labouring, wrote later of 'the caged quality of wartime' and how 'war was the dwindling of possibilities to single, unvariable desti-nies'. In him this induced 'a wild longing for change, for the possi-bility and prospect of *motion* that the war had brought to an end'.[23] In others apathy was its consequence. As Frances Partridge put it: 'I find one sinks or hurls oneself into this apathy, deliberately not thinking about the future, supposing nothing, wondering nothing, because one assumes it is "not for long".'[24] Thus did the changed character of the war continue to challenge the morale of Britain's 'homefront warriors'. The long haul that began about the middle of 1941 required stamina and patience. In both the British people showed themselves to have ample reserves.

Separations

No aspect of the long-term strain of war was as universally experienced as the enforced separation of people – of spouses, of lovers, of friends, of parents and children. Social survey material is notably thin in this area – as it is on the issue of wartime separation more generally: Home Intelligence and Mass-Observation are for once relatively unrevealing. The record has rather to be sought in the testimonies of individuals – diaries, letters and recollections – and in the creative work of writers and film makers of the time. Here, there is a patchwork of 'stories' each of which discloses the private anguish of one separation but which together represent the common lot.

The imperatives of war required that men were called away to fight, that workers had to move to where war industry was located, that the very young and the old were evacuated to safe areas. In the process personal relationships were brutally ruptured. Loneliness, anxiety and waiting became fixtures of daily life. When danger and deprivation in any case made that life more trying, the removal of the sustaining props of kinship and affection was a cruel aggravation. It is no surprise to discover that most of the songs of the time, and certainly the most popular among them, were sentimental ballads about the pain of separation, waiting and the yearning anticipation of reunion: 'We'll Meet Again', 'Lili Marlene', 'The White Cliffs of Dover', 'It's a Lovely Day Tomorrow', 'When the Lights Go On Again'.

No amount of well-meant help, of course, could change the reality of separation or more than briefly lift the nagging anxiety that millions of young wives and lovers were bound to have about men who were not just absent, but who were in places that were by definition dangerous: in the vulnerable bodies of Lancaster bombers over Germany, in ships crossing the U-boat infested waters of the Atlantic Ocean, under fire in the exposed wastes of the Libyan Desert. Only the unimaginative could find it easy to forget that their loved one was literally a hunted man, the deliberate target of

other men equipped and trained to kill him. Many have testified to
the cumulative strain of living with the dread of receiving the news
that their husband or lover was dead or missing. Marjorie Townsend
recalls her agonies waiting for news of her husband, missing in
Malaya: 'The post – Oh, how I looked for, yet hated the post. I used
to stand at the window when it was due and try to will the postman
to bring news, and my heart would sink when nothing came. But I
would pull myself together and think, there's another day tomorrow.'[25] And all the while a pretence of optimism and cheerfulness
had to be maintained. Dorothy Parker, who herself went through
this experience of separation from her husband in the First World
War, set down its essence in a short story she wrote in the Second.
In this, the waiting wife bitterly reminds herself of the 'rules' she
must keep to when she writes to her serviceman husband:

> never say to him what you want him to say to you. Never tell him how
> sadly you miss him, how it grows no better, how each day without him
> is sharper than the day before. Set down for him the gay happenings
> about you, bright little anecdotes, not invented, necessarily, but attrac-
> tively embellished. Do not bedevil him with the pinings of your faithful
> heart because he is your husband, your man, your love. For you are
> writing to none of these. You are writing to a soldier.[26]

Of course, the 'rules' were designed to help the men – just like Vera
Lynn's *Sincerely Yours*: the prime consideration here was *military*
morale and how civilians might help sustain it. The falsely cheerful
wife could see the sense of it and kept to the rules, if only because
she knew soldiers' mail was subject to censorship. But doing so
went against instinct and compounded the loneliness with the guilt
of deceit. The same duty for a wife attached to any periods of home
leave a serviceman husband might get. Above all, he must not return to his unit with his trained martial spirit impaired by anxiety
about the mental state of the woman he had left behind. He, for his
part, knew he must equally do what he could to be reassuring and
optimistic. The predictable result was often that the leave was spoiled
by an artificial gaiety struggling against the depressing reality of
the ineluctable approach of renewed separation. Ruth, the
serviceman's wife in Mollie Panter-Downes's short story *Goodbye,
My Love*, faces the final day of his leave feeling 'a little cold and
sick, as though this were the morning fixed for a major operation'.
And when the last moment arrives, 'One used the same words for a

parting which might be for years, which might end in death, as one did for an overnight business trip.'[27] For Lilian Borthwick, twenty-four years old and three years married, who always ended her letters to her absent soldier-husband, as he did, with 'Close to you' – the title of a popular wartime song – the leavetaking of August 1944 proved to be the last: 'I loved my husband so much. He was not a fighting man; he was so gentle and kind, and we were so happy together ... I was three months pregnant when the awful news came ... that Bob had been killed ... I lost the baby the same week ... I wanted to die – and have often wished I had then. I only wish I could have had his child. It would have been part of him for me to have.'[28] Like so many others Lilian had borne the strain of separation only to have her hope of a happy future dashed at the very time that the end of the war was in sight.

Whatever 'normal' family life had meant to individual families before the war, it was certain that the war would force changes upon it. Invariably, these changes were felt to be damaging and consequently were a potent source of strain on civilian morale, the more so for being long lasting. Here, too, the heart of the matter was separation – of wives and husbands, of parents and children, of grandparents and grandchildren, of brothers and sisters. Its agents were three of the war's big exercises in people management: evacuation, conscription (military and industrial) and war work.

Rather under half of the children eligible were evacuated in 1939, 40 per cent of these returning within four months. There were later, smaller, evacuations when bombing began in 1940 and again in 1944. Although it is impossible to say precisely just how many children were evacuated in total, perhaps a third of all families took part in evacuation during the course of the war; sufficient, that is, to make it a mass experience. Conscription and war work, too, affected millions. By 1945 there were 4,680,000 people in the armed forces, 437,000 of them women. One third of the male population of working age, half of them married, was in uniform and away from home. War work of one kind or another might require workers to live away from home, whether it was the 25,000 civil servants who, under 'Yellow Move', left London and set up their offices for the rest of the war in hotels in spa towns and seaside resorts, or the thousands of men and women who were brought to the centres of engineering and aircraft manufacture in the Midlands and who were housed in hostels or found billets in the local community. In their different ways, all three operations – evacuation, conscription and war work – conduced to the same result: the displacement of people and the consequent disruption of family life.

In most families before the war, periodic or long-term separation of parents and children was unusual. The loss of the shared intimacies and rituals of family life was therefore frustrating and depressing for parents who had naturally expected to have them. When evacuation was the cause, clearly the loss was absolute, mitigated in some instances if distance and work permitted parents to visit their evacuated offspring. When a father was on service overseas and unable, therefore, to get the home leave that home-based servicemen might have, his children might not see him for several years. Those on war work away from home would usually get back for weekends, just enough to keep the continuity of paternal presence, but itself accompanied by the stress of long-distance travel on a heavily overloaded and depleted railway network. To varying degrees, then, the qualities of family life that parents particularly value were impaired by the necessities of war. It might be not being together to celebrate a child's birthday, to go on outings together or attend the big events in a child's school year – the nativity play, a concert, sports day. Or, more basically, it might be simply not being there to witness the stages of a child's mental and physical growth and being unable to be a part of his or her nurturing environment. When the children were in distant reception areas, naturally, both parents had to endure this loss of parental experience. Frances Partridge recorded the effect on her friends, Phyllis and Philip Nichols who, after much internal turmoil had sent their children away to Canada: 'The absence of their children is evidently agony to them; they were always talking about them and one evening when Phyllis brought out their photos to show me, she trembled so violently that the sofa on which we were sitting shook beneath us.'[29] More typically, the children remained at home and in this case fathers were more affected than mothers, for military service or alternative war service was not required of mothers of infants or school-age children. Women might have the consolation of continuing to have their children with them, but the enforced absence of thousands of wartime fathers gave a like number of mothers the extra role of father substitute in the weeks, months or years of their husbands' absence. The difficulties of this dual role apart, it was an intrinsically melancholy burden, always accompanied by the feeling that it was second best and that as time passed and the children grew and developed, the fulfilling experiences of peacetime family life were being irrecoverably lost. Dorothy Griffiths' husband Griff was dispatched to India, leaving her at his parents' home in Yeadon with her eighteen-month-old son Stephen. In the two years that passed before Griff's return she diligently tried to keep alive their family spirit:

> All the time Griff was in India I would let Stephen hold his Daddy's picture at bedtime and kiss him goodnight. I was so afraid of him being a stranger when he came home. After all my efforts to get Stephen to remember Griff, even holding a pencil in his little hand and guiding it to form x's at the bottom of letters, when his Dad did come home there was friction. Stephen couldn't understand why this man was in Mummy's bed.[30]

Like Dorothy Griffiths, Marjorie Townsend set out to keep her husband in her children's minds but then fell prey to an additional worry: 'While he was away, I used to worry about the children. I wanted them to know and love their father when he came back home to them, so I used to talk to them about "Daddy" and show them his picture constantly. Then I would wonder, suppose he never did come back? Was I only making it harder for them?'[31] Such was the burden of many thousands of young wives struggling to hold together their diminished families. In an autobiographical short story, 'The Sailor's Wife', written in 1945, Ann Chadwick graphically conveyed the mental pressure on the lonely young wife. The woman tries unsuccessfully to find a room for her baby and herself in a port so that they can see her husband when he has leave. In a delirious state after being knocked down in the street by a lorry, her mind is invaded by the voices and scenes of her house-to-house search and of her growing sense of despair:

> You service wives should stick at home. Should. Ought … should stick. War won't last forever. One year. Don't marry before the peace. Wait. Don't start babies in wartime. Wait. Wartime. Four years. Don't live in wartime. Wait. Stick. Sorry I can't help. Can't give you eggs. Sorry, only for registered customers. Sorry no life going on in wartime. Wait … Only four or five years.[32]

For many such women there was an additional reason for bitter regret: long-term separation could wreck any plan they might have had for the number and spacing of their children. Most, being the wives of young men, were themselves young enough to at least achieve the former when their marital life was eventually restored; but for a minority there was no margin of time and they therefore had to bear the reality that the war was denying them maternal fulfilment.

No less difficult was the mental trial of parents whose adult children were in the armed forces and away at the fighting fronts of the war. Theirs was an intrinsically realistic dread: the middle-aged could remember the previous war and so would be under no illusions about the chances of their sons coming through the present war unscathed. Instead of the contentment of seeing their children building their married lives and of themselves being grandparents, this generation had to carry the burden of knowing that all such joys were under mortal threat. Mrs Joe Mallinson of Huddersfield faced multiple loss, for she had no less than seven sons, all eligible for military service. Her reaction to the outbreak of war was to gather her brood together and take them to a local photographer for a keepsake photograph, on the reasonable grounds that she was unlikely to see them all survive what was to come.[33] Clara Milburn, living near Coventry, suffered no less for having only one son to worry about – rather the reverse, for being past childbearing age, the loss of her beloved Alan would have been the end of her maternal or grandmaternal experience. Her trauma was weeks of dread-filled days and restless nights, waiting for news. Her agony ended only when she finally heard that her son, who was with the British Expeditionary Force in May 1940 and had gone missing, was a prisoner in Germany, but safe and well.[34] Nella Last succinctly summed up the situation of waiting people everywhere: 'It's such a cruel war: few escape. Bodily or mentally, we are "all in it".'[35]

Behind the separation of spouses and partners lay the understood, although largely unmentioned, misery of sexual deprivation. At a time of life when a settled relationship might normally be expected to have a sexual dimension, millions of people were constrained by events to a life where this was reduced or missing altogether. The luckier ones where those whose partner's work or service was in Britain, for there would always be periods of leave or short-term passes in which to meet. For those whose partners were in distant theatres of the war or, worse, held prisoner by the enemy, long-term sexual frustration was their lot. It had to be accepted as just one of the many ways in which normal life was put 'on hold' by the war. It remains a relatively secret facet of the common experience. While one of its consequences – the phenomenon known as 'drifting', or the striking up of extramarital affairs – was the subject of social surveys and magazine articles and advice, the deprivation itself went without public comment and has left virtually no trace in private record or recollection. It could be held that 'drifting' was a safety valve that sustained the morale of lonely wives.[36] Its downside was the negative effect it had on the morale of servicemen husbands – as German radio's propaganda services recognized and were only to ready to exploit.

In many cases the distance of separation was small enough to permit periodic reunions. The 70 per cent more passengers carried by the railways during the war years might be parents making visits to their children or their own elderly parents in the reception areas, billeted war workers returning home for weekends, or servicemen snatching the chance of a forty-eight hour leave to spend a few hours with their family. It could never be enough and often the time spent travelling would be as long as that spent with the family. People made the effort more or less resignedly, accepting the reality that the situation could not be helped, that it was the same for everyone and, in any case, it would not last for ever. Cheerful resignation was perhaps the most characteristic of responses to the adversity of wartime life. It appears to have been the way thousands of waiting mothers, wives and lovers were able to endure the prolonged absence abroad of their serviceman sons, husbands or lovers. Mass-Observation conducted a survey on happiness in the summer of 1943. Its findings confirm the ready resort of the waiting woman to self-imposed fortitude. A 35-year-old working-class woman responded:

> If your hubby's out in the Middle East, like mine, and you don't know when you'll see him again, you can't be *happy*, it stands to reason. But I think you ought to make the effort to be cheerful, it's better for yourself as well as other people. I made up my mind when he left England that the kids should never see me crying or worrying, and, well, they

seem to be growing up happy, the way they should, and that's worth every bit of effort I've made.[37]

The rationalization of being cheerful for the sake of others is characteristic. A 30-year-old working-class woman, whose husband was in the RAF, put it bluntly: 'Well, what I think is, you can't afford to let yourself go, because of other people.' For her, too, the first of these 'others' was a child: 'I have to keep going, just to keep him happy and contented ... I never have any trouble with him just as long as I don't let myself down.' This was the tough front she adopted to mask the instincts she admitted to: 'I *could* let myself be miserable all the time ... we were very happy together, and I miss him terribly all the time. Sometimes I want just to lie down on my bed and have a good cry.'[38] She might have been speaking for the millions of waiting women everywhere who somehow found the mental reserves to see them through their common trial.

A small but important initiative to mitigate the waiting was the use the BBC made of the capacity of radio waves to cross frontiers and oceans. On the Forces Programme and the short wave services, 'Message Programmes' became regular and popular features. Most of these were aimed at keeping up the spirits of men and women serving in the armed forces overseas and consisted largely of the broadcasting of messages, pre-recorded by relatives or read out by the presenter. But increasingly the Corporation recognized the importance of these link-ups to civilian morale, and for this nothing was better than two-way programmes. *Children Calling Home* and *Hello Parents*, which linked parents and their evacuee children in Australia and South Africa, were as much to do with cheering up the adults as helping homesick children, and short wave link-ups like *Greetings from Cairo* and *Calling Blighty* brought the actual voices of the serving men and women directly to their loved ones listening in their homes to the BBC. Two-way programmes took up a lot of resources, however, and so the one-way programmes continued. One of them, *Sincerely Yours, Vera Lynn*, devised specifically to help wives and servicemen to bear their separation, was among the BBC's most listened-to programmes.

It was upon women that the main burden fell of another common consequence of the men's departure for military service: poverty. An ordinary soldier's wife received seventeen shillings (85p) a week, with additions of five shillings for the first child, three for the second, one for any others. A further seven shillings would be contributed by the husband from his soldier's pay of fourteen shillings. Some employers made up the pay of their serving employees to what it had been before they were called up, but many did not, and there was no legal obligation upon them to do so. This meant that until 1944, when a big overhaul of the system greatly lessened the problem, soldiers' wives with young children lived in real hardship. A mother and three children getting the maximum allowance of thirty-three shillings would be existing on just one-third of the income that the average man in civilian employment was bringing home to his family in 1941.[39] Financial pressure drove many such women to find work to supplement their income. Since there were insufficient day nursery places, going out to work would force them to leave their pre-school children with neighbours. But Mass-Observation found that 80 per cent of mothers surveyed in an area of London were against having their children looked after by neighbours. Rather than do this they did not work at all, struggling on in hardship, or else they took in 'outwork' at very low rates of pay.[40] For too many young wives, then, the pain of separation was compounded by the anxiety of trying to make ends meet.

Restrictions, restrictions

The war had begun with a deluge of orders and regulations and the flow did not abate as the war progressed. What differentiated the civilian experience in the years after the end of the Emergency was not so much the greater intensity of officially imposed constraint but the feeling that the return of normal life was a long way off. Short-term inconvenience was something most could easily tolerate; accepting it as a way of life required the rarer qualities of the stoic.

One of the most onerous of the war's impositions was the wrecking of career plans. The demands of the uniformed services and war industry could only be met by the deflection of millions of people from the careers they had planned for themselves or had already begun. Conscription alone accounted for five million, very few of whom had welcomed it as a good career move. Among them would be apprentices perhaps halfway through their service, articled clerks preparing for professional examinations, or students whose degrees had yet to be completed. Most would spend the duration of the war in uniformed frustration. Some might even find themselves at the coalface, as one of the 'Bevin Boys', drafted by lot, to make up the shortfall in coalminers. Workers in certain occupations might find themselves obliged to remain in work they had wanted to give up. Research workers might see their funding withdrawn and their talents diverted to war-related projects. No man of working age could be sure he would not be uprooted for work away from home. Nor did women escape the Government's attention: by 1943 all single women between sixteen and forty were either in the auxiliaries of the armed forces or doing specified war work. While some might have welcomed this as a challenge or even something they really wanted to do, the fact that compulsion was introduced in December 1941 shows that most women were choosing to do other things with their lives. The power of the war to derail one's life plan was, then, for men and women alike, one of its most resented attributes. But it was the common lot, there was little one could do about it, and so it was grumblingly accepted as a regrettable necessity.

The narrowing of choices might be said to be the leitmotif of the civilian experience of the war. How it operated to limit the choice of whom one lived with and what work one did has already been shown. In all sorts of lesser ways, too, the imperatives of the war economy, translated into government orders and regulations, cramped the lives of the citizens as they lived through these years along 'the tunnel' to victory. After three and a half years of them the journalist E. H. M. Relton ruefully observed: 'Restrictions, discomforts, official supervision that smacks of Fascism – these we suffer but do not enjoy. Nor do we discuss them. But they are felt.'[41]

Every December from the beginning of the war, Mass-Observation asked its National Panel of Observers what they considered the six main inconveniences of the war. In all, nineteen items appeared in the cumulative lists. Top of the list, every year except 1942, when it came second, was the blackout.[42] No more need be said of this than was said in Chapter 2, save only that once the Big Blitz of 1940–41 was over and in most places bombing became a rarity, the blackout's limiting effect on social life was even more acutely felt and the requirement to maintain the nightly routine of putting up the blackout became a wearisome and seemingly pointless chore.

Never falling below third place in Mass-Observation's list – and in 1942 actually heading it – was transport. As we have seen, the need for people to travel was greatly increased by conscription, evacuation, office dispersal and industrial concentration – features of the war that all placed people at a distance from their homes and families. The effect of all these extra journeys on the railway system alone was to increase its passenger traffic by 70 per cent, despite a three-fold increase in fares. Railway posters might ask 'Is your journey really necessary?' but for these people it was a superfluous question. The increased demand would have been problem enough. What made the situation worse was a simultaneous rise of 50 per cent in goods traffic. This came from the need to transport men and materials for military operations; to service the war industries and the distribution of imports, rerouted to the west coast ports; and to carry bombsite rubble from London to locations in eastern England, where new airfields were being constructed for the escalating bombing campaigns against Germany. Finally, the system that was bearing all this extra work was itself becoming less fitted to do so: staff shortages had been caused by the conscription for military service of 100,000 railwaymen, a loss never fully made up; there was a shortage of spare parts because of the conversion of many railway workshops to munitions work; replacement rolling stock was not being made, so the existing stock became progressively rundown; and the infrastructure was damaged by targeted bombing.

Such was the context of travelling by train during the war. The actual experience was predictably stressful. Passengers had to expect much longer journey times than the schedule promised. Delays occurred when passenger trains were diverted into sidings to let more urgent military or munitions trains through, or when air raid alerts at night obliged drivers to dim the lighting and reduce speed to 30 mph. Confusion and inconvenience was caused, especially if the journey was unfamiliar or made after dark, by the absence of station names – removed in June 1940 as part of the steps taken to foil invaders. The trains were always overcrowded and at night the lighting was too weak to allow the mental diversion of reading. Restaurant or buffet cars were rarely provided and station buffets were invariably inadequate for the needs of their would-be customers. Harold Nicolson (overstating a little, perhaps) summed up wartime rail travel, in February 1944: 'St. Pancras station on a wet midnight, and after three hours in a packed corridor, makes one realise that this, in fact, a total war.'[43]

The stress and discomfort of train travel was matched by that of travel by bus. As with the railways, the demand for bus travel increased as the resources of the bus companies contracted. On reduced services, queuing, overcrowding, delays and diversions became part of the experience of getting to and from work or going anywhere beyond walking distance. In all sorts of ways ordinary social life was affected by the difficulty of getting about. When the last bus left the town centre at 9 p.m. many would have to forgo or cut short visits to the cinema or concert hall.[44] Even church attendance might depend on whether one was willing or able to get there on foot, so sparse were transport services on Sundays. Again, what might have been tolerated as an minor inconvenience had it been for a short time became a wearisome part of existence when it dragged on through the six years of war.

The 10 per cent of families fortunate enough to own a car might in theory have been spared the miseries of public transport. However, petrol was rationed for the private motorist at the outbreak of war: just four gallons a month for the smallest car, ten for the largest, with supplementary supplies for essential business or domestic purposes. This might have been just enough for some people. But petrol, like all things imported, was an increasingly scarce commodity and by March 1942 the basic ration had been withdrawn altogether, forcing motorists without essential user status to join the queues for the hard-pressed trains and buses.

The war had worse trials to set than difficulties over transport. Nevertheless, wartime travelling was usually a frustrating and fatiguing experience. Popular references to travel made at the time or in recollection characteristically concentrate on this aspect. But the reasons for the impairment of the services were obvious and generally well understood and, on the whole, the hardship was accepted with the resigned stoicism that people were so often called upon to display during this time. There were even those who insisted on looking for the silver lining to the drab coat of wartime transport. The novelist H. E. Bates, for instance, wrote of his pleasure at the ending of the traditional silence of the English railway compartment: 'The making of friends has never been so easy. In the whole history of the British railways there has never been, I should think, so much conversation and friendliness per mile as now.'[45] But instances of such good-humoured making the best of the situation are rather rare in the record. Only the fact that, despite all the inconveniences, people continued to travel and passenger revolt was not one of the system's problems, suggests that the written record might be misleading. Thus, in Zelma Katin's memorable account of her life as a tramcar and bus conductress in Sheffield, written in 1944, one has to search hard to find among her references to awkward and difficult passengers the rather grudging acknowledgement that the majority were only too obliging.[46] Similarly, Mass-Observation's surveys of public attitudes to transport tell us in great detail what people were grumbling about – overcrowding, bad timekeeping, inadequate heating, dingy and shabby waiting rooms, poor refreshment facilities, and so on – but mention almost in passing that there was 'acceptance that trains cannot run to schedule', that there was 'quite appreciable goodwill towards the buses' and that passengers were 'enthusiastic' about the drivers and conductresses.[47] In the recollections of train and bus travel assembled by Norman Longmate for *How We Lived Then*, one has to read between the lines of the lurid tales the fact that, at the heart of it all, people were making the best of the difficulties. A wartime railway poster read: 'Food, shells and fuel must come first. If your train is late – *do you mind*?' Longmate concluded that 'the public, once convinced the sacrifice of its comfort was necessary, *did not*'.[48]

The rationing of petrol was part of what came to be a near comprehensive system of goods rationing. In Mass-Observation's survey of wartime inconveniences, people put rationing and shortages high on their list, typically just below the blackout and transport. Rationing became more extensive when the efforts to curb waste, to increase home food production and to concentrate consumer goods production on necessities were not enough to make up for the extra needs of the war industries, nor to compensate for the imports lost through enemy action against merchant ships. The limited rationing that sufficed in 1940 had by July 1942 given way to a much more thorough system. Getting enough to eat was not the problem: in terms of quantity and nutrition the nation was probably better off than before the war, at least partly in consequence of the Ministry of Food's provision of welfare foods and its education of the public about nutrition. The problem was monotony. With food imports down by half, and the remaining half concentrated on basic foods, no amount of 'digging for victory' could replace bananas, lemons, cocoa, coffee, tea and all the others products that in normal times flowed into Britain from the tropical and subtropical parts of the world. Some exotic foods simply disappeared for the duration of the war; others appeared very occasionally at exotic prices. The rationing of most foods, moreover, meant that while no one could complain that they went short of calories, the makeup of meals that provided those calories had finite limits. 'Filling up' on bread and potatoes, especially when the greyish National Wheatmeal Loaf was to most people so unpalatable, turned too many meals into dreary boiler-stoking operations. Eating out was a relief for those who could afford restaurant prices; but even this became progressively duller as sources of imported items shrank and government-imposed price capping blunted the restaurateurs' resort to the high-priced offerings of the black market. Some foods – fish, chicken, fruit, vegetables – remained unrationed, but the snag was that their availability was at best intermittent. Fish supplies fluctuated greatly and there was a fall in the overall amount caught, due to labour shortage in the fishing fleets and contraction of safe fishing grounds. In consequence, whenever fish became available in a locality, there were queues, as indeed, there were for onions, oranges and other unrationed items when they erratically appeared in the shops. Queuing for food was one of the home front's characteristic activities, if standing still for hours can be so described. It followed not just from the fluctuations in the supply of certain foods but from the fact that retailers, wanting to appear fair, did not allow customers to build up stocks by buying a large amount at a time. If dietary variety was sought, frequent queuing for small quantities was unavoidable. While it was a chore for everyone, it naturally seemed more burdensome to the elderly, the infirm and those trying to manage the commitments of both work and family. It even robbed children of their leisure time. Ron Ellis, who was nearly seven when the war started, recalled having to forgo football or cricket most Saturday mornings to cycle from his village into Burton upon Trent and queue for whatever happened to be available. And though he was there an hour before Bird's the Bakers opened, he was joining a queue already 100 yards long.[49] In 1940 and 1941 food difficulties came second only to the blackout in people's concern. Mass-Observation reported in July 1941, when queuing was getting worse, that food shortages were causing 'disproportionate damage to people's emotions'. Tomatoes had disappeared from the shops as soon as the Minister of Food, Lord Woolton, announced price control. The same thing happened to strawberries, and potatoes as soon as price control was imposed. People were 'bewildered and annoyed', too, by the scarcity of eggs.[50] Clearly, not all food retailers were interested in being fair and cooperative. In 1942 food slipped to third place in the list and then to fourth in 1943. This indicates that although the food situation was perceived to be improving after rationing reached its fullest extent and that the Government was winning the battle to get food off the list of morale depressants, it was none the less always a cause of dissatisfaction. And yet, some could look back on shortages and the rigours of the food queue and remember its compensations. Elizabeth Smith, a housewife in Sunderland, recalled:

> Every day I used to meet my sisters in town and we would join the queues when a few oranges, fish – in fact, when anything that was unrationed was for sale. Oh, the laughs we used to have listening to the conversations of the people! The things some of them would have loved to do to Hitler and his gang ... In spite of our fears, we could always have a good laugh.[51]

If dull sufficiency characterized wartime food, of practically everything else there was dull insufficiency. One of the hardest shortfalls to take was that of coal, still the means by which most homes were heated. Coal output was falling at the same time that industrial demand for coal was increasing. The result was inadequate supply for domestic users. From July 1941 there were restrictions placed on household deliveries and in January 1944 these were tightened still further to no more than 4 cwt. a month for a household, and that only if the householder had less than 20 cwt. in stock. Wartime hearths were necessarily frugal affairs. It so happened that the first three winters of the war were unusually severe. The difficulty of keeping warm, especially if one's house had suffered bomb damage and was less than draught-free, was therefore just one more problem, one more obstacle to good cheer.

Progressively, the Government reduced the number of consumer goods it considered essential and then imposed on these, simple, basic standards of material content and design. In consequence all manner of 'luxuries' went into short supply or disappeared altogether and choice was limited in what remained. With the former, the problem for most people was that the line the Board of Trade drew between 'essential' and 'inessential' was too low. A large number of household and personal items were designated inessential and when these were used up or worn past repair people were obliged to do without or else begin the desperate and time-consuming search for replacements. Journalist George Beardmore, already having trouble finding cigarettes and bemoaning the quality of the sausages he had queued for ('mainly breadcrumbs'), wrote of razor blades, 'one simply has to marry a shopkeeper's daughter before one can get hold of new one'.[52] The same severe mind that classed a close shave as inessential came down on meeting the basic needs of babies. Production of feeding bottles and rubber teats was reduced, along with that of many other items of baby equipment such as cots, mattresses, cot sheets, baths, prams and pushchairs. For young father Ced Waters, the day he was sent out by his distracted wife to scour the chemist shops of Chester, following the breaking of the last remaining feeding bottle in the house, was carved in his memory as deeply as anything else that happened in the war.[53] A survey carried out by the Board of Trade itself in 1943 revealed the sort of difficulties people were experiencing; it showed that over a four-week period, of women seeking to buy a frying pan, more than half were unsuccessful, and of those trying to buy a saucepan, three-quarters had failed. One of the saddest casualties of the new austerity was the production of toys, or rather those toys that contained certain materials that had become scarce – kapok, hemp, rubber, cork, celluloid and plastics. Since balloons and crackers had gone entirely and sugar was in short supply for cakes and icing, parents had real difficulty in providing their children with anything like the traditional celebration of birthdays and Christmas. Richard Brown, like all the fathers he knew, spent the evenings of successive Novembers and Decembers crafting wooden toys from bits of wood saved from purchases made for house maintenance or for repairing bomb damage.[54] People were urged to use public transport less ('Is Your Journey Really Necessary?'), and yet bicycles and accessories like tyres, inner tubes and brake blocks were in short supply. Matches, torch batteries, alarm clocks, plates and teacups – the list of everyday things that became scarce was seemingly endless and constituted a real reduction in the material quality of life.

The imposition of rationing on clothes was as much an emotional as a physical deprivation. It was compounded, moreover, by the application, in 1942, of Utility standards to clothes, making manufacturers conform to stringent limits on the amount of material they used for every item. The resulting garments were for many people depressingly plain and spare-looking (although the system's blindness to the quality of the cloth, as distinct from its quantity, permitted those with higher incomes to purchase clothes that would last, using no more coupons than for clothes that would not – a perceived unfairness and consequently a grievance often voiced).[55] By denying to people the simple pleasure that could come from the purchase of an attractive new outfit, hat or pair of shoes, clothes controls contributed to the general drabness of wartime life, besides condemning women to spending much of their spare time darning and patching old clothes and making new ones from whatever bits of material they could come by. In doing so they were following the official advice, briskly sloganized as 'Make Do and Mend'. No one could deny that there was an absolute need for the demands of the fighting forces to take priority over those of the civilian sector, but while the intellect might acknowledge national necessity, the discomfort and inconvenience that was its corollary was nevertheless a real test of the individual's sense of material well-being.

One of the factors aggravating this sense was the gradually increasing presence in many parts of Britain of soldiers and airmen from the USA. Objectively this should have had an unqualifiedly positive effect on British morale, since it provided concrete proof of the likelihood of victory. After the early years of 'fighting alone', the arrival of the Americans was certainly a welcome development. But once people had the assurance of ultimate victory they tended to take it for granted, and then the negative side of hosting the three million visitors became more apparent. On their bases the young servicemen fed like peacetime princes and on the town they never seemed short of spending-money. George Orwell wrote about the resentment caused by the knowledge that precious shipping space was being used to import food luxuries for the GIs, even bulk items like beer, for they apparently would not drink English beer.[56] In essence it was a problem of relative deprivation: the conspicuous consumption of the GIs stood in stark contrast to the austerely plain lifestyle that most English people had been reduced to and it was difficult not to feel at best a little envious. In due course, the affluence of the visitors ceased to matter much in people's state of mind. The reason was the increasing participation of US soldiers on the fighting fronts, first in North Africa and Italy, then in the great invasion of occupied Europe in June 1944. And all along, increasing numbers of US airmen were joining in the strategic bombing of Germany. When Americans were sharing the real pain of war in death and injury their hosts found it hard to resent their privileges.

The impairment of material comfort tends to bulk large in people's memories of the war, disproportionately so, perhaps. Everyone who lived through this time has his or her tale of the trial of being short of or without a peacetime favourite, whether it was the taste of fresh lemons, the feel of silk stockings, the scent of French perfume or the warm glow of a large open fire. Whatever one was used to there was bound to be some loss. How much people were really depressed by this seems to have depended on the individual's disposition. Mass-Observation's surveys certainly confirm that most people grumbled about shortages and loss of choice and that, when asked, they put these things high on their list of complaints: 'Considerable lack of cheerful sacrifice' noted a report of June 1941.[57] And, in contrast to attitudes to food rationing (discussed further in Chapter 5), the perception that the system of clothes rationing fell well short of achieving 'Fair Shares for All', was widespread and persistent, featuring prominently in the reports of Home Intelligence and Mass-Observation. On the other hand, for every Mollie Panter-Downes, upset at the reduction in the number of pleats permitted in a skirt, there was a Richard Brown phlegmatically refusing to grumble about all the war's constraints: 'Clothes rationing announced today, to come into force at once. We'll be allowed sixty-six units a year. That seems plenty to me.'[58] In the final analysis, most people accepted the basic principle of rationing as the fairest way of sharing unavoidably reduced resources, and in consequence they complied more or less willingly with the system. There is too, the plentiful evidence of willingness to give 'Make do and Mend' a try. Anyone who had a garden could get a few vegetable seeds into the soil and most did, even authors like George Orwell and George Beardmore, who might have been expected to begrudge the time 'digging for victory' took from their writing. 'Grow your own onions' urged Lord Woolton, but the more enterprising went still further and took to keeping poultry or even a pig in their backyards. Some people eked out their coal stocks with supplements of coal bricks made from coal dust mixed with earth, pine cones and sticks gathered on country walks, driftwood collected from the seashore or timber from the rubble of bombed buildings. Others adopted the sociable solution of 'fire sharing', that is, groups of neighbours spending winter evenings together in one another's houses, each coming with some lumps of coal for the communal blaze. By such methods domestic coal consumption in the final year of the war was down to thirty-three million tons, three-quarters of the annual amount used before the war.[59] Not letting fuel shortages dominate one's outlook required self-discipline, none the less. Nan Fairbrother, alone with her two small sons in their Buckinghamshire farmhouse, recalled a testing time, when for three weeks in severe weather they had no fuel at all and how, after being miserable with cold at first, they rallied: 'we soon accepted the cold house, soon the children got used to being muffled up with layer upon layer of wool ... It had the advantage, too, that we lived as much out of doors as we do in Summer, for like Summer it was no colder in the garden than in the house, and the frosty country was a delight'.[60]

The rationing of clothes unleashed the national genius for invention and adaptation. Richard Brown cheerfully recorded in his diary in April 1944: 'I've been wearing a mac for work this winter which had been retired once', noting also that 'Housewives spend lots of time in cutting down and it is the rule, almost, for youngsters' things to be made from rejected grown-up things.'[61] All manner of materials were put to use in the making of clothes: cheesecloth, curtain net and butter muslin – all unrationed – for underwear, cleaning rolls for nightdresses, blackout material for skirts or evening dresses, surplus service blankets for 'blanket coats' or winter dressing gowns. Of course, by the final year of the war everyone looked comparatively shabby in their threadbare, patched or improvised garments, but since the deterioration was universal it was hard to feel deprived. The occasional wistfulness about the lack of new and

stylish clothes is more than outweighed in the record by the sense
of achievement people evidently got from rising to the challenge of
rationing and shortage. Such was the case of a young woman who
worked in a government drawing office. She had been given an old
linen map, which she decided could be turned into a blouse. Firstly,
she boiled it to remove the starch and printer's ink; then she dyed
and ironed it; and finally, using an old paper pattern and buttons
from an old dress, cut out and made up a wearable blouse that had
cost her only ninepence and used no coupons. As she recalled: 'I
was very proud of this blouse.' Another instance was the Hendon
family who through a friend came by salvaged material from a
bombed-out undertakers. A large bolt of purple material, used for
covering coffins going for cremation, was changed – by soaking –
into a shade of blue-gray and made into two longsleeved winter
dresses; another bolt of white muslin – used for lining coffins – was
transformed into pillow cases, handkerchiefs and curtains.[62]

The same resourcefulness and adaptivity was called upon to wage
war on the kitchen front and recalled later with the same sense of
accomplishment. In part, this was a case of being willing to try
previously neglected sources of food, like dandelion leaves and nettle
tips, cowheel, tripe and oxcheek, or new things that were on offer
like whalemeat and dried eggs; in part, it was a matter of finding
substitutes like carrots for almonds in puddings, dried elderberries
and chopped prunes for currants in cakes, and potatoes for practically everything. The lack of egg yolks and olive oil did not deter
Mrs K. Dent of Birmingham from trying to make mayonnaise; the
Daily Telegraph rewarded her with ten shillings and sixpence for
her version, which used reconstituted egg powder and margarine.
In Richard Brown's household, his wife's inventiveness, together
with the supplements from his carefully tended allotment, led him
to conclude: 'We don't feel the lack of meat ... In fact I sometimes
think the dishes we get now are more delicious than before the
war.'[63] This was probably putting on a brave face. Most people did
not welcome the shortages and loss of choice. But it must also be
noted that for a sizeable section of the poorer classes, wartime food
was actually an improvement on their pre-war diet in terms of both
quantity and nutritional value. The extent to which this was a consequence of government policy initiatives is discussed in detail in
Chapter 5. It will suffice here to say that the factors included greater

average disposable income in the average household, an increase in the consumption of school dinners, the provision of welfare foods – milk, orange juice, blackcurrant juice and cod liver oil – for infants and nursing mothers, a general rise in the average adult's milk consumption, communal feeding in workers' canteens and cheap British Restaurants and nutritional education from the Ministry of Food, put out by the press and radio. Better eating quickly translated into improved health and vitality. To the extent, therefore, that the nation's state of mind depended on how well it was being fed, while the war might have seemed to many a gastronomically bleak period, it was in fact a time of improvement. It is perhaps significant that most of the contemporary complaint about wartime food, and most of the later testimony, is from the relatively affluent, for whom the plain and restricted fare of shops and restaurants came as more of a change. For the average person, apart from the inconveniences of rationing, queuing and erratic supply, food was not problem enough significantly to depress the spirits.

Getting nourishment for the mind, as for the body, required effort, because, here too, there was contraction, restriction and loss of choice. Getting away for a holiday or short break was hemmed in with difficulties, as public transport struggled to operate, petrol became hard to get and resorts were blighted by barbed wire and tank traps. Even the alternative of day coach trips disappeared. The best one could hope for and, indeed, what one was officially encouraged to settle for, was a 'holiday at home': picnics and music in the park, trips to the zoo, boating on the river, and the like. Watching the star performers of one's favourite sport was the sort of mental refreshment that also effectively disappeared. Spectator sport, at the highest level at least, was badly impoverished by the call-up of many of the players, who, after all, were of the right age for military service and by definition fit enough for it. The biggest spectator sport of all, football, continued, but without most of its leading professionals, the league reorganized on a regional basis to save on travelling and some of the grounds given over to Civil Defence purposes. Even the teams of the leading clubs were often made up of schoolboys or part-timers from the forces or industry, occasionally strengthened by the guest appearance of a star player released by the forces for the day. The relatively low standard of the play compared with before the war, together with the increase in

Saturday working in many industries, led to a falling away of spectators, and many clubs closed down for the rest of the war. Cricket fared even worse. From 1940 to 1944 the county championship was suspended and first class cricket effectively ceased except for the irregular treats of one day fixtures between scratch sides, which included any professionals who might be available. Again, cricket grounds often fell victim to the needs of Civil Defence – barrage balloons, anti-aircraft batteries and searchlights – or to the necessity to render open spaces unusable to the aircraft of an invading enemy. Racing was suspended at the outbreak of war and when allowed to resume was restricted to just six racecourses, all in England, and to operating with only locally trained horses. Greyhound racing was limited to one day a week per track. The same factors that decimated the spectator sports enfeebled the participation sports. Golf courses, tennis courts, rugby pitches, parks and recreation grounds all made suitable places for conversion to food production or Civil Defence. When the All England Tennis Club at Wimbledon had become a Home Guard drill ground, the Oval cricket ground a prisoner of war camp, the rugby ground at Twickenham an allotment, Kempton Park racecourse an internment camp and Epsom racecourse a military training area, the chances of survival for the humble spaces of the amateur were slim. And as for energy consuming facilities like swimming pools and ice rinks, closure was virtually a foregone conclusion.

The level of restriction on sports owed much to government policy. At the outbreak of war all outdoor sports meetings were banned; during the Phoney War it allowed activities to be resumed; in the national crisis of mid-1940 sport was stopped altogether but again allowed to pick up again towards the end of the year; at the time of the fall of Singapore and Churchill's Cabinet changes in early 1942 tight restrictions were reimposed, only to be gradually eased as the war situation improved. Finally, in the last months of the war the Government placed no restraint at all on the efforts of authorities, clubs and associations to revive activity and as a result something approaching peacetime levels was achieved. The erratic nature of government intervention reflected ambivalence about the place of sport in war. There were many in official life and outside it who thought that the allocation of any resources at all to sport during a struggle for national survival was wasteful and that sport, moreover, served to distract the nation from the necessary war effort. In a Commons debate in February 1942, at a time when the *Daily Express* was running a campaign for much more drastic restrictions on sport, the Lord President of the Council and Leader of the House, Sir Stafford Cripps, referred to dog racing and boxing as 'completely out of accord with the true spirit of determination of the people'. They should 'no longer be allowed to offend the solid and serious intention of the country to achieve victory'.[64] But this was the extreme view. Most MPs backed the Government line that, on the whole, sport was valuable – even purely spectator sport of the kind Cripps and others condemned – because it helped to sustain popular morale. There was little argument about the usefulness of participant sports for the armed forces as an aid to physical fitness and team spirit, and a similar case could be made in respect of the civilian population. The Government kept its critics at bay by adopting a generally tolerant policy, periodically imposing restrictions on sport as and when the national situation suggested revision of priorities. Things might have been worse, then, but for all the efforts of the authorities to maintain some semblance of sporting recreation for the citizen, there was no concealing the impoverishment of both the spectator side and the participatory side of sport under the exigencies of war. For a sporting nation like the British, this was just one more way in which the war threatened to wear down the Dunkirk spirit and to nibble away at civilian morale.

Working and not working

As it happened, the effect of restrictions on leisure was less than it might have been. For a sizeable proportion of the civilian population there was in reality very little time for leisure activity at all. If it meant nothing else, total war meant work – work for every available pair of hands. By 1941 the drafting of young men into the armed forces, together with the huge expansion of munitions and food production, had created a demand for labour that could not be met simply by the pre-war pool of the unemployed. Additional sources of labour were found in married women and retired people, but there was still an absolute excess of demand over supply. One of the inevitable consequences of this situation was an increase in the average number of hours people worked and a with it an increase in industrial fatigue. In theory workers could choose whether or not to do overtime; in practice they were under strong moral pressure to do it, not only from employers but also from fellow workers making up the teams that characterized the working arrangements in many workshops. A survey of 160 factories conducted in the autumn of 1941 found that in more than half a fifty-five hour week was being worked. In just under half there were women working fifty-eight or sixty hours. Even after reductions in the working week, in 1944 women were typically still working fifty or fifty-five hours a week.[65] The figures reveal not just how great the burden of war work was, but that in falling on women as much as men it was loading an already hard-pressed section of the population. A report of the Council of Social Services in Liverpool in May 1941 observed: 'many of these workers have been subjected to unaccustomed strains both at home and at their work. The normal holiday and weekend arrangements have of necessity been interrupted and as a result there is a danger of a reduction in productive capacity due to persistent fatigue, in some cases leading to breakdown in health'.[66] The 'unaccustomed strains' referred to here were a series of devastating air raids; but even without air raids there was plenty of unaccustomed strain for women managing the double burden of home and work, finding time to queue for food, prepare meals and keep the house clean in the few hours spared from paid work. And just to add to the pressure, there was for women the bitter aggravation of unequal pay, for, as Eleanor Rathbone said in a Commons debate in February 1942, 'we often find that when a job is offered to a woman, changes are made in the processes to enable the employers to say it is not the same job that a man was doing before, but a different one. Then changes are made in the rate of pay.'[67]

The strain of long hours of work, often on a shift system, was universal, however. The fact that it was of necessity prolonged over months, then years, as the war dragged on, told on everyone. Nor did its routinization prevent particular groups from being subject to the additional strain of periods of intense activity in fulfilment of an urgent order. When the Huddersfield firm of David Brown and Sons, working at full-stretch pitch-testing gears for battleships, was given an order for a newly designed tank gearbox, inhuman demands were asked of the workers. An account of the routine of one of them, Jack Oldroyd, records:

Jack began work at 7.30 a.m. on Monday, working through until Tuesday midday. He was then taken home to rest; then he and others working on the job were up first thing Wednesday to begin again, working through the night until Thursday midday. Returning home to sleep, he was at Brown's on Friday morning, where he worked until Saturday dinnertime. This routine went on for three weeks, at the end of which Jack felt 'absolutely beggared'.[68]

No overtime was paid for this exhausting routine, and the timekeeping was so strict that even a visit to the lavatory required clocking in and out. Brown's was not typical of war industry as a whole, but the anecdote goes some way to explaining why by the middle years of the war there was talk of a general malaise affecting the industrial workforce. Workers – and not just at Brown's – felt, it was said, in the phrase of the day, 'browned-off'. Diana Murray Hill described the process of becoming browned-off:

> Scarcely perceptible at first, and then steadily and more steadily growing till, aided by other factors like lack of sleep, petty illnesses, and factory disturbances, it permeates and then predominates your whole life ... the browned-off man has his fingers on you and after he has had you in his insidious grip for a year, two years, or more, unless your morale and health are very sturdy, he can make you very poor shadows of the War Effort Girls.[69]

The way such feelings showed themselves was in an increase in industrial absenteeism and unofficial strikes. Records for absenteeism were not kept systematically in the period 1939–41; thereafter the Government gave the matter close attention and something like reliable national statistics were compiled. These showed that the average absence for men was 6 to 8 per cent of man-hours worked and for women an average of 12 to 15 per cent. This was double the pre-war rate, although there was no further increase between 1943 and early 1945, when there was a slight rise.[70] Despite the improvement of arbitration machinery through the establishment in 1940 of a National Tribunal, the number of strikes rose. In 1941 the number of days lost was 1,077,000 and this continued to rise to a peak of 3,696,000 in 1944.[71]

While no one imagined that the level of effort achieved during the crisis of 1940 was sustainable over the longer term, the falling away represented by the data on absenteeism and strikes was of grave concern to the Government and was the subject of a long-

running national debate in the press. If victory depended on continuing commitment and maintenance of the national effort, which
was how the official propaganda of the day had it, then the situation on the industrial front was worrying. In 1942, although there
were reasons for optimism about the final outcome of the war, there
was clearly still a long way to go and a continuing need, therefore,
to resist complacency and relaxation of effort. Judged on the figures, this need was not well understood among workers; rather,
selfishness and sectionalism appeared to be present in an increasing
proportion of them. In its 1942 examination of northern factories
Mass-Observation found no change in pre-war attitudes among
employers and workers: 'One looked in vain for any sign of a unity
binding all parties in the fight against Germany ... the real war
which is being fought here today is still pre-war, private and economic.'[72] Given the official view that high morale and a cooperative and committed attitude went hand in hand, was the slackening
off of the productive effort therefore a sign that civilian morale was
faltering?

In the matter of absenteeism, any attempt at gauging its significance for civilian morale must first recognize that, by later standards, the statistics produced were crude. Most firms had not kept
a record of absenteeism before the war and the few that had followed no common method. Comparisons between the war years
and pre-war, therefore, are little more than rough estimates. The
Ministry of Labour and the Ministry of Supply began to collect
information from 1942. This produced figures that were, for the
first time, anything like reliable; but even these suffered from the
conflation of avoidable and unavoidable absenteeism. The distinction is crucial, for no one could seriously argue that sickness or
fatigue were frivolous reasons for failure to report for work. Half
of all cases were accounted for by certified sickness. Of the remaining half, one half could be estimated to be unavoidable, the rest
avoidable absences. A telling facet of the figures reveals why: they
show that women had twice the rate of absence as men – even
higher if they were married.[73] The reason for this surely lies not in
the greater proneness of women to sickness but to the unequal way
in which the burdens of life on the home front fell on men and
women? Women workers with young children depended on the
availability of child care. Where there were day nurseries, this was

in theory a resolvable problem, for day workers, at least. But the provision of nurseries was patchy and insufficient, which meant that many women had to resort to the intrinsically less reliable willingness of older relatives or neighbours to act as minders. Again, it was on women that the time-consuming task of family shopping largely fell. Shop opening-hours actually contracted during the war. Unless a woman was fortunate enough to work in a firm that gave its women employees time off for shopping, the only times available to her were her lunch hours or Saturday afternoons, when the queues were longest. Mass-Observation recorded the views of some typical women workers at the end of 1941: 'We are expected to shop in the lunch hour, and that means either not having a proper lunch or not shopping properly'; 'The place where I work is away from the place where I live, and it takes too long to get back and shop even if I spend the whole lunch hour on it. I have to shop back there because those are my registered shops for rations'; 'having to shop at any odd hours, we who are working in factories are at a great disadvantage to the women who are not doing anything, and who get all the pick in the morning'.[74] Housework had somehow to be managed on Sundays or in what was left of the evenings. If a woman's work also entailed travelling time, it can readily be understood why, short of changing to part-time work, she had no alternative but simply to take off the occasional day to catch up with her other duties, thereby clocking up another 'avoidable' absence. Apart from the real likelihood that if women tried to manage everything without days off they would become ill with exhaustion, the relatively high incidence of female absenteeism reveals less about commitment to victory than about the failure of employers and other family members to adjust their thinking to take account of the unequal burden that fell on so many women. By the end of 1941, the Ministry of Labour was belatedly trying to persuade employers to give women time off for shopping. Where this occurred a difference was made, but the gap between what women needed and what they got forced many of them, in the interest of their own survival, to take their own measures.

Women were not the worst offenders, however. That label attached rather to juveniles – workers aged fourteen to eighteen. This group, moreover, also had the worst record for time-keeping. At the time it was put down to the effects of full employment on attitude formation. Too young for national service and free from fear of dismissal, this cohort of young people often felt differently about work, at least for the time being. They knew that at eighteen their choices would narrow or disappear entirely. These adolescent years therefore had about them the irresistible quality of a last fling, largely absent before the war, and many evidently seized the chance while they still had it.

Another aspect of absenteeism comes to light if the detail of the statistics is analysed. A Mass-Observation investigation in August 1941 at two shipyards on the Clyde, Fairfield's and Denny's, showed that within the overall absentee rate of 6 to 8 per cent, which was twice or three times the pre-war rate, the figure for overtime absenteeism was no less than 35 per cent. The explanation, the investigators discovered, was that the men objected to paying tax on overtime – especially when this was weekend work – and that, in any case, the new income tax assessment made many workers feel it was financially not worth working beyond a certain point. These were men, moreover, who in many cases had known years of unemployment and who were thoroughly pessimistic about the prospect of their current jobs being still there once the war was over. For these men, and by extension those in like situations elsewhere, there were limits to the power of the appeal for national sacrifice on behalf of a country that had treated them so poorly in the past.[75]

When the global figures on absenteeism are adjusted to take account of the female element, if not that of the juvenile, they look altogether less significant as an indicator of the patriotic commitment of the workforce. None the less, they do suggest some slackening of enthusiasm for the national project as the war went on. Moral reproof would be misplaced, however. What happened was no more than the entirely predictable outcome of straightforward war-weariness, the susceptibility of ordinary human beings to cumulative fatigue. The whole outlook of the war, moreover, was in mid-1943, say, fundamentally different from that of 1940–41. When the sense of threat was relatively weak and ultimate victory seemed assured it was not surprising that the average citizen's readiness for self-sacrifice abated to some degree, and that his or her effort accordingly failed to match that of the days of crisis. Even trade union leader turned Minister of Labour, Ernest Bevin, while recognizing that there was 'no defeatism and very little evidence of war weariness' and that 'hard work, alterations in mode of life and various inconveniences are accepted as a necessary part of the war effort', complained that 'in the absence of military operations close to the country there is no fiery enthusiasm or sense of urgency among workers collectively'.[76] And yet, despite the crucial change in the psychological environment, when one might have expected the national effort to have gone on slackening, in the last three years of the war, for all but the final phase, the rate of absenteeism remained constant.

Many of the factors that gave rise to absenteeism were also behind industrial disputes. But as we have seen, the number of days lost through disputes, in contrast to those lost through absenteeism, more than tripled between 1941 and 1944, with a parallel loss in production. What at first sight might be taken to indicate the existence of widespread and unprecedented industrial malaise at a time of national need, however, looks less damning when the picture is clarified. Firstly, a comparison with the figures for the First World War shows that the record was appreciably better in the Second World War. Although the number of stoppages between 1939 and 1945 was nearly twice that of 1914–18, fewer workers were involved directly or indirectly – 480,000 compared with 632,000. Also, the number of days lost was fewer – 1,900,000 compared with 5,360,000; and the yearly average of time lost in the second war was only 35 per cent of that lost in the first.[77] Secondly, the figures for industry as a whole conceal the fact that a sizeable part of the problem concerned a single industry: coalmining. No less than 46.6 per cent of the strikes, 55.7 per cent of the working days lost and 58.5 per cent of the workers involved were accounted for by coal. There were special reasons why industrial conflict was so much worse in this industry than in others. Until late in the war, despite its exhausting and hazardous nature, it was relatively ill paid: in 1944 miners came fourteenth for pay in a list of one hundred occupations. For the greater part of the war, therefore, miners felt relatively deprived, especially when they compared themselves with munitions workers, who earned more money in less dangerous work.[78] Even had pay not been an issue, the pre-war legacy of employer–worker relations in coalmining was largely negative. The bitter disputes of the interwar years had created an adversarial mindset on both sides. An American mission to the British coalfields in mid-1944 commented on 'the bad feeling and antagonism which pervades the industry and which manifests itself in low morale, non-cooperation and indifference'.[79] It was here referring to the miners, but it elsewhere criticised the failings of managers, from their reluctance to invest in new technology to their dictatorial management style. The charge against the miners is that they put self-interest ahead of patriotic effort: on all counts – absenteeism, strikes and output per man – their record is certainly poor, relative to other workers. But it should be borne in mind that the problems of the industry could not be simply spirited away when war came. The official historian summed up his explanation of coal's wartime troubles: 'Many of the most unsatisfactory features of the war record of the coal industry arose from the fact that in 1939 the industry had been a sick industry and the mineworking community, with all its abundant reserves of vitality, a sick society.'[80] The depressing wartime figures relating to coal were, in fact, better in some respects than those for the pre-war period. Between 1929 and 1938 the average number of days lost through strikes was two million, whereas in every war year except 1944 the number was less than 900,000; between 1935 and 1939 52 per cent of the days lost by all industry were accounted for by coalmining, a percentage only exceeded in the war years by that for 1944; and whereas 62 per cent of all industrial disputes in the 1935–39 period involved the 6 per cent of the insured working population who were miners, in the war years, when miners accounted for 5 per cent of insured workers, the figure was down to 46.6 per cent. Criticism of the miners has concentrated on negative attitudes, but other factors affecting productivity were of some account. It was a fact that in this traditionally young man's industry the average age of the workforce was rising: in 1931 it was 34 years 6 months, in 1941 it was 37 years 1 month and the proportion of the workforce over 40 years of age rose from 33.5 per cent in 1931 to 40.6 per cent in 1941.[81] Dr H. S. Houldsworth, Fuel and Power controller for North East Region, reckoned in 1942 that much of the absenteeism was due to 'the poor physique of some of the older men'.[82] It should also be borne in mind that three-fifths of Britain's coal output came from districts where the mines were old, more difficult to work or were under-capitalized and where it was therefore impossible to match the productivity achievements of the modern mines of the Midlands Amalgamated District.[83]

The charge that the miners failed to meet their patriotic obligations but rather exploited the national crisis to their own advantage is exaggerated, therefore. It should also be emphasized that
miners constituted *only* 5 per cent of the working population. For
the vast majority of workers the charge does not even arise; they
did all that was asked of them. And if national productivity was
disappointing in the war years, it was nevertheless an improvement
on pre-war: in 1945 output per worker was 4 per cent above the
level of the last year of peace. This improvement, moreover, was
achieved despite the drag of several adverse factors: the dilution of
skilled labour in the workforce; the ageing composition of the
workforce; disruption to production caused by air attack; production delays due to interruption of supplies and design modifications; management deficiencies; and, perhaps most important of
all, a decline of 13.1 per cent in the capital-to-labour ratio.[84] While
lack of commitment cannot be discounted as a factor in low productivity – especially in the coal and shipbuilding industries – it is
not at all clear that it should be accounted the prime cause. If civilian morale is in any way to be equated with performance at work,
the verdict must be that morale was sound enough. It was always
possible to cite examples of bad behaviour; the press would from
time to time feature scandalous instances of lazy or malingering
workers, and everyone had a tale to tell of some slackness they had
come upon. The much-quoted journalist J. L. Hodson told of a
doctor acquaintance's bitter complaint about the workmen sent by
the Ministry of Labour to repair his hospital's roof. They hung about
and did no more than two hours work a day. When he told them so,
one said 'Well, what about it?' But Hodson went on to comment
that such tales were negligible 'set against the mass of fine and solid
work being done', underlining the point that the repute of the many
should never be tarnished by the transgressions of the few.[85]

The rise in crime during the war might at first sight be taken to be
evidence of an increase in selfish and anti-social behaviour that
reflected badly on the state of civilian morale. The statistics for the
war years show an increase of 57 per cent in the number of recorded crimes. This compares with an increase of only 21 per cent
in the previous five years. At the same time the number of accused
found guilty rose by 54 per cent. The story behind the figures,

however, shows that the obvious inference – that civilian morale was poor and getting worse – would be the wrong one. In his monograph on wartime crime, Edward Smithies showed that much, if not all, of the increase can be accounted for by the greatly expanded range of behaviour classified as criminal under emergency regulations.[86] No less than 300,000 people passed through the courts in 1940, charged with offences against the blackout regulations. One might assume that many of these were otherwise law-abiding citizens whose only real offence was carelessness. The rationing system created a whole new area of illegal activity, the black market, which also made pitfalls for the unwary. And for a time the police took a much more serious view of certain offences; the public expression of extremist political views, for example, was judged to be damaging to public morale; or 'careless talk' which threatened national security. Conscription and labour law could also make criminals out of otherwise law-abiding people. In short, the regime of wartime tended to criminalize many who were strangers to the courts. One does not have to insist that people behaved like angels to make the point that the statistics on wartime crime are, to say the least, ambivalent in the light they throw upon the state of civilian morale.

At the very opposite end of the spectrum of human behaviour to industrial absenteeism was a response to the pressures of war that deserves at least as much notice: volunteering. Few behaviours demonstrate more unambiguously active commitment to the national purpose and arguably, few serve so well as litmus test of the state of civilian morale. As has been shown, in 1940 official calls for voluntary effort, from joining the Local Defence Volunteers or ARP to donating cooking pots for aircraft manufacture, were resoundingly successful, more than fulfilling the hopes or expectations of the ministers who made them. In the phase of heavy bombing that followed, volunteers were the essential auxiliaries of the post-raid services, at a time of manifest national crisis. The long haul was an intrinsically severer test of unselfish commitment. Was the surge of freely-given effort sustained through the four remaining years of the war?

As the call-up drew more and more young men into the armed forces, it became clear that the war effort required many more workers than could be provided by the pre-war pool of unemployed. Every alternative source was surveyed by the Ministry of Labour. A temptingly large reserve of untapped labour was identified in the adult female population. Accordingly, the Government launched a campaign to get women to come forward for work of national importance, either moving from less essential work or entering work for the first time. The results of this campaign were disappointing; too few women answered the call, and the consequence was the introduction of female conscription. Under the National Service (No. 2) Act of December 1941 unmarried women aged between twenty and thirty (the lower limit being reduced to nineteen in 1942 and the upper to forty in 1943) had to register for work, choosing between the armed services, civil defence and industry. Married women up to forty (later raised to fifty-one) who were without big family responsibilities had to register for war work. This resort to compulsion might seem to be clear evidence of female apathy towards the war effort: despite all the moral chivvying they were subjected to, they were apparently unmoved. But before so harsh a judgement is pronounced it should be recognized that taking up war work was problematical for many women, a fact insufficiently understood by a largely male officialdom at the time. Even for the category of women that was targeted most in the initial appeals – young single women – it was not a straightforward matter. Most of those already in paid work were in domestic service, shops and offices, or the textile, clothing, boot and shoe, food and drink, and light engineering industries. For these, transfer to a working life in the armed forces or in the engineering, metals, explosives, chemicals and shipbuilding industries, clearly meant more than a change of scene. At the very least, it meant entering a traditionally male environment, where, at least initially, women would be in a minority and where fitting in might be difficult. Efforts were of course made by the authorities to persuade them that they would be warmly welcomed and given every possible assistance towards learning the job, and that a happy sense of fulfilment would be their reward. But this presumed that women in their own lives had no experience of male prejudice and resistance to change and were incapable of extrapolating from it. As Eleanor Rathbone said in a Commons debate: 'Many trade unions, especially in the engineering industry, have opposed the admission of women ... They have objected to women as women.'[87] No amount of propaganda, moreover, could prevent potential volunteers from discovering or simply hearing about what life was really like in the services, in heavy industry or on the land. It could turn out to be a liberating and happy experience, and many have testified that it was; but others encountered mockery or sexual harassment from male colleagues, or were given the hardest, dirtiest or least interesting jobs to do. Mary Fedden, a 'Land Girl' in her early twenties, recalled: 'The farmer was absolutely dyed in the wool, and thought no woman could be any use on the farm. He had to take me because his chaps had gone to war, and he had only two old men. So he had to accept me, and he gave me all the toughest jobs he could to try to prove I was no good.'[88] Everywhere women were paid less than men, for even in firms on government contracts, where the principle of equal pay for equal work was established, employers often classified the work either as 'women's work', or 'men's work' that required additional supervision, so that in practice they could pay the women less than the men. The average wage for women in 1944 was only 53 per cent of that for men.[89] To the extent that the attractiveness of work related to the prospect it opened up of training and a career, few women had reason to be drawn. Most of the work was unskilled, and even where some skills training was offered, it did not imply long-term employment. 'Dilution' agreements between employers and trade unions, with Ministry of Labour approval, bound the signatories to the restoration of pre-war trade practices when the war was over. Such 'safeguards' for men meant absolute job insecurity for the women taken on during the war. High profile disputes like the women's pay-strike at the Rolls Royce aero engine factory at Hillington, near Glasgow – even when, as in this case, they were apparently successful – only served to warn women that they could expect no favours in the workplace and that they would at best be regarded by employers and male colleagues as temporary interlopers, to be laid off at the first opportunity. Such inducements as the Government did contrive to make hardly concealed their short-term nature. While many who did come forward appreciated the temporary improvement to their financial position, they had good reason to share the feelings of those who did not that the exhortation 'Women of Britain, Your Country Needs You' was a form of moral blackmail.

There were other reasons why women did not volunteer for war service or war work. In many cases the decision was effectively not theirs to make. Young unmarried women might be dissuaded or prevented from doing so by their parents or boyfriends, married women by their husbands, either for reasons of prejudice about the suitability of the work for women or simply out of genuine concern for their welfare. Mass-Observers recorded some typical remarks among married Class C (artisan) women in Worcester: 'My husband says it would degrade him in his position. He had quite an argument about it. He wouldn't mind me being in an office.' (50-year-old); 'I don't think it's very nice work, not for a woman like me, my husband is in the civil service. I have to think of him.' (35-year-old); 'My son wouldn't let me do work in a factory, the terrible types you find there.' (55-year-old).[90] In the case of women with family responsibilities, the decision was effectively dictated by the extent of those responsibilities. A woman with pre-school children, for instance, could only contemplate working if there was a nursery at the workplace or if she was willing to put her children into the care of relatives, friends or childminders. Even then, she had to make a judgement about whether she would be left with enough time for the rest of her domestic duties – shopping, cooking, housework. In the case of a woman whose husband was living at home and whose children were of school age, there was theoretically scope for work, at least part-time. But again, as we have already observed, the reality of wartime life was that many tasks, such as shopping, took longer to do, and new ones were added, such as putting up the blackout, repairing or remodelling clothes or tending a vegetable plot. If the prospective work also entailed travelling anything more than walking distance, then this alone – because the transport services were so slow and overburdened – might be decisive in ruling it out. The Wartime Social Survey in late 1941 found that one third of a sample of women 'apparently free to go into war work' were unwilling to do so because of their domestic commitments.[91] The willingness of other family members to help with the domestic work was not something that could be taken for granted; for every man whose attitude to the sexual division of labour was changed by the war, there was another who resisted its assault on what he took to be the natural order of things. As one part-timer in Coventry put it:

'The Employment Bureau could give us full-time work, but we would get war in our homes if we took it.'[92]

There were, then, many reasons why the appeal for women volunteers was relatively unsuccessful; enough to dismiss the suggestion that among the female population there was a patriotic deficit. It may be fairer to assume that those who could, did. 'Relatively unsuccessful' in fact masks volunteering on a scale worth recognizing. From the start of the war to the time conscription for women was introduced in December 1941, 105,000 women volunteered for the armed forces and auxiliary services and 20,000 for the Women's Land Army. And of the one million more women who entered civilian employment in the same period, 871,000 chose the heavy sector – engineering, metals, shipbuilding, chemicals and explosives. The volunteering did not stop, moreover, with the start of compulsion: all sectors continued to recruit from among women who were exempt from conscription. Finally, it should be remembered that working women were not necessarily reluctant workers; on the contrary, most wanted to continue in paid work when the war was over. A survey made in 1944–45 by the Amalgamated Engineering Union of women in the engineering industry (three-quarters of whom had entered it during the war) found that no less than 68 per cent of them wanted to stay on.[93] The wider-ranging Government Social Survey anticipated this picture in 1943: it found that 55 per cent were determined to continue in paid work and only 20 per cent determined to leave. Here was further evidence that those who could work, mostly did.

Women also made a significant contribution to the wider field of volunteering – the many ways in which civilians gave up their spare time and energy to unpaid voluntary work. The phenomenon of unpaid volunteering throughout the six years of the war was one of its characteristic features and surely one of the most striking indicators of the robust state of civilian morale. Of the one and a half million civilians who made up ARP's 'fourth arm' of wardens, firefighters, rescue workers, ambulance drivers, medical staff, telephonists and messengers, no fewer than four-fifths were unpaid volunteers. So, too, were the vast majority of the two million members of the Home Guard, all of them giving up several hours a week to improving and practising their military skills. When Richard Brown volunteered for the Home Guard in October 1941 this was by no means the first time he had given up some of the little spare time he had over from his full-time job as a draughtsman. As he noted, mock-modestly, in his diary: 'I have done, am doing rather, warden's work and have taken on the maid-of-all-work senior's job, have taken up First Aid, have become fairly efficient at plane spotting, am digging for victory and, after all, am working on war work. Also I have given blood at the hospital. Suppose I am doing my bit now. Swank.'[94] Far from seeing the end of the Emergency as a chance to relax a little, he sought to increase his participation. He was probably an exceptionally dutiful citizen – indeed, he elsewhere writes of acquaintances who were not 'doing their bit' – but his example, nevertheless, was repeated many times over, right through the war. No more so than in the millions of women who belonged to the Women's Institutes, the Townswomen's Guilds, the YWCA, the Salvation Army, the Red Cross, the St John Ambulance Brigade, the Co-operative Women's Guilds, the Citizens Advice Bureaux and, above all, the Women's Voluntary Services – 500,000 strong in November 1939, increasing to 843,000 in February 1941.[95] In a moving entry in her diary, Nella Last, reflecting on the fact that her local WVS committee consisted, apart from herself, entirely of elderly women – the youngest sixty-four, the oldest seventy-three – wrote: 'such gallant old troupers, who think it's a sign of weakness to complain of tiredness or strain'.[96] While women's role in bolstering post-raid services in 1940–41 has rightly dominated descriptions of their work, their continued voluntary effort in less spectacular work, like staffing British Restaurants, organizing social centres for evacuees and running day nurseries for the children of working mothers, was no less heroic: the very stuff of the 'people's war' and a palpable testimony to the persistence of commitment to the national project.

The women's organizations might be taken as symbolic. Volunteering on the scale witnessed in the Second World War far outweighed the negative features of civilian behaviour on the home front – absenteeism, strikes, looting, blackmarketeering, and the like. The sheer bulk of volunteering should stand as a reminder to commentators that most people behaved well – many of them outstandingly well – in the trying conditions of war. The failings of the few are, of course, part of the social history of the war, but they should never be allowed to obscure the merit of the many. Most people did not slack at work, steal and loot, waste resources or withhold cooperation from the authorities. J. B. Priestley, speaking in 1970, observed: 'The British people were at their best in the Second World War. They were never as good before it and, I'm sorry to say, they have never been quite as good since.'[97] In other words they rose to the occasion. To a remarkable degree, in a nation not known for slavish conformity, people *did* 'Dig for Victory', Make Do and Mend', 'Walk Short Journeys' and 'Buy Defence Bonds'; to a remarkable degree people *did* 'Carry On', 'Go To It' and 'Fight For It Now'. By their behaviour they showed they believed in the necessity of the war and the justice of the cause, in the competence of their leaders and in the ultimate certainty of victory. These were the behaviours and attitudes of a people whose morale was in good heart. Peaks and troughs there certainly were, but overall, the traditional picture of a spirited and resilient people is a valid one.

At the end of Chapter 2 reference was made to the relaxation of official anxiety about civilian morale when the Blitz seemed to be petering out and the worst threat to Britain's survival seemed to have passed. As things turned out, the men of the Ministry of Information had no cause to regret their belatedly discovered optimism about the resolve of the British people: they came as well through the test of the long haul as through that of the crisis year.

The phrase 'finest hour' implies the existence of less glorious times. No one would deny the sinew straining heroism of 1940–41. But 'carrying on' through the different strains of the long haul required of ordinary citizens qualities that were in their own way no less demanding. And by and large they were not found wanting.

In the final year of the war, within a week of the heartening vision of victory that was represented by the success of the D Day landings in Normandy, a final test of endurance was hurled at the civilian body: the V-weapons. The people had mentally disarmed themselves for air raids and had got used to a life without them. It was a body blow. In the first week of the V1 raids Herbert Morrison told his Cabinet colleagues of his anxiety on this score: 'After five years of war the civil population were not as capable of standing the strain of attack as they had been during the winter of 1940–41. If flying bomb attacks were supplemented by rocket attacks ... there might be serious deterioration in the morale of the civil population.'[98] He was right about what the enemy would do but largely wrong about the consequences. Rockets (V2s) were added to the assault and although by August fighter planes and anti-aircraft guns were destroying two-thirds of the pilotless planes (V1s), there was no answer to the V2s. One and a quarter million people left London and about nine thousand of those who remained were killed. A Gallup poll taken in August 1944 revealed that 50 per cent of the public found the effects of the flying bombs more trying than the Blitz of 1940–41; 31 per cent found them less trying.[99] George Beardmore noted in his diary in January 1945: 'We are all suffering here at home, the worst period of the war. We are all – all of us, at the office, in the shops, and at home – weary of war and its effects.'[100] He doubtless spoke for many. But gruelling though it was, this devastating trial did no discernible damage to the morale of the population living in the target area of London and the South East. The old alert routines of the Blitz were restored and life carried on. The final trial of the war thus served to confirm the broader story of wartime civilian morale.

Notes

1 F. Partridge, *A Pacifist's War* (Phoenix, 1996) p. 159; M. Panter-Downes, *London War Notes 1939–1945* (Longman, 1972), p. 168; M-O, File 783.

2 M-O, File 729; H. Millgate (ed.), *Mr Brown's War: a Diary of the Second World War* (Sutton, 1998), p. 100.

3 S. Orwell and I. Angus (eds), *The Collected Essays, Journalism and Letters of George Orwell* (Penguin, 1970), vol. 2, p. 480.

4 R. Wybrow, *Britain Speaks Out 1937–1987* (Macmillan, 1989), p. 13.

5 HMSO, *Fighting with Figures* (HMSO, 1995), p. 231.

6 M-O, File Report 729.

7 E. Bowen, *The Heat of the Day* (Jonathan Cape, 1949), p. 87.

8 Millgate (ed.), *Mr Brown's War*, p. 148.

9 M-O, File Report 1545.

10 Wybrow, *Britain Speaks Out*, p. 13.

11 N. Longmate, *How We Lived Then* (Hutchinson, 1971), p. 108.

12 H. I. Weekly Report, 2–9 February 1943, INF 1/292.

13 I. McLaine, *Ministry of Morale: Home Front Morale and the Ministry of Information in World War II* (Allen & Unwin, 1979), p. 169, citing H.I. Weekly Report, 17–24 November 1942, INF 1/292.

14 M-O, File Report 1522, 30 November 1942.

15 Memorandum to the Cabinet, 27 November 1942, CAB 66/31.

16 Panter-Downes, *London War Notes*, p. 256.

17 Wybrow, *Britain Speaks Out*, p. 16.

18 The chart forms the endpapers of I. McLaine's *Ministry of Morale*.

19 Partridge, *A Pacifist's War*, pp. 191–2.

20 *Ibid.*, p. 112.

21 Panter-Downes, *London War Notes*, p. 353.

22 *Ibid.*, 5 July 1942, p. 235.

23 E. Blishen, *A Cackhanded War* (Thames & Hudson, 1972), pp. 113, 141.

24 Partridge, *A Pacifist's War*, p. 77.

25 Recalled in C. and E. Townsend, *War Wives: a Second World War Anthology* (Grafton Books, 1989), p. 73.

26 D. Parker, 'The Lovely Leave', in *The Portable Dorothy Parker* (New York, Viking Penguin, 1973).

27 M. Panter-Downes, 'Goodbye, My Love', 1941, reprinted in *Good Evening Mrs Craven* (Persephone Press, 1999).

28 Recalled in Townsend, *War Wives*, pp. 290–1.

29 Partridge, *A Pacifist's War*, p. 104.

30 Recalled in Townsend, *War Wives*, pp. 101–2.

31 *Ibid.*, p. 74.

32 A. Chadwick, 'The Sailor's Wife', in W. Wyatt (ed.), *English Story, 6th Series* (Collins, 1945).

33 H. Wheeler, *Huddersfield at War* (Alan Sutton, 1992), p. 6. Against the odds, all did survive.

34 C. Milburn, *Mrs Milburn's Diaries* (Fontana/Collins, 1980), p. 48.

35 R. Broad and S. Fleming (eds), *Nella Last's War* (Falling Wall Press, 1981), p. 251.

36 As much, indeed, was implied by the unregretful women who recalled their wartime affairs for a television programme, *What Did You Do in the War Granny?* made by Leanne Klein and Emma Willis, Channel 4, 1999.

37 Tom Harrisson, 'Happiness in Wartime', M-O, File 1947.

38 *Ibid.*

39 Average weekly earnings of men aged twenty-one and over were 99s 5d in July 1941, 124s 4d in July 1944. HMSO, *Fighting With Figures*, p. 236.

40 M-O, File Report 1151, March 1942.

41 *The Spectator,* 2 April 1943.

42 M-O, File Report 2085, April 1944.

43 *The Spectator,* 2 February 1944.

44 In the case of cinema-going, however, people were reluctant to concede defeat: Mass-Observation found that it was the last pursuit to be relinquished. File 486, 8 November 1940.

45 *The Spectator*, 18 October 1940.

46 Z. Katin, *'Clippie': the Autobiography of a War Time Conductress* (John Gifford, 1944).

47 M-O, File Reports 914 (trains), 1040 (buses).

48 Longmate, *How We Lived Then*, pp. 293–320.

49 Personal communication with the author, April 2001.

50 M-O, File Report 775.

51 Townsend, *War Wives*, p. 1.

52 G. Beardmore, *Civilians at War: Journals 1938–46* (Oxford University Press, 1986), 3 June 1941, p. 114.

53 Personal communication with the author, December 1994.

54 Millgate (ed.), *Mr. Brown's War*, p. 211.

55 See, for example, M-O, File Report 756, *Clothes Rationing: First Reactions*, June 1941; INF 1/292, 16–23 March 1942; INF 1/292, 2–9 March and 13–20 April 1943.

56 G. Orwell, 'Letter from England' to *Partisan Review*, in Orwell and Angus (eds), *Essays, Journalism and Letters*, vol. 2, pp. 319–21.

57 M-O, File Report 738.

58 Millgate (ed.), *Mr Brown's War*, 1 June 1941, p. 98.

59 HMSO, *Fighting with Figures*, Table 5.4, p. 90.

60 N. Fairbrother, *Children in the House* (The Hogarth Press, 1954), p. 184.

61 Millgate (ed.), *Mr Brown's War*, p. 211.

62 Both examples drawn from Longmate, *How We Lived Then*, p. 251.

63 Millgate (ed.), *Mr Brown's War*, p. 114.

64 Hansard, 25 February 1942, vol. 378, cols 311–20.

65 H. M. D. Parker, *Manpower* (HMSO, 1957), pp. 444–5.

66 Council of Social Services (Liverpool), Bulletin No. 51, 'Rest Breaks for Women Workers', 17 May 1941.

67 Hansard, 3 February 1942, vol. 337, col. 1114.

68 Wheeler, *Huddersfield at War*, p. 94.

69 'Ladies May Now Leave Their Machines', in Y. Klein, *Beyond the Home Front* (Macmillan, 1997), p. 148.

70 P. Inman, *Labour in the Munitions Industries* (HMSO, 1957), pp. 227–8.

71 HMSO, *Fighting with Figures*, Table 3.30, p. 64.

72 Mass-Observation, *People in Production: an Enquiry into British War Production*, Part I (John Murray, 1942), p. 15.

73 Mass-Observation's own survey produced figures that almost exactly confirmed those of the Ministry of Labour. See *People in Production* , pp. 235–6.

74 *Ibid.*, p. 227.

75 M-O, File Report 932. In *People in Production* (p. 220) M-O showed that Sunday absenteeism was a common feature in firms that ran a ten-day shift system. It suggested this was simply a result of fatigue.

76 'Industrial morale', memorandum by Ernest Bevin, 6 October 1942. CAB 71/10, LP (42) 222.

77 Parker, *Manpower*, p. 457.

78 C. Barnett, *The Audit of War* (Macmillan, 1986), p. 80.

79 Cited in W. H. B. Court, *Coal* (HMSO, 1951), p. 220.

80 *Ibid.*, p. 332.

81 *Ibid.*, p. 119.

82 Cited in Barnett, *The Audit of War*, p. 66.

83 *Ibid.*, pp. 66–7.

84 HMSO, *Fighting with Figures*, p. 221.

85 J. L. Hodson, *The Land and the Sea* (Gollancz, 1945), p. 170.

86 E. Smithies, *Crime in Wartime: a Social History of Crime in World War Two* (Allen & Unwin, 1982), p. 2.

87 Hansard, 3 February 1942, vol. 377, col. 1115.

88 Cited in M. Nicholson, *What Did You Do in the War Mummy?*(Chatto &

Windus, 1995), p. 52.

89 Inman, *Labour in the Munitions Industries*, p. 374.

90 Mass-Observation, *People in Production*, p. 152.

91 Wartime Social Survey, 'An Investigation of the Attitudes of Women, the General Public and ATS Personnel to the Auxiliary Territorial Service', New Series, No. 5, October 1941.

92 M-O, File Report 952.

93 P. Summerfield, *Women Workers of the Second World War* (Croom Helm, 1984), p. 160.

94 Millgate (ed.), *Mr Brown's War*, p. 114.

95 *The Times*, 14 November 1939, 19 February 1941.

96 Broad and Fleming (eds), *Nella Last's War*, p. 98.

97 'Home Fires', *World at War*, Thames Television, 1970.

98 War Cabinet Conclusions, 16 June 1944, CAB 65/42.

99 Wybrow, *Britain Speaks Out*, p. 16.

100 Beardmore, *Civilians at War*, p. 187.

PART II

EXPLANATIONS

4

Persuading the people

MANY OFFICIAL and semi-official words and images were devoted to sustaining civilian morale during the Second World War. The attempt to explain the state of mind of the British people in this period might begin, therefore, with a consideration of the nature of these words and images, the thinking that lay behind them and what effect, if any, they had on the targeted audience. As discussed in Chapter 1, the importance of modern mass communications to the state of public morale in time of war was recognized by the Government of the day in 1935 in its initiative to create, at least in 'shadow' form, a Ministry of Information, charged with the task of maintaining morale. And we saw how, when war came, the duly established Ministry entirely failed to fulfil its brief, instead incurring public ridicule and earning for itself the unflattering sobriquet of 'Ministry of Disinformation'.[1] Over the course of the war, however, the Government learned from experience. The simplistic notions about communications and popular morale with which it began the war, symbolized by the closure of cinemas and Chamberlain's contemplated shutting down of the BBC, were gradually replaced by a more sophisticated understanding of the nature of the relationship between what people were told and how they felt and behaved. The Head of the Home Intelligence Division at the Ministry of Information, Stephen Taylor, believed that the factors determining morale could be divided into the 'material' and the 'mental'. The material factors were: food, warmth, work, leisure, rest and sleep, a secure base, and safety and security for dependants. The mental factors were: belief that victory was possible, belief in equality of sacrifices, belief in the integrity and efficiency of the leadership, and belief that the war was necessary and just.[2] It is the efforts the Government and its allies in the media made to promote the 'mental factors' that form the subject of this chapter.

Controlling the news

At the Ministry of Information the brief to sustain the morale of the people was translated into a three-fold policy: firstly, the replacement of free availability of news and information with a regime in which these would be controlled and managed; secondly, to provide reassurance of the certainty of victory and of official concern for the people's needs; thirdly, to stimulate patriotic commitment to the war and the war effort. This policy in turn led to the delineation of four main activities: the censoring of the supply and transmission of news and information; the setting of guidelines for the output content of the BBC and the film industry; the monitoring of civilian morale; the production and commissioning of propaganda. Since what people heard and saw – and how they felt and behaved in response – is the main consideration here, the focus of this chapter will be on the last of these, the propaganda products of the Government and its proxies in the form of speeches, posters, advertisements, pamphlets, films and broadcasts. But first, some consideration, further to that given in Chapter 2, needs to be given to the news of the war as it reached the public via newspapers, radio bulletins and newsreels.

It will be recalled that during the Phoney War the hapless news editors of the newspapers, the BBC and the newsreel companies were obliged to depend entirely on the official sources for their raw material on the war and that the resulting meagreness and sketchiness of what they were then able to transmit was a cause of public frustration and resentment. When the war finally started to catch fire, literally, in April 1940, the public demand for full and accurate coverage of what was happening on the fronts – in Norway, in the Low Countries and in France – was naturally much greater than for the 'non-fronts' of the Phoney War. However the demand remained unsatisfied. The pattern was set by the confused and misleading reporting of Anglo-French efforts to counter the German occupation of Norway. Mention of difficulties and setbacks was withheld and an impression thereby created that the campaign was going well – an impression furthered by some unjustifiably optimistic statements by the War Minister, Sir Samuel Hoare and the First Lord of the Admiralty, Winston Churchill. The subsequent decision to withdraw from Norway, leaving the Germans in possession, took the public by surprise, therefore. And in relation to morale, the whole affair was damaging. After being so misled over Norway, people were naturally even more sceptical about what they were being told by the media when the action moved closer to Britain in May. In a Mass-Observation survey on the news, 56 per cent stated that they were tired of the BBC because it kept repeating the same news and distrustful of it because it seemed no longer an independent voice. And although newspapers were considered the best source of information (the BBC the second best), 84 per cent of men and 89 per cent of women were critical of the press's reliability.[3] This situation was no fault of the media people, for their information sources had hardly improved. The Service departments were as parsimonious with the facts as before and what they did release was misleadingly sanguine about the way the war was going. On the other hand, even allowing for the restrictions on what they might show, the newsreel companies – apparently in their anxiety to win official approval – were putting together material in a way that fell far below the standards of objective reporting. Gaumont-British's coverage of the Dunkirk operation, for example, was like a parody of blinkered, partisan triumphalism. The images of British withdrawal were unavoidable, of course, but the blaring patriotic music, accompanied by the sound of exploding shells, implied that breast beating was not in order. On the contrary, Dunkirk was an occasion for celebration, as the commentary made clear: 'A miracle of fighting genius ... most brilliant withdrawal in military history ... the navy has earned our undying gratitude, the army is undefeated, its spirit unbroken ... shots taken entirely at random all show laughing faces ... this is the epic of Dunkirk.'[4] Mass-Observation found much public criticism of this sort of reporting. Small wonder that this was a time when rumours were rife, one of which had it that at Dunkirk officers had fought to be evacuated before their men.[5]

Few would now deny that Dunkirk was a humiliating reverse for British arms and a disaster that brought Britain face to face with outright defeat in the war. The subsequent capitulation of France objectively made this a probability. And yet, this was not what the people were being told. Gaumont-British was not unique in its upbeat presentation of what was happening. Nowhere in official pronouncements or in the output of the media was there any acknowledgement of the true seriousness of Britain's position – of the parlous weakness of its armed forces and the vast power at the enemy's command. For the reality was that the truth was too alarming to be told. If the Government began the war with the intention of releasing to the public only such information about the war as could be presented in a positive light, its resolve was only reinforced by the turn of events from May 1940. For at least twelve months after Dunkirk the people were shielded from the full story of what was happening, even on the home front. The explanation is straightforward enough: in its wisdom the Government decided that the people could not take the whole unvarnished truth.[6] For all that Churchill in his Commons speeches and his broadcasts to the nation warned against assigning to the 'deliverance' of Dunkirk 'the attributes of a victory' and gravely asked the nation to prepare itself for the bigger test to come, an impression was given that the odds on a British triumph were at least even. Britain, he said, had on its own soil 'incomparably more powerful military forces' than ever before 'in this or the last war'; and he declared himself confident that 'we shall prove ourselves once again able to defend our island home, to ride out the storm of war'. And on the prospect of bombing: 'I do not at all underrate the severity of the ordeal which lies before us, but I believe our countrymen will show themselves capable of standing up to it.' The news media took their cue from Churchill. The *Evening Standard* was ready, after the fall of France, to print a Low cartoon showing a lone British soldier standing on the cliffs of Dover, shaking a fist at the menace across the Channel, with the caption: 'Very well, alone'; but if it knew of the huge disparity in British and German strength, it did not disclose it. Nor did the BBC offer more cautious appraisal; its thirty-four million listeners would have noticed little difference in its interpretation of events from that of Gaumont-British. They were not told about the dejected and demoralized state of the men of the BEF as they disembarked at Dover but rather that: 'they have come back in glory ... their morale is as high as ever ... they are anxious only to be back again soon – as they put it – "to have a real crack at Jerry" ... Cheering crowds were there to greet them.'[7]

When the Battle of Britain and the Blitz brought the war literally onto the home front it was theoretically more difficult for the authorities to hide from the public what was really happening. None the less, the official tendency towards glossing over bad news and exaggerating favourable news persisted. The Air Ministry's figures for German and British losses during the Battle of Britain, ineluctably passed on by the media, are a case in point. A post-war calculation put the overstatement of the British case at 55 per cent.[8] As for the bombing, the public was denied all but the most sketchy details of the location of raids and the extent of the casualties and damage. In radio bulletins and newspaper reports casualties were given as 'slight', 'considerable' or 'heavy' and in newsreel coverage damage to buildings was shown but the sight of dead or badly wounded people was excluded. Unusual care was taken by all the media, moreover, to present the performance of the ARP services and the demeanour of the ordinary citizens in the most positive light. Fire and rescue squads were invariably 'promptly on the scene' and the shelterers and bombed out were 'orderly', 'cheerful' and 'defiant'. Harold Nicolson had heard that the King and Queen were booed when they visited the East End in the second week of the Blitz. But the *Daily Mirror* reported that bombed-out people stood and cheered the royal visitors.[9]

Naturally enough, the news media were not happy with the level of censorship that forced them into this disingenuous presentation of the news. Even when owners and editors accepted the basic need for security controls and, too, the general proposition that they should put out nothing that might undermine public morale, they bridled at the emasculation of their competitive reporting instincts. The case for fuller disclosure of war news was always being advanced by media representatives, but progress in this direction only came when the Ministry of Information itself actively lobbied for it. In fact the News Division at the Ministry had been from the outset in favour of giving the public the maximum possible information. As its Deputy Director, Tom Clarke, a former editor of the *New Chronicle*, put it: 'Frankness will give all the more emphasis to bulletins announcing our successes. Our civilian population is not afraid of an occasional dose of bad news, and would not be cast into panic by it ... Detail kills the public distrust of vague announcements.'[10] Brendan Bracken's appointment as Minister of Information in June 1941 consolidated this view, in effect making it the position of the whole department. 'This is a people's war', he said, 'and the people must be told the news about the war because without them and their spirit, we cannot achieve victory.'[11] Bracken believed there was a direct connection between good public morale and the fullest possible supply of news. 'When the public is bewildered by something new', he argued, 'a failure to explain means the risk of driving a wedge between government and public and this fact must be given full weight when security risks suggest withholding information ... Harm can be done to public confidence by failure to allow for this.'[12] Here was the nub of the matter: a regime of too little information on the grounds that security required it and that in any case the public must not be alarmed, was itself a threat to civilian morale. The problem for the Government was to balance the needs of security and morale, both essential for the success of the war effort. Clearly, in the first eighteen months of the war, at least, it tilted too far towards the former: every survey undertaken revealed discontent about the insufficiency of information.[13]

With some abatement of official anxiety about civilian morale after the 'performance' of Londoners in the autumn of 1940, there was a perceptible improvement in the supply of information to the media. The evidence suggests that the change of approach had the desired effect. To the extent that popular morale was to be discerned in the credibility people accorded to the news, the situation was improving even before Bracken's arrival at the MoI. The BBC had largely reversed the public's distrust of radio news that had marked the first year of the war. In a Listener Research survey of February 1941 almost two-thirds of respondents thought BBC news '100 per cent reliable' and only one in 1,200 thought it 'completely unreliable'.[14]

Censorship did not disappear, however, and certain aspects of the war news continued to be withheld from the public. For example, the long and costly struggle with German submarines, which Churchill called the Battle of the Atlantic, went largely unreported because of the advantage to the enemy almost any information about this theatre might have given. Since the public was in any case scarcely aware of its existence, let alone its toll in lives and ships lost, this was not a problem for home front morale.[15] The reporting of air raids was a different matter: a significant proportion of the population had – albeit in varying degrees – actual experience of them, so complete concealment was not possible. Security considerations arose here, too, and weighing the necessity of giving away nothing that might help the enemy against that of sustaining the people's spirits by telling them what they wanted to know, was no easy task.

The established policy on the release of information about air raids was discussed afresh in the Cabinet but remained in place. Despite the MoI's advocacy of full and prompt disclosure, on the grounds of maintaining civilian morale, Churchill was not persuaded. He said he had not observed any depressing effect on morale resulting from the policy and he would 'strongly deprecate its abandonment'.[16] Here, the price of national security, that is, the encouragement given to rumour and to 'listening in' to German sources of information, was evidently judged worth paying.

Most people seemed to accept the official policy of not publishing air raid casualties. An early Mass-Observation survey found that 45 per cent approved the policy, 25 per cent disapproved and 32 per cent were indifferent. 'I think it's a very good thing', one 'approving' respondent said, 'we don't want to tell the Germans anything'.[17] And when the bombing spread out to include places other than London, there was about the same response to the policy of not naming the raided towns until at least twenty-eight days after the attack. Indeed, when for propaganda purposes, a well-meant news item was included, perhaps in the course of reporting a royal or prime ministerial visit to a particular town, telling of life and work getting back to normal, there were sometimes mixed feelings among residents. This was the case in Plymouth, which was visited by the King and Queen on 20 March 1941, four months after a bad raid; just one hour after they had left the town, another serious raid was suffered.[18] In the same way, the BBC's reports of the failure of particular air attacks seemed to some to be encouraging the *Luftwaffe* to have another attempt.[19] On the other hand, as Mass-Observation discovered, when a town felt that its own suffering or achievements under fire had been neglected alongside, perhaps, the limelight treatment that was accorded the East End or Coventry, there was often a feeling of injustice, which was not good for morale, either.[20] None the less, the public largely went along with the official policy: the reasons for it were, after all, readily comprehensible to the average citizen, however scornful he might be of the idea that it was partly conceived out of official doubts about his morale.

The selection of what it was safe or desirable to report remained a matter of judgement for the Government and the news media. On some occasions concealment backfired. In 1942 there were two notable instances, the fall of Singapore to the Japanese and the fall of Tobruk to Rommel's Afrika Corps. In both, the media repeated the mistake of their Norway coverage, that is, they gave out optimistic reports that failed to prepare the public for the possibility of reverses; so when they happened they came as a surprise and the blow to morale was all the greater. The assumption that the people had to be shielded from depressing news was probably false, anyway. There was, of course, rather a lot of bad news for most of 1942. This did not prevent Mollie Panter-Downes from joining in the criticism of the BBC over its reporting of the affair of the German warships *Scharnhorst*, *Gneisenau* and *Prinz Eugen* in February. These ships had slipped undamaged through the English Channel to home waters despite the attacks of British bombers and torpedo boats. The BBC reported the episode as 'more like a triumph for the RAF than the humiliating disappointment all thought it to be'. Panter-Downes doubtless spoke for many when she concluded that 'the public isn't taken in for a minute by any soft pedalling of bad tidings'.[21] In the case of the disastrous Dieppe Raid of August 1942, in which an Allied force of 6,000 men (mainly Canadian) was met by strong and well-protected German defenders who repelled the attackers, killing or capturing more than half of them, the news reports were less than honest, focusing as they did on the relatively successful air and naval aspects of the operation and glossing over what happened to the troops. Frank Gillard, who reported the raid for the BBC, had forever after a conscience about his part in this deception, even though he fully recognized that the truth might have had a damaging effect on national morale at a time when the war was not going very well.[22]

In retrospect it was fortunate that as something closer to the real story of what happened at Dieppe began to come out, it was overtaken by the morale-boosting good news of military success in North Africa. Since the improvement in the military position turned out to be more than a false dawn, there was from this point simply more good news to report. In consequence, the Government allowed a further relaxation; censorship became less rigid and the media were able to say more. People gradually became aware of a better match between what they wanted to know and what they were reading in their newspapers, hearing in the radio bulletins and even seeing in the newsreels. This extended even to the battle fronts. Already, by El Alamein, the BBC was allowed to record dispatches from the front line ready for broadcasting the next day. The culmination of this process came in the live radio reporting of action on the fighting fronts, beginning with the breakout campaign that followed the successful landings in Normandy in June 1944. The enormous popularity of such actuality reporting, testified by the soundings of the BBC's Listener Research Department (which showed that over half the population was listening to the nine o'clock news and to the nightly *War Report*) helped to convince the Government of the value to home morale of more informative coverage of the war news.[23]

Inevitably, the broadcasters sometimes judged wrongly. There were occasions when the military were unhappy about what had been put out, as, for example, in August 1944, when the United States commander General Bradley expressed anger that soldiers' lives had been endangered by the BBC's anticipatory announcement that the Falaise Gap was about to be successfully closed. For the most part, however, the Government and its informal agents of news transmission came to feel that in the way they controlled the news they had found the sought-for balance of objectives and that the needs of neither security nor morale were achieved at the expense of the other.

The propaganda of reassurance

For the propagandist it was axiomatic that an essential precondition of high civilian morale was the certainty of victory. If the citizens were convinced that they were on the winning side, they would bear the burdens their leaders imposed on them and make their own effort to realize the objective. It followed that, for their part, the leaders must give every possible assurance that the ultimate outcome of the war was in no doubt; for if ever a sense of futility took possession of the people's minds, apathy or dissension would quickly set in and the downward spiral of undersupply and military failure would become established.

The changing contours of Britain's military position during the Second World War imposed their own pattern on this basic requirement. Before the fall of France there was no reason to suppose that Chamberlain was wrong when he gloatingly announced (on 4 April 1940) that Hitler had 'missed the bus'; nor Churchill when, a week later, he said that in invading Norway Hitler had committed 'a strategic error comparable to that of Napoleon's invasion of Spain'.[24] Time was apparently on Britain's side and Hitler had overreached himself. Within a little over two months things were clearly very different: the German armies had triumphed and Britain, without powerful allies, itself seemed about to be invaded. Never was reassurance more necessary. But reassurance at this time, and for at least a year to come, was an uphill task. It became a little easier as the invasion threat receded, the bombing slackened off and thoughts of outright defeat were dispelled. But it was only with the first signs of the turn of the military tide that reassurances about ultimate victory could sound convincing. The Government's problem, then, was that reassurance was needed most in the period when it was most difficult, when its premises were least credible. And even after the period of standing alone came to an end, it was many months before the existence of powerful allies was seen to translate into military success and the fear of invasion and defeat was banished.

Reassurance propaganda had just two basic themes. The first was the strength and virtue of the leadership, fighting forces and popular resolve of Britain and her allies. The second was the obverse: the inherent weaknesses that lay behind the apparently invincible might of the Axis.

From the day he became Prime Minister, Churchill set a tone for his addresses to the nation that was sober, honest and realistic, as in his first speech to the Commons: 'I have nothing to offer but blood, toil, tears, and sweat'. But it is noteworthy that in his speeches at this time and throughout the year of crisis to come, he invariably took care to mention factors that remained in Britain's favour and which could yet lead her to victory. He thus reminded his audience of the previous occasions when Britain's enemies had tried to invade her and had been repelled; and he underlined the importance of Britain's control of the waters, across which any invasion had to come, and of her mastery of the air above them. When the Battle of Britain was fought and won, alongside his famous tribute to 'the Few' he made sure that the true significance of the victory was made explicit. And by himself remaining in London during the Blitz, his demeanour cheerful and defiant, he personally demonstrated the confidence in victory that he was asking others to have. As we have seen, Churchill's popularity ratings remained high, even when satisfaction with the Government's performance fell; he was a subtle reassurer, but he was also himself a factor of reassurance.

Official propaganda took its lead from the Prime Minister. The message of reassurance came in the form of pamphlets, leaflets, press advertisements, posters and postcards.[25] 'Friends overseas', for example, was readily resorted to during the anxious months when Britain stood alone. The message was really that 'alone' was an inaccurate term for Britain's actual position – from the beginning the four Dominions of Australia, Canada, New Zealand and South Africa were in the war and making contributions of troops and equipment. The Ministry of Information naturally made as much of this fact as possible, despite the reality that the contribution, particularly on the military side, was rather slight, for like Britain, none of these countries had conscription or a large standing army in peacetime.[26] A publicity campaign was organized in the autumn of 1940, drawing the people's attention to the Dominions' role in the struggle against the Axis. A linked series of press advertisements and radio broadcasts was devised, highlighting the contributions of each country and emphasizing the strength of the Commonwealth bond that made it more than the sum of its parts. 'There has been nothing like it in the world before', ran one advertisement, 'it is a Commonwealth, a family of free nations linked together by loyalty to one King'. The well-known fecundity of the Empire and Commonwealth in meeting much of Britain's peacetime needs in food and raw materials was underlined as a guarantee of a material lifeline in war. An advertisement on India, for example, was typical: 'DO YOU KNOW THAT INDIA supplies all the jute for making sacks and handbags, that more than half Britain's needs of livestock foods come from India, as well as tea, rice hides, skins, cotton and manganese? THESE ARE THE SINEWS OF WAR'. And, as if anticipating the question 'But will they reach us?', the Ministry ran a concurrent poster campaign extolling Commonwealth naval strength. Borrowing for its title a phrase from *Land of Hope and Glory*, 'MIGHTIER YET', one of these described the navies of the Empire as 'the most powerful seaforce in the world' and that it was being added to all the time in the shipyards of Britain.[27]

In the long wait for good war news the Ministry had to make the most of what meagre successes Britain's offensive forces achieved. The discrete theatre of Anglo-Italian fighting in Africa was the most productive of these. The recovery of British Somaliland and the expulsion of Italian forces altogether from East Africa in May 1941, for instance, was celebrated in a postcard headed 'The Decline of the Roman Empire', in which a map of the Middle East and North Africa in 1939 is contrasted with one for 1941. The smug face of Mussolini in the first becomes bruised and bewildered in the second, while British troops stand where Italians had once been and British ships dot the entire Mediterranean. Another is headed by Mussolini saying in June 1940: 'We take up arms against a sterile and decadent nation', its middle section has a pictograph showing the huge numerical superiority of Italian forces over those of British and Imperial forces, the lower section shows a British 'Tommy' booting Mussolini out of the picture. The idea of using the enemy's words against him was also the inspiration behind a series of postcards drawn by Nicholas Bentley; and the weakness of the Rome–Berlin Axis was again a fruitful subject. One shows an Italian soldier, his weapon abandoned, running for his life before the advancing bayonet of a grinning British 'Tommy'; the words below quote an Italian press release of March 1941: 'Italy's main function consists in drawing the best British imperial forces like a magnet.'[28]

Of course, everyone knew that the Italians were not the enemy that the Germans were and successes against the weak end of the Axis were not hugely significant. So the Ministry made what it could of the fact that the Germans were feeling the sting of the RAF. Another Bentley card shows a portly German burgher taking a stroll and becoming aware of a peculiar noise behind him; it is a British bomb, about to hit the ground. Beneath runs a quotation from the Official German News Agency in October 1940: 'Danger from British air attacks, according to experience so far, does not make any action necessary.' The reassuring implication is that the war is far from over, the enemy is not all-powerful, and the fight back has already begun.

When the long-expected entry into the war of the USA came at the end of 1941, the Ministry was ready with materials that drew out its significance for a nation that had weathered the enemy's assault but which was feeling literally battered by the experience. A leaflet excitedly called *A Giant Awakes* catalogued the immense industrial preponderance of the country that was now formally Britain's ally: 'OIL is the lifeblood of mechanised war. The U.S. produces nearly two-thirds of the world's oil. It produces, too, over two thirds of the world's sulphur, vital to arms production ... United States STEEL industries are huge, modern efficient ... The U.S. makes three out of every four of the world's automobiles.' American industrial might tipped the balance in the war of resources in 1917–18; only the ignorant could fail to draw the conclusion that something of the same was now in prospect. Being able to remind the people about their new ally's potential, was nevertheless a valuable and much-used weapon in the Government's reassurance propaganda during the first half of 1942, when there was little else to report from the war that was reassuring.

Among the hundreds of HM Stationery Office pamphlets produced during the war was a series that ostensibly provided an official record of particular aspects of the conduct and progress of the war. In 1940–41, for example, titles like *The Battle of the River Plate*, *Bomber Command*, *BBC at War* and *Fire over London* were published. Informative though they were, however, in many of them the aim simply to inform can be seen to have been compromised by other, more urgent imperatives. George Orwell was irritated to find that the best-selling *The Battle of Britain*, which, for his part, he had read for information, had rather the whiff of a tract, intended more as 'a cheer-up' than an objective record. But then, it was the wider public rather than exacting critics like Orwell that the Government had in mind as readers of these pamphlets, and its aim was more to do with morale than with education.[29]

In May 1940, as the general outlook worsened, the press was as active in the reassurance business as the Government could have wished. It is true that there was some handwringing in certain quarters – the 'soft liberal' defeatism of the *News Chronicle*, for example – but for the most part the press took a responsible, steadying line. Others, it might be added, were overzealous: the journalist J. L. Hodson wrote of the director of a daily newspaper (he did not say which) ordering the paper's astrologer to interpret the movements of the stars to show that while Britain must expect heavy knocks in the short run, in the longer term she would be victorious.[30]

For the historian casting an eye over the daily record of events in the newspapers, one of the striking aspects is how much of the general tone is conveyed by the cartoons. As Roy Douglas has said, the cartoonist 'exaggerates and oversimplifies situations', but at the same time, the cartoon 'preserves a vitality which has been lost from factual accounts of events'.[31] Two 'Zec' cartoons from the Emergency of 1940 show how at that time the Press tried to point up Britain's advantages and get as much as was possible from the meagre bits of good news. The first, from 23 May, vaunted the new leadership. It shows a giant nutcracker, embossed with a swastika, held by an ape-like hand; the 'nut' in its jaws bears the smiling, cigar-smoking face of Churchill and the caption runs: 'Much Too Tough a Nut!' The other addressed the problem of popular fear of invasion. It shows Neptune, sitting on a rock in the shallows beneath the Dover cliffs, over the caption: 'The Old Ally Remains!'[32] Since the fear of invasion was still present in September, the cartoonists continued to work at dispelling it – George Whitelaw in the *Daily Herald*, for example, on the last day of the month. His cartoon has invasion represented by a hot-air balloon in which the passenger (Hitler) is waiting for the cast-off, an event that looks doubtful, for the hoarding that stands alongside shows the departure date as 1 September, crudely altered fourteen times by the furious-looking promoter (Goebbels).[33] In other words, the invasion was off, at least for the present; Britain now had the chance to recover from Dunkirk and build up its strength against future invasion threats.

In the meantime, the heroic achievements of the RAF were exploited for every last ounce of comfort they afforded – not merely the defence of Britain in the summer of 1940, but also the bombing raids on Germany, which Goering had unwisely boasted could never be achieved. The Royal Navy, too, was repeatedly shown as a formidable component of Britain's strength, its actions against Vichy France's navy at Oran in July, against Italian naval power at Taranto in November and Cape Matapan in the following March, serving as authentic demonstrations. Other crumbs of comfort were played up for all they were worth. In its daily 'Thanks a Lot' spot, for example, the *Daily Mirror* informed readers that New Zealand was stepping up its food production in order to make good Britain's loss of European suppliers, adding: 'Hitler has no such friends who will grow his food for him. In the long run that will tell.'[34]

In the early years of the war a potential source of reassurance lay in the hope that the USA would enter the war rather than let Britain succumb to the Axis. When Congress repealed some of the arms sales restrictions in the Neutrality Acts and, through the 'Cash and Carry' arrangement, made America – in Roosevelt's words – 'the arsenal of democracy', the British newspapers applauded and reminded readers that the same facilities were not being offered to the Axis powers. The uncertainty that the pro-British Roosevelt might fail to win a third term as President in November 1940 was especially alarming in the perilous autumn months of that year. But the press made the most of the fact that Roosevelt's opponent in the election, Wendell Willkie, was every bit as hostile to Hitler as he. And when Roosevelt won and the Lend-Lease Bill was enacted soon after, an increasingly confident tone infused the newspapers. A Vicky cartoon in the *News Chronicle* for 18 May 1941, captioned 'Thumbs Down on Hitler', shows Roosevelt at the presidential desk about to press a button marked 'CONVOYS'. Two other such buttons are visible, marked 'LEND-LEASE BILL' and 'NEUTRALITY PA-TROLS', reminding readers of the steady progress of the USA's abandonment of strict neutrality. This progress towards the hoped-for day when the Americans would throw in their lot with Britain was charted with mounting excitement, culminating in the formal entry of the USA into the war in December. At that point Vicky came up with a resonant echo of David Low's famous May 1940 cartoon of the members of Churchill's newly formed coalition government, marching shoulder to shoulder, rolling up their sleeves for action. Here, the coalition of united and determined men are Roosevelt, Willkie, La Guardia, Hoover, Hearst and others, advancing on an amazed and alarmed Hitler and Tojo.[35] Just as Britain rallied under Churchill to block the onward march of fascism, Britain and a 'united' USA together would throw it into reverse.

Germany's attack on the Soviet Union in June 1941 had significant implications for Britain's position as the only country in Europe still in the fight against the Axis. At the very least it reduced some of the pressure on Britain; and if the Russians proved able to absorb the assault and tie down German armies in a longer struggle, the prospect for offensive operations and an ultimate roll-back of German conquests markedly improved. Diplomatically, it was a delicate situation for Britain to handle. The Nazi–Soviet Pact had been damaging for Britain's position from its inception two years before and of great value to Hitler in accomplishing his victories. And Stalin, too, had been as aggressive as Hitler against his smaller neighbours Poland, Latvia, Estonia, Lithuania and Finland. Britain had every reason to resent the role that the Soviet Union had played and every reason to distrust Stalin as a possible comrade-in-arms. But the fact was that Britain was beleaguered and could not afford to be over-particular about her associates. So Churchill extended the hand of friendship, pledged material assistance and persuaded the USA to include the Soviet Union in the Lend-Lease scheme. This opened the door to the propagandist to exploit the unexpected morale-boosting potential of Russian entry into the war on the anti-Axis side. In their role as unofficial propagandists the newspapers seemed happy enough to go along with this idea, although the cautiousness of the Government's welcome for the turn of events was reflected in the Fleet Street response. No rash assumptions were made about the strength of the Soviet Union or about German abandonment of plans to attempt an invasion of Britain. Indeed, the *Evening Standard*, which had been saying in the first half of June that Hitler must invade Britain within eighty days, did not abandon this view in the light of Operation Barbarossa.[36] The most popular way of using the situation for the purpose of reassurance was to emphasize the problems that Hitler had given himself by taking on the Russians. Thus a *Daily Express* cartoon in July, captioned 'Blunting the Blitz', shows in comic strip form a German tank, driven by Hitler, on which is mounted an enormous Blitzkrieg spear, advancing on a Russian tank. As the German tank advances the Russian tank retreats; but the Blitzkrieg spear becomes progressively blunter and Hitler becomes more and more frantic.[37] The Anglo-Soviet Treaty and Stalin's dissolution of the Comintern are treated in the same fashion, the emphasis being on the consternation these developments were supposedly causing in Berlin, Rome and Tokyo.

The technique of gleaning reasons for optimism from the internal strains in the Axis alliance had a good basis in fact, of course, but the press found it as difficult as the Ministry of Information to get much mileage out of this until things actually started to go wrong for the Italians in the Horn of Africa, Libya, and Greece, when Mussolini could be shown as a military liability to Hitler, repeatedly getting into difficulties that obliged him to mount rescue operations. And as and when British successes in Africa eventually came, the newspapers did not fail to point out their implications for the faltering Rome–Berlin 'Pact of Steel'. As for the third partner, Japan, it was the evident absence of any real substance to its Axis role that the press tried to exploit. Strube's cartoon for the *Daily Express* in July 1941 depicts a telephone conversation between a peevish-looking Hitler and the Japanese Foreign Minister, Matsuoka. 'When are you coming in Matsuoka?', asks Hitler, 'I've already entered my third week in Russia.' 'What's the hurry, Adolf?, an impassive Matsuoka replies, 'We've just entered our fifth year in China.' This one scores a double by not only showing readers that the Berlin–Tokyo alliance was mere words, but also suggesting to them that Hitler's assumption of a quick victory in Russia was premature.[38] In this way, Fleet Street sought to prick the bubble of Axis unity and invincibility in the minds of the public.

More difficult to mock was the frightening appearance of German rocket bombs, at a point in the war where the ordinary citizen might well have assumed the worst was over. The cartoonists' answer was again to reassert the invincible strength of Britain's allies, and the unstoppability of the advances that were in progress against Germany. Illingworth's cartoon 'Overshadowed' in the *Daily Mail* was typical. Here, Hitler and his aides are admiring a huge V2 rocket on its launching platform, oblivious of the giant boots, one labelled 'the Normandy advance' the other 'the Russian advance', which are descending on them and will crush them, rocket and all. For once, there was no exaggeration or wishful thinking involved: short of physical penetration of the launch territory, there was no military answer to these weapons. Fortunately, this penetration was manifestly about to happen, as Allied forces east and west closed in on the German homeland.[39]

The theme of reassurance is prominent in the films, official and unofficial, that were made during the crisis period of April 1940 to June 1941, and then, decreasingly, in those made to the end of 1942.

Britain at Bay, an eight-minute MoI documentary film released in July 1940, was typical of the genre. In this, cinema audiences were given visual reminders, reinforced by the commentary (written and read by J. B. Priestley) of Britain's actual strengths at this time of high danger. First it emphasizes Britain's island position, and how on many previous occasions, such as in 1804, when Napoleon amassed an invasion force, Britain had been menaced by a continental enemy who had failed to effect a bridge over the guarded moat of the Channel. It goes on to parade the supposedly undiminished strengths of the armed services: the warships patrolling the coastal waters, the hordes of fighter planes patrolling the skies, the army, now supplemented by the Local Defence Volunteers, guarding the coasts. The audience is then reminded of the elaborate ARP preparations that have been made; and a brief spotlight falls on the surge of civilian activity to produce the weapons of war. Finally, the unnerving notion of 'Britain alone' is comfortingly qualified by a reminder that the Empire is behind her – the countries are listed, accompanied by shots of marching troops from Canada, Australia and India. Throughout the film the stirring music soundtrack is punctuated by the bugle call for 'Stand To!', implying that Britain is ready and on the alert. Other documentary shorts echoed these attempts at reassurance. *Miss Grant Goes to the Door*, which went out in July 1940, shows, in dramatized form, the successful countering of a German parachute invasion in which, once alerted, the defence forces spring impressively into vigorous action. *Squadron 992* showed the work of a barrage balloon team on the Forth Bridge and the failure of a German bombing raid in the face of the combination of balloon protection and British fighter planes; *Dover Front Line* showed that town's defences blunting the effectiveness of German attacks; *Sea Fort* depicted a garrison in a fort at sea warding off attacks by sea and air; *London Can Take It!* reminded people reeling from the onslaught of the Blitz that the enemy was not doing this unanswered: 'every night the RAF bombers fly deep into the heart of Germany, bombing munition works, aeroplane factories, canals, cutting the arteries which keep the heart of Germany alive'.

Supplementing the documentary shorts were a series of feature length fictionalized narrative-documentaries that focused on the strength of the various services, all in their different ways successfully meeting the challenge of the national crisis. *Merchant Seamen* showed the necessary supplies of food and materials getting through; *Fires Were Started* showed the Auxiliary Fire Service's answer to the menace of incendiary raids; *Target For Tonight* showed the public that Britain was not just on the defensive but was taking war to the enemy. It followed a night mission by Bomber Command to destroy an oil depot in Germany. *Coastal Command* did a similar job on a flying-boat of Coastal Command, which in the course of carrying out convoy escort duties, attacks a German warship and sinks a U-boat.

The commercial film makers, whose principal purpose was to provide entertainment that was good for box office receipts, none the less echoed the reassuring message of the official films. The first to be made (released in October 1939) was *The Lion Has Wings*, co-directed by Michael Powell, Adrian Brunel and Brian Desmond Hurst. An associate producer of the film, Ian Dalrymple recalled that at this stage in the war, when fear of massive air attack was pervasive, the main aim of the film was 'to reassure the British public they weren't all going to be blown to pieces in five minutes: the Royal Air Force would prevent it'.[40] The film therefore culminated in a set piece in which an imagined night attack by the *Luftwaffe* is thwarted by a combination of anti-aircraft guns, barrage balloons and Spitfires of '301 Squadron'. The raiders turn back and make for home, their mission unaccomplished. As the commentary put it, Britain's air force was 'second to none, ready for anything, no matter how difficult and dangerous'.[41] *Convoy* (1940), dedicated to 'the Officers and Men of the Royal and Merchant Navies', drove home the message that supplies were in safe hands and that the enemy's attempt to starve Britain out was doomed. Another, *49th Parallel* (1941), reminded audiences that the Commonwealth countries, in this case Canada, were in the war and were as committed as Britain herself to the defeat of the Axis powers.

For its part, the BBC contributed to active reassurance through the medium of its features and talks. *War Commentary*, listened to by over seven million, offered weekly analysis of the events of the war, in which speakers – mostly military figures – were able to use their inside knowledge to blunt the effect of the more alarming popular constructions on military setbacks; *Marching On*, a programme that presented dramatized reconstructions of episodes in the war, maintained a predominantly optimistic tone; and a series of features on the armed services reinforced the message that Britain was fighting back: *The Battle of Britain*, *Spitfires Over Britain* and *Bombers Over Germany*, for example, showed the RAF active in both defensive and offensive operations. *Balloon Barrage* and *Watchers of the Sky* were radio counterparts of the documentary films mentioned above, as were *The Patrol of the 'Salmon'* and *Swept Channels*, which were about the strength and vigilance of the naval defence forces. And picking up one of the themes of *Britain at Bay*, an October 1940 feature *Napoleon Couldn't Do It* once more celebrated Britain's unique advantage of the possession of a natural moat, one guarded, moreover, by naval forces that Hitler could not match and over which air superiority had been successfully maintained. Like the Press, the BBC kept its audience abreast of the ever-increasing involvement of the USA in the war, beginning with the preferential 'Cash and Carry' arrangement for war supplies, which started in the first month of the war, and reporting as they happened the key events in the process by which US support grew: the 'destroyers-for-bases' deal of August 1940, which transferred fifty US destroyers to Britain; the passage through Congress of the Lend-Lease Bill, which guaranteed supplies to Britain regardless of her capacity to pay for them at once; the arrival of US forces in Iceland and the institution of US Navy escorts for convoys across the North Atlantic as far as Iceland; and finally, the entry of the USA as a formal belligerent, following the Japanese attack on Pearl Harbor in December 1941. For over two years the USA's formal neutrality remained unchanged and the BBC had to observe due caution on the matter. While it certainly played its part in making the case for regarding the war as a common cause in its broadcasts to the USA, it did not want to be accused of encouraging complacency in Britain about the prospect of American entry, the more so since there were those who assumed it to be ultimately inevitable. But if the BBC did not explicitly forecast American entry, the tone and cumulative effect of its reports, talks and features *implied* it – mere factual reporting of the USA's creeping interventionism was alone enough to do that, since this was a type of war news for which there was *always* space.[42] Once the USA had formally become a belligerent and ally, the BBC put into operation a range of programmes that it had been readying for this eventuality. Their tone was understandably tributary and celebratory, a contented cataloguing of the awesome strength and still greater potential of the power that was now unequivocally with Britain in its struggle. Listeners could draw no other conclusion: the worst may be yet to come, but ultimately the war would be won.

Stimulating patriotism

Since the existence of national sentiment was a fact – and, in modern times, once the national armies had taken the field, there was always an extra surge of partisan feeling – no government felt it could look this particular gift horse in the mouth. As elsewhere, Britain's leaders did their best to exploit love of country for what it could yield for the project of winning the war. How people felt – and, especially, how they behaved – it must be stressed, was the litmus test of the health of civilian morale. It followed that a policy to stimulate the sentiments that were known to increase active commitment should form part of the Government's strategy. The policy that emerged took two principal forms, which were naturally linked: appeals to patriotic feelings and calls for patriotic behaviour. And like so much else in policy, it reflected the broad division of the war into the phase of crisis and the period of the long haul.

As discussed in Chapter 1, social developments before the war, particularly the growth of class antagonism, pacifism and regionalism had occasioned some anxiety among the political elites about the state of national feelings. The Phoney War period had done little to lay this anxiety to rest. In the propaganda of the Emergency, therefore, there was, initially at least, some diffidence about content and method, as if the successful formulas of the previous war were not guaranteed to work this time and a subtler touch was needed. For one thing, popular attachment to the British Empire could not be taken for granted. George Orwell acknowledged that as long as Britain itself was under threat of invasion, ordinary people would do whatever the Government required of them. But he was doubtful that they would respond as well to a patriotic call to bear danger and privation for the defence or recovery of distant bits of the Empire or even feel that 'fighting in Africa, or in Europe, has anything to do with the defence of Britain'.[43] The Emergency was the most favourable of testing grounds, then, though not necessarily indicative of what might be needed when the time came for the rolling back of German power.

At this time two voices, which also happened to have by far the largest audiences, stood out among the appeals to patriotism, and came almost to symbolize it: the voices of Churchill and Priestley. Perhaps because he was himself a historian, Churchill's concept of patriotism was imbued with a profound sense of Britain's history, especially what he saw as its unique role in establishing parliamentary democracy as a modern ideal for all humanity and its achievement in planting its civilized and civilizing system in every continent. In the crisis of 1940 he confidently assumed these feelings were widely shared and so made unabashed appeal to them. The 'island race', as he characterized his compatriots, was aroused and on its mettle. 'We shall defend our island, whatever the cost may be', he announced on 4 June. He used the island theme again two weeks later, as France fell: 'Hitler knows he will have to break us in this island or lose the war.' On 14 July he again assumed an unswerving 'no surrender' mentality: 'we would rather see London laid in ashes and ruins than that it should be tamely and abjectly enslaved'. And in the historic role of defending civilization: 'Neither by material damage nor by slaughter will the British people be turned from their solemn and inexorable purpose.'[44]

Priestley, too, also played on the national myth of an island people, protected from its foes by the sea and the men of the sea. As it happened, the very first of his fifteen-minute talks, called *Postscripts*, which followed the nine o'clock news bulletin on Sunday nights, was entirely on this theme. 'Nothing, I feel, could be more English than this Battle of Dunkirk' ... (and when I say "English" I really mean British) in the way in which, when apparently all was lost, so much was gloriously retrieved'. Appealing to the national love of the idea of the underdog amateur foiling the mighty professional, he affectionately evoked the role of the 'little ships' – the pleasure steamers that joined the warships in the rescue operation – 'so typical of us, so absurd and yet so grand and gallant'. His final words fitted in perfectly with the BBC's own positive slant on the setback: 'our great-grandchildren, when they learn about how we began this war by snatching glory out of defeat, and then swept on to victory, may also learn how the little holiday steamers made an excursion to hell and came back glorious'.[45] Was the phrase 'and then swept on to victory' inserted more in hope than conviction, one wonders? Either way, it served its rallying purpose by excluding the very thought of defeat – by assuming there would *be* a time when one would be able to look back on the present as yet one more test of Britain's mettle, passed like all the others. In subsequent talks Priestley called up images of England and Englishness calculated to evoke in his audience feelings about what these notions represented and to promote modest pride in them. On the English landscape: 'the lush fields and the round green hills dissolving into the hazy blue of the sky … It's as if this English landscape said "Look at me, as I am in my beauty and fullness of joy, and do not forget".' On 'ordinary folk', on night duty with the Local Defence Volunteers: 'There we were, ploughman, and parson, shepherd and clerk, turning out at night, as our forefathers had often done before us, to keep watch and ward over the sleeping English hills and fields and homesteads.' And on Churchill: 'this is the kind of man the English, and the Scots and the Welsh, and for that matter the Irish, want at this challenging hour'. Shakespeare, Dickens and Hardy were pressed into service in these affectionate evocations of the land and the people.[46]

One other individual voice made an impression at this time, that of George VI. Although he could not match Churchill and Priestley, the King could naturally expect a reasonably large and attentive audience. Like them, when he addressed the nation, he assumed its steadfastness and made much of England's wider standing: 'The walls of London may be battered, but the spirit of the Londoner stands resolute and undismayed … There'll always be an England to stand before the world as the symbol and citadel of freedom.'[47]

Speeches like these had their echo in the tone adopted by the press. When Chamberlain stood down and the Churchill coalition was formed, hearts-and-flowers poet Patience Strong used her 'Quiet Corner' spot in the *Daily Mirror* to indulge in a typical bit of lionising: 'We know that we can trust them / for we know they will not fail … Although the ship of state may roll and tack upon the sea / They will steer her safely to the ports of Victory.'[48] Zec, too, was in heroic-poetic mode on 19 June 1940; alongside a visual of a defiant Britannia ran an (unidentified) quotation, the last line of which provided the caption: 'All our past proclaims our future / Shakespeare's voice and Nelson's hand / Milton's faith and Wordsworth's trust / in this our chosen and chainless land / Bear us witness: come the world against her / England yet shall stand.'[49]

Zec could be the sharpest of critics and the most relentless of conscience prickers; here, however, he was using his skills simply to ask people to identify with their roots, to remember they were British.

In the Government's printed publicity nothing more exactly illustrates the official appeal to patriotic sentiment than the series of posters painted by Frank Newbould, an assistant designer at the War Office, issued by the Army Bureau of Current Affairs. Under the common title, 'Your Britain. Fight for it *now*', these depicted different places in Britain: Salisbury cathedral, seen across meadows, where haymaking was in progress; the South Downs, with a shepherd and his dog in the foreground; Alfriston fair – merry-go-rounds and sideshows set against a backdrop of trees and parish church; 'Village Green' – inn, church and thatched cottages, clustered around a green adorned with duckpond and spreading oak tree. Idealized and Anglo-centric though they were, these scenes were chosen, presumably, because they were thought to represent the essence of Britain in the imaginations of ordinary people, whether they lived in such places or, like the majority, in the towns and cities of the industrial areas.

The tendency to use the cliché of rural England to represent Britain appeared, too, in films, especially those made under official sponsorship. In *Britain at Bay*, for example, although there are images of industrial towns and factory workshops, these are outweighed by those of the cliffs of Dover, the Yorkshire Dales and other country locations. It starts with a sequence of such scenes, accompanied by oboe and strings playing suitably idyllic music. The commentary breaks in with: 'For nearly a thousand years these hills and fields and farmsteads of Britain have been free from foreign invasion.' And after acknowledging that 'not all of us live in such peaceful solitudes' – brief shots of the 'other Britain' – it quickly gets back to the rural with: 'and never far away from even the blackest towns was always one of the most beautiful, peaceful countrysides in the world'. It was the Nazi threat to *this* Britain that – or so the propagandist hoped – would call up a patriotic anger in the minds of the people and which they would fight to defend.

Feature film makers appeared to be happy to fall in with this rather unbalanced picture of the country everyone was fighting for. Throughout the war films were made in which it was implied, as Orwell put it, ' that England is an agricultural country, and that its inhabitants derive their patriotism from a passionate love of the English soil'.[50] The first of these, *This England* (1941), takes the form of a chronicle of English history, focusing on four occasions when, as in 1940, England's independence was threatened: by the Normans in 1066, the Spanish in 1588, the French in 1804 and the Germans in 1914–18. Again, 'England' is represented at each of these points in time by a village – the same village – and the English by its inhabitants. Rural England was likewise the chosen backdrop for the dramas enacted in *Went the Day Well?* (1942), *A Canterbury Tale* (1944) and *Tawny Pipit* (1944). All three films implied that in the countryside was to be found, unchanging, the very essence of the English character – 'the principles of balance, peacefulness, traditionalism and spirituality'.[51] And as the production dates show, this perspective was by no means confined to the early years of the war or to the period of the Emergency.

Alongside the myth of rural England, the other main component of *This England* was national history. History was a productive seam, wherein stereotypes of Englishness could be mined; and in the early years of the war several directors hewed out some choice nuggets, in the form of famous individuals thought to embody the concept: Admiral Nelson, in *Lady Hamilton* (1940), Disraeli, in *The Prime Minister* (1941), William Pitt, in *The Young Mr Pitt* (1942). Olivier's *Henry V* – history via the imagination of Shakespeare – was essentially of the same genre. Behind such films was the hope that ordinary citizens in the 1940s would connect with their country's past and feel proud to be members of a nation that had produced such stalwarts and heroes.

However, it was fully recognized at the MoI and among film makers that the supposed national virtues of 'stoicism, humour and dedication to duty' might be easier for ordinary citizens to identify with if a film's characters were of less elevated stations in life.[52] For all the mileage that could be got from 'mobilizing the past', moreover, it was probable that contemporary role models would be yet more effective.[53] Films were made, therefore, that depicted people in every sort of occupation and situation, displaying essentially the same 'English' qualities that distinguished the likes of Henry V, Nelson and Pitt. *Pimpernel Smith* (1941), *49th Parallel* (1941), *In Which We Serve* (1942), *Fires Were Started* (1943), *The Gentle Sex* (1943), *Millions Like Us* (1943), *This Happy Breed* (1944), *The*

Way to the Stars (1945), and many others, were vehicles for the transmission of an ideal of Britishness that might make those who saw them feel borne up and sustained in a time of stress. Happily, there were occasions when fact was as inspiring as fiction: the War Office and the film industry did not let the news of El Alamein speak for itself. Rather, they collaborated to capture the whole operation on celluloid in *Desert Victory*, which was released in March 1943, just as the last Axis forces in Tunisia were being defeated. Against a real life context in which the virtues of the British were being seen to be rewarded, the national self-promotion of the fictionalized dramas stood to gain in credibility.

Apart from giving Priestley his *Postscripts* spot, where, as already noted, he consciously made appeals to patriotic sentiment, the BBC more generally in its programmes joined in the loosely coordinated operation, following the same broad pathways of landscape, history, culture and national character. In the early months, there were features such as *For Ever England* and *The Land We Defend*, the very titles of which conjured up the pastoral idyll – Siân Nicholas described the latter as 'portraying Britain as essentially one vast and picturesque village, with the British people characterised above all by their love of the countryside'.[54] However, the BBC gradually moved away from this idealized picture of Britain, (conceived, like the films, essentially as England), towards a focus on the people who made up the British – Welsh, Scots, Irish and all – in programmes like *Everyman and the War*, *My Day's Work* and *We Speak for Ourselves*. Like the film makers, the programme makers of the BBC sought to sustain popular morale by reminding people that the national character was something to be proud of and worth fighting to preserve.

In one particular field the BBC was uniquely positioned: it was the largest provider of music in the country, and it reached by far the largest audience for music. BBC Managers were well aware of the possibilities this position gave them to fulfil their brief from the MoI to help sustain the morale of the civilian population.[55] In fact, they had been thinking about it even before the war. In the mid–1930s the Director General, referring to radio as an instrument of morale maintenance, wrote: 'It is conceived that the broadcasting of programmes of music may be a valuable factor in this field.'[56]

The well-known power of music to arouse human sentiments made it an immediately obvious way of releasing and enhancing patriotic feeling. For the men in charge, patriotic music implied mainly the 'serious' sort, initially, at least. In time they came to accept that for most listeners, popular songs like *The White Cliffs of Dover* and *There'll Always Be An England* had more patriotic resonance than Parry's *Jerusalem* or Elgar's *Pomp and Circumstance Marches*; but in the early months they gave to the Music Department rather than to the Variety Department the brief of putting music to work for the morale of the nation.

Since the BBC had already an established practice of commissioning new works from composers, it was a simple matter to attach to future commissions the requirement that they should have 'patriotic' flavour. Following a prompt from the MoI, four composers; Ralph Vaughan Williams, John Ireland, George Dyson and Roger Quilter, were approached in 1940 to write a patriotic song, the invitations being accompanied by a suggestion that they might seek out suitable words in the works of Masefield, Blunden, Binyon, Read and Dunsany. The MoI was also behind an initiative to get a new patriotic march composed. Inviting John Ireland to write it, the Director of Music, Adrian Boult, wrote: 'I know they have in mind something of the "Pomp and Circumstance" pattern, with an attractive title which has a bearing on the present mood and general outlook today.'[57] Ireland fulfilled the brief with professional efficiency: his *Epic March* effortlessly recaptured the spacious 'Edwardian' idiom of the Elgar marches and he provided a piquant bonus by inserting into the opening bars the rhythm of the Morse code for 'V', thereby anticipating the BBC's adoption of this as its call signal for its broadcasts to occupied Europe. To William Walton went a commission to write a suite from the music he had composed for the film about the making of the Spitfire fighter plane, *The First of the Few*. His *Spitfire Prelude and Fugue* was the result; a more perfect evocation of the spirit-stirring mood of 1940 than its commissioners had dared to hope for. More commissions followed. For example, an invitation for a brass band suite based on traditional British tunes went out to eight composers, all of whom accepted and fulfilled the brief: Vaughan Williams, Jacob, Bax, Walton, Quilter, Ireland, Dunhill and Bantock. This project was clearly aimed at yielding music that would explicitly celebrate the 'diversity within unity' of the United Kingdom, matching the documentary features that were being put out by the Talks Department and the Features and Drama Department.

There was, of course, plenty of music already in the repertoire that could do service in arousing patriotic sentiments, and the obvious pieces were given extra prominence in the schedules. More generally, however, the Music Department sought simply to put out a greater proportion of British music, allowing its intrinsic national resonances to speak for themselves. British music as a proportion of 'serious' music in general accordingly increased its share of air time. It was 16.8 per cent in December 1939, 20.9 per cent in April 1940, 27 per cent by October 1943.[58] With more space at their disposal for British music, the programme makers devised new series tailored to the new regime, such as *British Composers of Our Time*. Besides the classical repertoire, there was the large field of folk music, which not only had the desirable 'national' resonance but was more likely to appeal to a mass audience. Again, it was the MoI that nudged the BBC towards its duty. It asked the BBC explicitly to broadcast more programmes of English, Scottish, Irish and Welsh national and folk songs, 'particularly if they have a touch of the sea about them'.[59] The series *Britain and its Music* did this by bringing into studios or catching on location in outside broadcasts a colourful variety of folk singers, choirs, fiddlers, pipers and accordion players. At the same time the managers worked at the theme of 'strength in diversity' by bolstering the output of programme makers in the regions. North Region's *Strike a Home Note*, for example, concentrated on the vigour of popular culture in northern England, giving listeners the sound of children's choirs, singers of northern folk songs, colliery bands and works orchestras. These sounds, homely and amateur though they were, were going out across the land because they had the power to evoke the atavistic, tribal feelings that total war demanded.

It was this very power that lay behind the decision of BBC managers to reduce the amount of 'enemy' music in BBC programmes, following the logic that what was capable of arousing *German* patriotism had no place on British radio when Germany was the enemy. The explanation given, eventually, was that the banned music was that for which the copyright was in enemy hands – German or Italian – since it would be wrong for performance royalties to be accumulated in Britain for countries with which it was at war. In reality, there was a much more extensive blacklisting, unannounced and secretly operated, for which the criterion was 'music infected by the German spirit'.[60] On this basis selected items were deleted from the repertoire of BBC orchestras and given no place in record programmes: much of Wagner, for example, some of Richard Strauss, even Sibelius's 'Finlandia' – for once Finland became an ally of Germany, its music, too, was vetted for the 'wrong' sounds.[61]

The BBC's 'Alien Composers' policy was itself a contribution to a wider policy adopted by every propaganda agency as part of the attempt to stimulate patriotic feelings in the public, that is, the policy of denigration of the enemy. The hate propaganda of the First World War had given such tactics a bad name and, with few exceptions, nothing so crude was attempted this time round. But it was deemed too productive a tactic to forgo altogether. War had something primitive and tribal about it, after all, and the mobilizing of hatred against the out group was intrinsic to it.

Much of the anti-German propaganda that ordinary citizens encountered (and also anti-Italian, anti-Japanese and, until June 1941, anti-Soviet propaganda) appeared more or less spontaneously in the media, without any obvious official coordination. None the less, it is quite clear that the Government wanted it and promoted it from the start, at least in respect of anti-German propaganda. This was wholly within the domain of the Ministry of Information, and it was effectively left to itself to work out ways and means. The only restraint was in the short period when Chamberlain was Prime Minister. He never really gave up hope that the German people would rise up and overthrow the Nazi regime, and so he would not allow propaganda that depicted the Germans as all equally depraved. Churchill had no such delicacy. In any case, by the time he took over, the case for resting hopes on the 'good Germans' was so much weaker. Dunkirk and the defeat of France finally removed all restraint: from this point the distinction between the Germans and the Nazis effectively disappeared from official propaganda. Hitler was 'the embodiment of the German lust for power in the most evil guise it has ever taken'.[62] At the MoI there were true believers in the doctrine that the Germans were a psychologically damaged people who were constitutionally unable to live at peace with their neighbours, who always coveted what was not theirs and who would stoop to any barbarity to acquire it. The British people must be shown that there was no compromise to be had with such monsters, that submission to Hitler meant slavery and that there was therefore no alternative to armed struggle and the attainment of unqualified victory. These men never changed their beliefs and since their position went unchallenged at the Ministry – frequent changes of Minister notwithstanding – theirs was the policy that was adhered to throughout the war. The language used in the MoI's attacks on the Hitler Youth, the persecution of Jews and other minorities, the brutal occupation policies, and other targets, cumulatively gave the impression that the Germans were, always had been and always would be a barbarous, uncivilized people. In mid–1940 it launched what it called an 'Anger Campaign', designed to counter incipient apathy and defeatism and arouse people against the threat to their way of life posed by the expansion of German/Nazi power. The pamphlet *What Would Happen if Hitler Won* warned that, in the event of a successful invasion of Britain, ordinary people would not simply be left alone by the Germans: 'If Hitler won you couldn't make a joke in the pub without being afraid that a spy may not get you run in or beaten up; you could not talk freely in front of your children for fear that they might give you away (in Germany they are encouraged to); if you were a worker you would be at the mercy of your employer about hours and wages, for you would have no trade union.'[63] In a booklet simply titled *No!* the MoI catalogued the crimes perpetrated by the Germans (no longer simply 'the Nazis') against the peoples of Europe. It luridly described their behaviour in Poland: 'Hitler has visited the most spectacularly savage oppressions known to European history … An entire people is being exterminated … Ruthless slaughter … indescribable brutalities.' By 1942, in a probably unintentional parody of Nazi propaganda about the Russians, the Ministry was resorting to crude representations of the enemy as sub-humans. In a leaflet entitled 'The Battle for Civilization', for instance, a raging battle scene is dominated by a foreground figure of a snarling gorilla-like creature equipped as a German soldier.

The mass communications media followed the Ministry's lead more or less wholesale. Images of the enemy as petty criminals with a low respect for other people's property and a propensity for stabbing one another in the back, tended to give way to more serious representations in which their character and behaviour is perverted, sinister and brutal. *Picture Post*'s July 1940 feature 'What Are We Fighting For?' for example, used the device adopted by many propagandists, of contrasting the virtues of British society and the British character with the faults of Germany and the Germans, making much of the latter's current manifestations under the Nazis – the concentration camps, the perversion of children's minds in the Hitler Youth, and the like.

The BBC avoided the cruder methods of the popular press but its line did not differ fundamentally. In features like *The Shadow of the Swastika* and *Under Nazi Rule* and talks in the series *The Voice of the Nazi*, the denigration simply came dressed up in the clothes of serious inquiry informed by expert opinion from the disciplines of history, sociology and psychology. Listeners hoping to find in drama productions relief from tendentious features and talks, were quite often served more of the same: plays like *They Call it Peace*, which imagined Britain under Nazi rule, or drama-documentaries like *Escape to Freedom* and *It Might Happen Here*, which used real stories about Occupied Europe to give verisimilitude to dramatic scenarios in Britain.

In the cinema, too, audiences often encountered material that set out to persuade them of the special iniquity of the Germans. For obvious reasons there were practical limits to what could be done in newsreels and documentaries, so the main burden of the propaganda in this field fell on the makers of feature films, who used film drama for imaginative, though informed, constructions of German behaviour. An early film, Roy Boulting's *Pastor Hall* (1940), told the story of the persecution of a Christian minister in Germany who spoke out against Nazi policies. Like Anthony Asquith's *Freedom Radio*, which followed in 1941, Boulting's film pulled no punches about the brutal nature of the regime, but it did make a distinction between the Nazis and 'good Germans'. By 1942 this sort of nicety had disappeared from feature films; all Germans were presented as equally bad. This was invariably the case in the many films, such as *Secret Mission* (1942) and *The Flemish Farm* (1943), that used Resistance in Europe as the subject or the background. The film makers also used the theme of Britain under German rule. *Went the Day Well?* (Alberto Cavalcanti, 1942) contained several scenes in which the occupiers acted ruthlessly and brutally against civilians as well as uniformed defenders. Humphrey Jennings's *The Silent Village*, made for the Crown Film Unit in 1943, told the story of the Germans' destruction of the Czech village of Lidice, following the assassination by partisans of the *Reichsprotektor*, Reinhard Heydrich. It overcame the problem of lack of real footage by transposing the action to Wales under an imagined German occupation. Thus the horrors inflicted on the inhabitants of remote Lidice were made believably real for people who must be persuaded, or so it was thought, that there was no future in a compromise deal with Germany.

Making people feel proud to be British was one thing; getting them to behave patriotically was another. Since the latter was not an inevitable consequence of the former, propaganda was needed, or so it was believed, to prompt the sort of behaviour that would maximize the potential of the home front. There must be no wastage of human resource; every individual who could contribute must do so. In achieving this the role of propaganda was deemed quite as important as the carrots and sticks of labour policy, for there would always be a proportion of the population – women at home with children, the elderly, and others – whose voluntary effort was needed; in any case, proceeding by consent was obviously more desirable and more effective than by coercion.

Some of the attempts to persuade people into patriotic behaviour took the straightforward form of exhortation. At first the Government's efforts were often ineffably dull and vague, as in the poster that had a crown as its only visual element and the words: 'YOUR COURAGE, YOUR CHEERFULNESS, YOUR RESOLUTION WILL BRING US VICTORY'. Other appeals suggested specific behaviour, as in the poster showing evacuees arriving in the countryside under the message: 'Women wanted for Evacuation Service' and the subscript: 'Offer Your Services to Your Local Council'. Or simply, a uniformed head and the words: 'Join the ATS'. A more subtle ploy was to prick the viewer's conscience. Thus a poster of September 1940 showing five RAF pilots contemplating a sky cleared of raiders, under Churchill's memorable words: 'Never was so much owed by so many to so few'. Or, more practically, a poster issued by the Ministry of Health showing a bombed-out mother and children against a background of wrecked houses, under the caption: 'It might be YOU!' and the message: 'Caring for Evacuees is a National Service'.[64] Similarly, campaigns were conducted to get people to match the efforts of those in the armed services by cooperating with the policies to curb waste of food and materials, to save fuel and to boost National Savings. Government propagandists could usually rely on backup for this sort of exhortation from the press. A page of the *Daily Mirror* on 20 May 1940 was typical: the cartoon is worked around a quotation from Shakespeare – 'But screw your courage to the sticking place, and we'll not fail!' – and the leader first quotes a speech by Ernest Bevin – 'Every man and woman in this country must give a bigger output' – then goes on to give its own rallying call: 'Into battle! We are all in the line of fire, civilians and fighters alike. If every man and woman strive their hardest, victory is certain and Nazism will perish.'

Right across the media, the most-used method of persuading people into patriotic behaviour, whether they were in work or not, was to present them with civilian models or exemplars. 'Heroes of the Home Front' stories could be found most days in the newspapers, some lending themselves to striking photographs, such as those of humorous homemade notices put up by owners of bomb-shattered shops, informing customers that it was more or less business as usual, or that of a milkman nonchalantly picking his way over mounds of bomb rubble to deliver milk to his customers.

But it was the medium of film that perhaps lent itself best to the technique of persuasion by example. Cinemagoers – most people, that is – were generously served with role models, real and fictional, at every stage in the war, for there was never a time when the need for patriotic effort of one kind or another diminished. In the MoI's 1939 short *Westward Ho!* people in safe areas were shown their duty as welcoming hosts to evacuees. In mid–1940 everyone was shown how to act if German paratroops landed; in *Miss Grant Goes to the Door*, a ten-minute 'instructional drama', two middle-aged women living alone foil the efforts of a German soldier disguised as a British officer. The implication was that no one should think their services were not needed or that they had nothing to offer. As an army officer says in the closing scene: 'The front line runs through every household now'. During the period of heavy bombing, most people became familiar with how to 'carry on' under the most trying circumstances, simply by seeing the newsreels.

Typically, these gave an impression of ordinary people as resilient – defiant even – in the face of death and destruction, cheerfully making the best of their situation and acting like good citizens. In addition, there were MoI-sponsored documentary films like *Britain Can Take It* and *Christmas Under Fire*, which gave more polished projections of citizen virtue in this time of greatest trial. In the former, the images of London in the Blitz are accompanied by a commentary that purports to describe, but really prescribes. The people of London are held up as exemplars of right-thinking, right-doing citizens:

> This is the London rush hour. Many of the people at whom you are looking now are members of the greatest civilian army ever to be assembled. These men and women who have worked all day in offices or in markets, are now hurrying home to change into the uniform of their particular service ... They are the ones who are really fighting this war ... Brokers, clerks, pedlars by day – they are heroes by night.

Not everyone could be a hero in this sense. But it was broadly true to say that the Government wanted people to do more than survive and remain of good cheer. Active commitment to the war effort was the objective, and films could show them what this meant.

Once the true emergency phase of the war was over, the prime target of this sort of propaganda was women. Tom Harrisson explained why in 1942: 'As this war gradually moves towards its fourth year, more and more does it become, on the Home Front, a war of women ... Now every available female body is required in a war factory or in uniform.'[65] By this time the simple arithmetic of military conscription and the war economy had created a demand for labour that exceeded the supply. Women constituted the last resource that had not already been exhausted. This was the context for documentary films like *Night Shift* (1942) and feature films like *Millions Like Us* (1943). Jack Chambers' fifteen-minute telescoping of the twelve hours of nightshift work in a factory making guns for tanks, is seen through the eyes of a new female recruit. The noisy, dirty, male world of a heavy engineering works is shown in fact to be a community of largely female workers of all ages, who get through their physically tiring stint at lathe and drill in a spirit of good-humoured and comradely endeavour and who leave for home in the morning suffused with a sense of wellbeing from knowledge of a job well done in the home front war. The film is honest enough about the strain of the work, but it systematically dispels the misconceptions potential recruits might have had that such factories were suitable only for men. Frank Launder and Sidney Gilliat's *Millions Like Us* also focused on women in factories, using the same device of following the experiences of a new recruit, this time at a factory making aircraft. The newcomer has not chosen the work, being a 'mobile female' directed by the Ministry of Labour. But the message of the film was really aimed at women who were not liable for the call-up, but who might nevertheless be willing to come forward. As the Ministry official explains to the new recruit: 'Mr Bevin needs another million women, and I don't think we should disappoint him at a time like this. The men at the front need tanks, guns and planes. You can help your country just as much in an overall as you can in uniform these days.'

One of the most striking features of surviving Second World War ephemera is the large proportion of it that relates to a propaganda campaign of one sort or another. There is no doubt that the civilian population of that time was subjected to a veritable barrage of official and semi-official exhortation, injunction, instruction and advice throughout the period of the war. The question remains of whether civilian morale was sustained or improved by all this endeavour. Did it succeed in making people feel and act in ways any different from how they would have felt and acted anyway?

An answer to this question might begin with some general observations about human responses to propaganda. Human beings typically feel and act the way they do from a multiplicity of causes. Calculated attempts by others to influence them will always be inextricably mingled with other influences, operating in infinitely variable proportions. It follows that any attempt to discover the discrete effect of a particular propaganda campaign is inherently impossible; the total effect of all campaigns not much less so. This is not to say that propaganda is without effect, merely that its effects, if any, are unmeasurable. Propaganda, in short, is an inexact science. In the totalitarian regimes of the time this truth was imperfectly understood. Rather the dictators thought they knew better and, in the belief that the minds of the masses could be precisely manipulated by modern methods of communication, centrally controlled, they allocated a large amount of resources to the operation. In Britain, although there were enthusiasts for mass manipulation through propaganda, some of them in the Ministry of Information, on the whole the official attitude was sceptical – Chamberlain totally, Churchill not much less so. Neither man was willing to rule propaganda out altogether as a supplement to the substantive policies that would win the war, but nor did they expect great results from it. Indicative of this scepticism among elites, was a Penguin Special *Science in War*, published in June 1940, in which a group of scientists advocated, among other things, an input of psychological and sociological science into the assessment of morale and the construction of propaganda. In other words, there might be something in this propaganda business, but let judgement be suspended until it has become more science-based and scientifically measured. On the other hand, there were occasions when Government leaders displayed an anxiety about certain messages reaching the general public that suggests they were not wholly sceptical about the power of the modern media to influence attitudes and behaviour. The Government's muzzling of troublesome newspapers – the warnings given to the *Daily Mirror* and the shutting down of the *Daily Worker* – was surely a sign of concern about their negative effect on popular morale. Churchill complained to Cecil King, a *Mirror* director, that the paper's hostile editorials in early 1941 created a spirit of 'despondency and resentment, of bitterness and scorn', that might be 'suddenly switched over to naked defeatism'.[66] Similarly, J. B. Priestley was silenced when in his radio talks he began to ask awkward questions about war aims and reconstruction (see Chapter 6), and Churchill attempted to prevent the showing of Powell and Pressburger's film *The Life and Death of Colonel Blimp*, on the grounds that it undermined confidence in the army. Ambivalence persisted: while it is clear that the Government attached less importance to mere words and pictures than to other aspects of managing the war, the sheer scale of its propaganda suggests it was unwilling to take a gamble on the matter, choosing rather to play safe and churn it out, anyway. In the final analysis, it was the impossibility of proving any cause-and-effect relationship between propaganda and behaviour that determined the official attitude.

Establishing the objectives of the wartime persuaders is straightforward enough, then; gauging precisely what they achieved, however, is difficult and uncertain. Much of the evidence relating to the public effect of particular propaganda campaigns – and even to whole genres and media – is anecdotal. Where there were systematic attempts to monitor the effect of individual films, broadcasts, advertisements and the like, the procedures do not, by later standards, have a high degree of social-scientific credibility. For both kinds of evidence, moreover, it is an uneven picture, made up of more or less random fragments. With these caveats in mind, then, what does the evidence suggest?

In the area of news about the war, the picture is characteristically equivocal. On the one hand, according to Mass-Observation at the end of 1940, every survey it had undertaken revealed public discontent about insufficient information in the newspapers and in the newsreels on what was happening in the war.[67] By this reckoning, not being told the worst did not sustain or improve people's morale, and it may even have been counterproductive. Margery Allingham, writing in 1941 of the 'extraordinary anxiety in official circles not to alarm the public', thought (like Mass-Observation) that this merely served to feed rumours, such as that about the building of a chain of super-mortuaries to cope with bomb victims.[68] On the other hand, Mass-Observation's summaries of morale showed big swings daily, from wild hope to despair, depending, it seemed, on the nature of the news.[69] If morale really was suffering when bad news was released, the implication is that the Government's policy of keeping such items to a minimum was wise, and that total frankness would have been more damaging still. But people, it seemed, resented being treated as though they could not be told the truth about the war, and were suspicious that 'national security' was sometimes used disingenuously. On balance, the evidence suggests that most thought knowledge was preferable to ignorance, and that their mental state was their own affair.

When it comes to assessing the effect of attempts to reassure the public and to stimulate its patriotic feelings and behaviour, Churchill's speeches stand out as playing a unique role. Was he telling the people what they wanted to hear? A fight to the death? No surrender, come what may? It would seem so. Many contemporary accounts – not just the fancy of retrospect – testify to the very real sense in which he both inspired and personified the people. Molly Weir told of how her mother responded to him: 'She loved, above all things, listening to Churchill ... "Here he comes. The British bulldog. By God, he puts new life into you".'[70] 'What they

like most', wrote Mollie Panter-Downes, 'is his great gift for making them forget discomfort, danger and loss and remember only
that they are living history'.[71] His 'blood, sweat and tears' speech,
she thought, 'struck the right note with the public because it was
the kind of tough talk they wanted to hear after months of woolly
optimism'.[72] Churchill's own view on this was characteristically
modest: 'I was very fortunate: I did nothing more than give expression to the opinion of the people of this country, and I was fortunate in being able to put their sentiments into words.'[73] The
implication is that the speeches were not primarily attempts to persuade at all. Frances Partridge was not sure about this: 'I remember, how loathsome his early speeches seemed to me and wonder if
it is I who have changed, or Winston? Have we all given in now
and become war minded, where once we stuck our toes in?'[74] George
Beardmore, while coolly objective about the oratorical skill being
deployed, was none the less happy to admit that this was a voice
both for and of the people: 'A marvellous speech and a long one by
Churchill last Sunday in his appeal to the Americans .... His closing
passage "Give us the tools and we will *finish* the job", was so intense that it kept a roomful of us silent for three minutes after he'd
gone .... His genius is that while he puts into magnificent words
what we ourselves are thinking, he manages at the same time to
inspire.'[75] Isaiah Berlin, too, noted Churchill's ability 'to impose his
imagination and his will upon his fellow countrymen ... [He] lifted
them to an abnormal height in a moment of crisis', turning them
'out of their normal selves, and, by dramatising their lives and making them seem to themselves and to each other clad in the fabulous
garments appropriate to a great historic moment, transformed cow-
ards into brave men, and so fulfilled the purpose of shining armour'.[76]
As to whether he *needed* to remind people that there was no future
worth having in a compromise with Nazism, we might, with benefit of hindsight, say that he did not. The evidence is abundant
enough that contempt for Hitler and all his works was widespread
and that this attitude hardened as the war increasingly revealed his
true character.

   In assessing the effect of films, the main evidence lies in the findings of the occasional surveys on certain films, undertaken by Mass-
Observation, and in the popularity of particular films, as suggested
by audience attendance figures. In July 1941, Mass-Observation

asked its panel of 142 observers their opinion of fifteen MoI short films. Of the 56 per cent who had actually seen enough of these to comment, only 10 per cent thought them 'bad' or 'very bad'; the rest were positive – 17 per cent rating them 'mixed to fair', 25 per cent 'good' and 4 per cent 'very good'. The best-rated film was *Britain Can Take It!*; *Men of the Lightship* received only praise; *Miss Grant Goes to the Door* and *Home Guard* aroused interest, praise and criticism. The ratio of praise to criticism was 96:66, that is, about three appreciative comments for every two critical comments. *Britain Can Take It!* and *Miss Grant Goes to the Door* were the most frequently mentioned films of the fifteen. This exercise predictably showed that straight 'public information' films failed to arouse enthusiasm, whereas any film containing an element of drama brought favourable comment. From this it would appear that boredom thresholds were typically low, even when the information being made available related to matters that might cause anxiety, such as gas drill or the air raid routine. But of course, it revealed nothing of the actual effect of the films, however rated, on civilian morale. More relevant to this were the occasional attempts made to assess audience reaction during the showing of a film. For instance, when an audience was studied watching *Miss Grant*, there was close attention, 'some grunts of approval' and an absence of laughter or jeers. When some were questioned afterwards, these impressions were confirmed in responses like: 'We went to see a film *Typhoon*. There was an awfully good short all about invasion. It was exciting and told us a lot.'[77] In a report made in Worcester on reactions to *Britain at Bay*, there was a 'good audience response' – applause for the RAF, Navy and Churchill and eight seconds of applause at the end.[78] Again, as with the replies of the observer panel, the recording of a positive audience response can at best give only an indirect indication of effect on morale. It might reasonably be *inferred* that the propagandist's objective was more likely than not to have been achieved in such circumstances of approval; but clearly, this does not amount to positive proof.

No one went to the cinema primarily to see the short films. Box office receipts reflected the demand for the main picture that was showing and tell us nothing of the general popularity of the shorts that happened to be in the programme. Box office figures for 1940–43 do tell us, however, that of all British films released in that period the most popular were those with MoI-approved propaganda content: *Convoy*, *49th Parallel*, *The First of the Few* and *In Which We Serve*, and that the third most popular film of 1943 was the feature-length documentary *Desert Victory*. But box office success was no better guide to effects on civilian feelings and behaviour than the approval of Mass-Observation's panel. For more meaningful evidence of this, we would have to turn to the more detailed reports that Mass-Observation made from time to time on the reactions of audiences to particular films. Its reports on *The Lion Has Wings* (directed by Michael Powell, Brian Desmond and Adrian Brunel, 1939) and on *Ships With Wings* (directed by Sergei Nolbandov, 1941), for instance, would certainly have satisfied those who made them that their effect on morale was positive. On the latter film, Mass-Observation found that in a large number of cases people's emotions and feelings were stirred by seeing it. It recorded far more favourable than unfavourable comment, citing remarks like: 'Proud of our oldest Service', 'I felt I ought to do something to help them', and 'I felt as though I'd like to join it when I saw it'. However, Mass-Observation thought that many of the people who went to see the film did so 'because they liked the Navy and had an interest in it'. The film therefore 'preached mostly to the already converted'.[79]

Taken together, box office statistics and the patchy and piecemeal reports of Mass-Observation do not allow anything conclusive to be said about the effect of propaganda films on civilian morale. At best, they suggest that such films made some positive, although intrinsically unquantifiable, contribution to attitudes and behaviour and that – since by the end of the war no less than thirty million people attended the cinema every week – this contribution involved a large proportion of the population.

The BBC had its own in-house means of finding out what audiences thought of its programmes: the Listener Research Department, whose activities were in fact greatly expanded during the war. From LR's regular soundings, together with the figures on size of audiences for particular programmes, it was possible to say with some accuracy which programmes were popular and what it was about programmes that listeners liked and disliked. Thus the BBC's managers learned that while more than a third of the adult population (twelve million people) listened to the series *The Shadow of the Swastika*, and could therefore be presumed to approve of it, patriotic 'tribute' programmes were not much regarded; and that listeners to serious music, far from welcoming the shift of emphasis to British compositions, yearned to hear more Wagner and Richard Strauss! The BBC also had the benefit of occasional Mass-Observation reports on programmes, learning, for instance, that the response to Priestley's Dunkirk *Postscript* was 'not really favourable'; 'too romantic', 'too unreal', 'overdoing the sentiment', were typical listener comments.[80] But detailed though Listener Research and Mass-Observation reports were, as a guide to the public's state of mind and behaviour, they suffered from much the same limitations as surveys of film audiences. Although a presumption of positive effect might be made about programmes that were popular, ultimately the BBC as propagandist was no more able to say with certainty what kind of effect its propaganda programmes were having than the film makers were of their films.

What has been said about film and radio propaganda can, by extension, be said of propaganda through the printed word. One can note that the *Daily Mirror* and *Picture Post* were very popular, numbering their readers in many millions; and then argue that since these organs, although often critical of the Government, were decidedly 'on side' in the national project of winning the war, then they might be presumed to have been an influence in this sense on a sizeable section of the population. Doubtless the concerted efforts of editors, columnists, photo-journalists and cartoonists to get people to rally to Churchill's stand in the crisis of May–June 1940, for example, had some positive influence. But any more precise linkage of medium, message and recipient is not possible to make.

Like their counterparts in films and radio, those working in the print media discovered, if they did not already know, that there was an inbuilt resistance in the British public to being told what they should think and how they should behave. Readers and audiences knew when they were being targeted and at best found it amusing and at worst irritating. As Mass-Observers and Listener Researchers discovered again and again, respondents often made a point of telling them when they detected tendentiousness in a film, a radio programme or a newspaper article. With remarks like: 'you got too much propaganda stuck down your throat', 'propaganda, pure and simple, don't you think?', 'they're overdoing the propaganda – it's not necessary', ordinary citizens seemed to relish the chance to show they were nobody's fools.[81] The reality was that in British society there was little scope for hard sell propaganda, and not much more for the soft sell. With such limitations so firmly entrenched, therefore, the effect of propaganda was bound to be at best marginal. Tom Harrisson, speaking, as it were, from the inside, thought so. In iconoclastic mood, he told a conference of historians in 1973: 'Looked at in the short term, on the spot, in the war, neither films nor posters nor leaflets, nor any other form of *deliberate* propaganda directed at the home front really mattered at all. The war, morale and all that was going on was at another level.'[82] It is to this 'other level', or more properly, 'levels', that this study now turns.

Notes

1 The MoI was doubtless partly in the mind of Tommy Handley, the leading performer in the immensely popular radio comedy show *ITMA*, when he created the fictitious character of 'Minister of Aggravation and Mysteries'. Another stimulus to creative renaming was William Joyce ('Lord Haw Haw'), who referred to the MoI as the 'Ministry of Misinformation'.

2 S. Taylor, Memorandum, 1 October 1941, INF 1/292.

3 M-O, File Report 90, 30 April 1940.

4 M-O, File Report 215.

5 Cited in I. McLaine, *Ministry of Morale: Home Front Morale and the Ministry of Information in World War II* (Allen & Unwin, 1979), p. 81. Orwell also recorded hearing the rumour – see S. Orwell and I. Angus (eds), *The Collected Essays, Journalism and Letters of George Orwell*, vol. 2, (Penguin, 1970), p. 399.

6 Nicholas Harman described the disingenuousness of the version of the Dunkirk evacuation put out by the authorities and the media as 'the necessary myth ... whose poetic strength sustained the morale of the nation'. N. Harman, *Dunkirk: the Necessary Myth* (Hodder and Stoughton, 1980), p. 239.

7 Home News Bulletins, 31 May 1940.

8 P. Fleming, *Invasion 1940* (Hart-Davis, 1957), p. 131.

9 H. Nicolson, *Diaries and Letters 1939–45* (Collins, 1967), p. 114; *Daily Mirror*, 14 September 1940.

10 10 September 1939. Cited in McLaine, *Ministry of Morale*, p. 64.

11 *Daily Express*, 29 August 1942.

12 Memorandum to the War Cabinet, 24 April 1942, INF 1/679.

13 M-O, File 486, Sixth Weekly Report for Home Intelligence, 11 November 1940.

14 BBC Listener Research, 10 February 1941, R9/9/5.

15 An Odhams Press book *The British People at War*, was published in late 1942,

when losses to U boats were still rising. It contained a chapter called 'Guarding Britain's Lifelines', which eulogized Britain's convoy system but gave no indication of the scale of shipping losses or the critical nature of the situation.

16 Letter, Churchill to Duff Cooper, 7 March 1941, INF 1/846.

17 M-O, File Report 266, 12 July 1940.

18 M-O, File Report 626, Report on Plymouth, 1 April 1941.

19 S. Nicholas, *The Echo of War. Home Front Propaganda and the Wartime BBC* (Manchester University Press, 1996), p. 200.

20 For example, in Bristol and Liverpool. M-O, Files 626, 706. Orwell recorded this phenomenon as early as 3 September 1940 at Ramsgate. Orwell and Angus, (eds), *Essays, Journalism and Letters,* vol. 2, p. 420.

21 M. Panter-Downes, *London War Notes 1939–1945* (Longman, 1972), p. 210.

22 Gillard spoke of his anguish in the documentary programme on the wartime BBC, *What Did You Do in the War Auntie?* produced by Jeremy Bennett and shown by BBC1 in May 1995.

23 Nicholas, *The Echo of War*, p. 205.

24 *The Times*, 12 April 1940.

25 For this aspect of MoI work see HMSO, *Persuading the People: Government publicity in the Second World War* (HMSO, 1995).

26 For obscure reasons, little was made of the significant contribution to the Battle of Britain made by fighter pilots from Commonwealth countries, nor, indeed, of that made by escaped Czech and Polish air crew.

27 HMSO, *Persuading the People*, p. 25.

28 *Ibid.*, pp. 28–9.

29 Christopher Hitchens, in a recent book, described Orwell as 'a great contrarian'. *Letters to a Young Contrarian* (Perseus Press, 2001).

30 J. L. Hodson, *Towards the Morning* (Gollancz, 1941), p. 210.

31 R. Douglas, *The World War 1939–1945: the Cartoonists' Vision* (Routledge, 1990), p. xi.

32 *Daily Mirror*, 23 May 1940; 20 June 1940.

33 *Daily Herald*, 30 September 1940.

34 *Daily Mirror*, 19 June 1940.

35 *News Chronicle*, 10 December 1941.

36 Orwell typically saw conspiracy in this, the 'plot' being to frighten people into working harder. Orwell and Angus (eds), *Essays, Journalism and Letters*, vol. 2, p. 47.

37 *Daily Express*, 28 July 1941.

38 *Daily Express*, 10 July 1941.

39 *Daily Mail*, 29 July 1944.

40 Cited in S. P. Mackenzie, *British War Films 1939–1945* (Hambledon and London, 2001), p. 28.

41 *Ibid.*, p. 29.

42 A significant agency of reassurance about the USA was the series of programmes, simply called *USA*, which began in January 1941.

43 Orwell and Angus (eds), *Essays, Journalism and Letters*, vol. 2, p. 440.

44 Hansard, 8 October 1940.

45 From the published transcripts of *Postscripts* (Heinemann, 1940), pp. 1–4.

46 *Ibid.*, pp. 5–6, 9–10, 12, 28.

47 Radio broadcast, 23 September 1940, cited in *Daily Mirror*, 24 September 1940.

48 *Daily Mirror*, 20 May 1940.

49 *Daily Mirror*, 19 June 1940.

50 Review of the film *This England* in *Time and Tide*, 31 May 1941.

51 J. Richards, *Films and British National Identity* (Manchester University Press, 1997), p. 97.

52 *Ibid.*, p. 85.

53 The phrase 'mobilizing the past' was coined by A. Aldgate and J. Richards in *Britain Can Take It: British Cinema in the Second World War* (Edinburgh University Press, 1986), p. 138.

54 Nicholas, *The Echo of War*, p. 233.

55 In 1934 the proportion of programmes devoted to music was 65.5 per cent, all other material 34.5 per cent. From the Report of the Broadcasting Committee, 1935.

56 J. Reith, Memorandum: 'Protection against Air Attack', (undated, probably 1935), in A. Briggs, *The Golden Age of Wireless*, vol. 2 of *The History of Broadcasting in the United Kingdom* (Oxford University Press, 1965), p. 629.

57 Boult to Ireland, 27 November 1940, BBC Written Archives Centre, R27/55/1.

58 Figures in letter from Arthur Bliss (Director of Music from April 1942) to *The Sunday Times*, 24 October 1943.

59 Request passed on by Nicolls (Controller of Programmes) to Thatcher (Deputy Director of Music), Directive No. 9, 19 June 1940, BBC R34/953.

60 Nicolls to Thatcher, 24 April 1940, BBC R27/3/1.

61 For a full discussion of the 'Alien Composers' policy, see R. Mackay, 'Being Beastly to the Germans: Music, Censorship and the BBC in the Second World War', *The Historical Journal of Film, Radio and Television,* vol. 20, no. 4, October 2000.

62 MoI Policy Committee Paper, 17 June 1940, INF 1/849.

63 Cited in HMSO, *Persuading the People*, p. 21.

64 Examples of these and other posters discussed in this chapter are in the Imperial War Museum, London, poster collection.

65 T. Harrisson, 'Appeals to Women', *Political Quarterly*, 13/3 (July–September 1942), cited in J. Chapman, *The British at War: Cinema, State and Propaganda, 1939–1945* (I. B. Tauris, 1998), p. 201.

66 H. Cudlipp, *Publish and be Damned!* (Andrew Dakers, 1953), pp. 163–8.

67 M-O, File Reports 90, 486.

68 M. Allingham, *The Oaken Heart: the Story of an English Village at War* (Sarsen Publishing, 1987 edn), pp. 179–80.

69 M-O, File Report 169 (June 1940).

70 M. Weir, in M. Nicholson (ed.), *What Did You Do in the War, Mummy?* (Chatto & Windus, 1995), p. 143.

71 Panter-Downes, *London War Notes*, p. 137.

72 *Ibid.*, p. 58.

73 Lord Woolton, *Memoirs* (Cassell, 1959), pp. 261–2.

74 F. Partridge, *A Pacifist's War* (Phoenix, 1996), p. 79.

75 G. Beardmore, *Civilians at War: Journals 1938–46* (Oxford University Press, 1986), pp. 109–10.

76 I. Berlin, *Mr. Churchill in 1940* (John Murray, 1949), (written in 1940).

77 M-O, File Report 338.

78 M-O, File Report 341.

79 M-O, File Reports, 967, 1059, 1204, 1218.

80 BBC Listener Research, 15 April 1942; M-O, File Report 173.

81 See, for example, audience reactions to *The Lion Has Wings*, in J. Richards and D. Sheridan (eds), *Mass-Observation at the Movies* (Routledge & Kegan Paul, 1987), p. 318.

82 T. Harrisson, 'Films and the Home Front – the evaluation of their effectiveness by Mass-Observation'. Reprinted in N. Pronay and D. Spring (eds), *Propaganda, Politics and Film 1918–45* (Macmillan, 1982), pp. 234–48.

5

Easing the strain

THE CAPACITY OF HUMAN BEINGS not under military discipline to withstand danger and endure deprivation had been put to the test in the First World War. Governments could take some comfort from the remarkable results of that test. Yet there was at the same time a warning in the experience: the capacity had limits. When tested beyond those limits the result that could be expected was at best crippling apathy and defeatism, at worst revolution. In Britain, as shown by Stephen Taylor's views (discussed at the beginning of Chapter 4), this reality was well understood by those in charge of the nation's affairs and consequently, the understanding was translated into policies favouring the 'material factors' of morale. For certain groups, these amounted to real improvements on pre-war conditions; but in general they were implemented in the knowledge that, for the most part, they could only offer mitigation of the worsened conditions brought by war. Their object was to so manage the stresses of war on the home front that defeatism was banished, war-weariness was held in check and the productive effort was sustained.

Protection

Nothing was more fundamental to this outcome than protection from bombs; the pre-war ARP plans testified to recognition of this fact in governmental circles. The Blitz was the proving ground of those plans. And as we have seen, it revealed many defects both in the umbrella of protection and in the post-raid services that together the Government and the local authorities had put in place. Mindful of the possible consequences of neglecting to act, during the period of intensive bombing itself and in the following months, both took steps to remedy these defects. Even had the threat to morale not been so palpable, a strong stimulus to action came, in any case, from the prospect of political trouble. This spectre was raised by a vigorous campaign for better shelter provision in which the Communist Party played a prominent part. The problem as the Government saw it was complicated by the implications for morale of adopting solutions that departed from its considered policy of dispersal – for this was the thrust of the demands being made by the campaigners. There was a case for arguing, in the light of experience, that greater harm would be done to morale by resisting the demand for the building of large, deep shelters than by conceding it. Doing nothing was not an option, however, and the Government, to its credit, acted with dispatch. It instituted a review of shelter provision and set up a committee under Lord Horder to examine and report on shelter conditions. By the end of September 1940 improvements to shelter conditions were already taking place and decisions had been made to enhance protection.

The changes in shelter conditions aimed to tackle the misery and squalor caused by overcrowding and the unanticipated use of shelters as overnight accommodation. A green light was given to local authorities to incur expenditure to install lighting, seating and bunks in street shelters. For the larger public shelters – those holding over 500 people – they were additionally encouraged to appoint a full-time paid warden, to introduce a ticket system for places, and to install first aid equipment, toilets, heating and catering facilities. Provision was to be made for both street shelters and public shelters to be regularly cleaned and inspected. This was quite an ambitious programme involving large inputs of labour and materials – resources on which there were many other calls at this time. The Government hit on an ingenious way of maximizing the deployment of these limited resources: it divided the entire country into areas, according to the urgency of local shelter needs. Top priority was given to areas that had experienced heavy and repeated bombing and to areas of similar national importance that had so far escaped; a rather lower priority was accorded to large industrial areas of dense population, together with some areas in the south east, the south and the south west of the country, which were considered especially likely to be attacked; and a lower priority still was given to the rest of the country. In this way the people who were actually experiencing raids were the first to see the improvements.

Nights spent in communal or public shelters became less of an ordeal. Squalor was greatly reduced, if not entirely banished – most
did not get running water and WCs – and in many cases the shelter
came to have an agreeable social atmosphere, with organized entertainments, discussions and even educational courses taking place.
An observer approaching one of the improved large public shelters
in the capital at night would typically hear the sound of music,
laughter, applause and the rattling of teacups, and at the door his
nostrils were likely to be assaulted less by the stench of sweat, urine
and excrement, than the homely smells of soup or cocoa.

But important though such improvements were to people's sense
of well-being, still more important was the extent of shelter provision and the effectiveness of the shelters against bombs. The Blitz
showed that locally what had seemed a sufficiency sometimes turned
out to be a shortfall, since many of the surface street shelters were
failing to withstand bomb blast, let alone direct hits, and were consequently being under-used by shelterers. This simple fact had the
effect of falsifying the calculations of the authorities as to the pre-
paredness of their districts for air attack, and instead presented them
with the problem of large numbers of people seeking unplanned
places of cover like the Underground railway, railway arches and
the cellars and basements of any large buildings. Since it was evident that many people seemed to feel safer in these self-chosen
'people's shelters', especially the Underground, it made sense to recognize the value of this to general morale and to endorse it. One of
the first things the authorities did, therefore, was to regularize their
use, establishing in them the same standard of conditions that was
being created in the official shelters – toilets, bunks, first aid posts,
and the like.

An urgent need was to put right the structural defects of the
street shelters. It emerged that one of the reasons why some had
collapsed merely from the impact of bomb blast was that they had
been built with mortar 'stretched' with lime, and in some cases
with sand and lime only. This was a consequence partly of cost-
saving by firms contracted to build the shelters, and partly of misleading Ministry of Home Security instructions to local authorities
in April 1940, which led some borough engineers to believe that
cement-less mortar had official approval. Another defect that had
come alarmingly to light was that when a bomb caused the ground

under or near a shelter to move, the concrete roofslab lifted from the walls and then crashed down on them. People who had survived such an experience from the inside were naturally unwilling to trust a street shelter in future. The Government's solutions were threefold: to close (and ultimately demolish) those shelters that could not be made safe; to strengthen those that had proved reasonably safe; to build more shelters of improved design.

As this programme moved ahead, other measures were taken to reinforce and extend shelter provision. Trench shelters were strengthened with precast concrete linings and basement shelters with extra strutting. Experience had shown that large, steel-framed buildings were very resistant to the effects of bombing and that shelters in their basements were very safe, provided measures were taken to protect them from blast. Although to do so did not really conform with the dispersal policy, since every basement shelter in a large building would bring hundreds of people together in one place, the Government gave the go-ahead to local councils to require the owners of industrial and commercial buildings to make their basements available as public shelters outside business hours. In London, by the middle of October 1940, 340 extra basement shelters sufficient for 65,000 people had been acquired.[1]

A yet more radical departure from the dispersal policy came with the Government's decision to look again at the issue of deep shelters. By October the public agitation for deep, bombproof shelters was getting support from many quarters, including the more moderate sections of the press. The controversy was itself becoming a potential threat to morale. Against this background the Cabinet quickly reached a decision: authorization was given for the boring of a new system of tunnels linked to the London Underground and for tunnel boring to be carried out in locations in the regions where features like caves and quarries permitted it to be done without enormous cost. The London scheme alone created 64,000 extra bombproof places for shelterers and tunnelling schemes went rapidly ahead elsewhere: in Nottingham some of the many caves in the city were improved and strengthened; in the chalk of the North Downs in Surrey the county council bored five tunnels; in Birkenhead a shelter tunnel was made at the old Tranmere Quarry; in Portsmouth an old tunnel at Egg Buckland was converted and a new tunnel was made in Portsdown Hill.

This did not amount to an abandonment of the dispersal policy, for there was no decision to build deep shelters everywhere, but it was, like the earlier decision to give way on the use of Underground stations as shelters, clear evidence of a government anxious to do whatever seemed best for the preservation of civilian morale. It was a decision, moreover, that was virtually dictated by the politics of the moment: nothing less than the public's confidence in the Government seemed to be at stake. When the first surveys of public opinion – as distinct from the views of those claiming to represent it – were made in late November 1940, confirmation came of the wisdom of the concessions made towards deep shelter provision. In a nationwide survey, Mass-Observation asked: 'Do you think the Government has been wise or unwise in favouring the building of surface shelters rather than underground shelters?' While 14 per cent said they were wise, 71 percent said unwise. This confirmed a Gallup poll in London and the South East, in which 74 per cent said 'unwise'. When Mass-Observation asked about surface shelters, 67 per cent gave unfavourable answers and only 19 per cent gave favourable answers.[2] Public distrust of surface street shelters persisted even after the official attempts to rehabilitate them by reinforcement and design changes. Mass-Observation found, in a survey of August 1941, that for every one person in favour of them three were still critical.[3] In other words, rehabilitation alone would not have been enough to allay public fear of under-protection.

Once it had defused the deep shelter issue, the Government was able to consolidate an aspect of its policy that was quintessentially dispersive – the production and distribution of more domestic shelters. In the five months to the end of March 1941 another 184,000 Anderson shelters were made, giving home protection to about 1,100,000 people; and in the year to December 1941, 1,080,000 of the newly designed indoor domestic shelter, the 'Morrison', were manufactured, giving protection to a further 4,320,000 people. Cramped though it undoubtedly was if used by more than two people at once, the great virtue of the 'Morrison' was that it enabled users to bed down for the night within the relative comfort of their own home.

While it is true that the greater part of this ambitious programme of protection was yet to be realized by the time the Big Blitz ended in May 1941, there is no doubt that as a potential source of low morale, the problem of inadequate protection from bombing was solved. If anything, the country came to seem overprovided, for the bombing was never again as bad as it had been in the nine months from September 1940. In another sense, too, there was over-provision. A survey conducted during the Blitz in early November 1940 revealed that only 40 per cent of the capital's population actually used shelters during air raids.[4] Although more probably did so in September and October, when the bombing was worse, these figures are very revealing. Put another way, 60 per cent of people were so unalarmed that they chose to keep to their beds, at most moving those beds to the ground floor. The gap that campaigners pointed to between the number of shelter places and the population of the city was a purely paper affair: in reality, there was, and – with some few local exceptions, like West Ham – had been from the start, enough shelter for those who wanted and would actually use it.[5] While bombs were falling, shelters might be half-empty. It was a paradox, but for morale's sake it had to be. The true value of the enhanced physical protection was measured not so much by how much it was actually used but by the feeling of security that its presence imparted.

In the matter of shelters the Government continued to have 'Be Prepared' as its motto. Intelligence about Germany's V-weapon programme led to a decision to manufacture another 100,000 Morrison shelters and to move the national reserves of this type of shelter near to London, the presumed target. There were, as it happened, sufficient of these for distribution to meet demand when the conventional bombing campaign known as the Little Blitz unexpectedly erupted onto the capital early in January 1944 and carried on for three months. The stocks of Morrisons held in London Region during these raids never fell below 27,000. When the V-weapon raids finally came in June 1944, people did start sleeping again in the Underground and in the public shelters, but the demand was not sufficient to cause the Government to open up the new Underground deep shelters, which it had by this time designated as a reserve for operational purposes.[6]

In retrospect, the start of the bombing was a difficult time for the Government in maintaining public confidence in its policy of protection. But on the matter of shelters it recovered the position well. By a judicious mixture of concession and spending it was able to satisfy the popular demand for subterranean shelter without completely abandoning the policy of dispersal, which it continued to believe better for morale. In consequence there was never again the morale-threatening clamour that had momentarily unnerved officials at the start of the Blitz. People felt as safe as it was possible to be in the circumstances of modern war and came to take for granted the protection that the authorities had provided.

The other main way of providing protection – evacuation – was tried, as we have seen, with equivocal results at the start of the war. Evacuation seemed to many people not such a bad idea, after all, once they had experienced the realities of bombing. The Government exploited this sentiment by renewing its propaganda campaign to get people in the *bouches inutiles* category to leave the danger zones and by improving the financial incentives for them to do so. In fact, the prototype of this initiative was already in operation as part of the scheme to reduce the civilian population in the vulnerable coastal areas of the east and south – vulnerable, that is, not so much to bombing but to invasion. After the fall of France, the Government announced the 'Assisted Private Evacuation Scheme'. This offered free travel vouchers for mothers with children under five who had made their own arrangements for a billet in a safe area, and extended billeting allowances to the householders who received them, even where they were relatives or friends. While this scheme originated in the army's wish to rid the security zone of as many civilians as possible, its appeal for the Government lay partly in giving it a practical way of responding to popular fear of invasion, which was potentially damaging for morale. Under the scheme, 56,000 accompanied children and 49,000 unaccompanied children left the coastal belt and were billeted in reception areas.[7] When bombing of the capital began in earnest in early September the Government's initial response was to use the successful assisted evacuation arrangement. There was one small departure from this policy, which came as a result of a near panic demand by councillors and officials in West Ham for the wholesale evacuation of the borough, or at the very least, the worst-hit district of Silvertown. The Minister of Health, Malcolm Macdonald, visited the area on 11 September and took what Titmuss described as 'a brave and imaginative decision': transport would be provided the next day to evacuate anyone who wanted to leave Silvertown for billets in safer parts of London.[8] On the following day about 2,900 people, a small fraction of the population, presented themselves for removal. The Government's willingness to move with the tide of feeling was not only brave and imaginative; it was also shrewd, politically, and because it quickly told them that morale was better than the alarmists were saying. Panic and hysteria could be discounted; most people, even in this terrible cauldron of dockland, wanted to stand their ground and fight.

But as the murderous weeks passed the cry for evacuation again went up and the Government knew it had to do more. On 22 September, therefore, it offered an organized evacuation for homeless mothers and their children, limiting the scheme to the worst-hit boroughs of east London. After the Silvertown experience, it was not surprised that the take-up was small – only about 2,600 in the last week of the month. It seemed that there was no danger of the scheme cutting across the coastal evacuation process by using up all the available billeting places, so the Government extended it to all mothers and children in the London boroughs and even to several areas that were technically outside the county of London. This produced a sizeable, although manageable, evacuation of about 89,000 in October, followed by 11,200 in November and just 1,300 in December.[9] Once again, as with the question of shelters, there was a gap between the noise that the media and other groups were making and what the people actually wanted. When it came to it, the desire to stay close to home was for most people stronger than the wish to escape the horrors of daily life on the front line. While it probably helped to have the lifeline there to be grasped, it seemed that morale was less fragile than it had at first appeared to be. Titmuss has argued that the morale of people who chose to risk the bombs in order to keep the family together may well have been better than those who opted for a safe but separated existence, and that this was particularly the case among the poorer sections of the population, 'for among those with little property and social esteem, family members and family relationships are extremely important. With his own family the individual is, and what is more feels like, "somebody".'[10]

For those who stayed, the Government – or rather the army and the RAF – found an easy, though expensive, way of keeping up spirits: hitting back at the enemy. We have already noted how the raids on Germany were given maximum publicity to this end, but this was something rather remote from people's own lives and in any case had to be taken on trust. For the beleaguered people of the capital during the sustained bombing of 1940–41 there was the much more tangible – or rather, audible – evidence of strikes at the enemy's bombers, using anti-aircraft guns and nightfighter planes. There was naturally nothing the authorities could do about the noise of bombs; but the colossal racket created by the anti-aircraft barrage was a conscious choice. The effectiveness of the guns in actually bringing down enemy planes was slight but it was judged worth doing because the noise countered the impression fearful civilians might otherwise have that nothing was being done to parry the attack. The Ministry of Home Security had in fact noticed and recorded that the people's morale during an attack was 'noticeably improved by the effectiveness and ... the visibility and the audibility of both the active and the passive defences'.[11] In the first few days (7–10 September) London's AA batteries were little used because of the risk of shooting down the RAF's nightfighters. Since the latters' operations were not very obvious to the public, the decision was made to withdraw them for a while to enable the AA batteries to treat *all* planes as targets. On 11 September the head of Anti-Aircraft Command, General Sir Frederick Pile, had positioned 199 AA guns in London. That night (and throughout the Blitz) they set up a huge barrage that forced the raiders to fly higher and to avoid the inner artillery zone. Few actual 'hits' were made and the enemy was clearly not being prevented from continuing to drop many bombs. But this was not really the point of the exercise: in strictly military terms the advantage, at least at this stage in the development of interception methods, lay with the attacker. The real value – and purpose – of the AA barrage was its psychological effect on the civilian population. 'It is difficult to express how enchanting the roar of these big guns is to the dwellers of London', recorded the US military attaché, General Lee, when some large naval guns were added to the barrage.[12] The noise of this barrage made sleep difficult for millions, of course, thereby adding to the problem of fatigue, and anyone outside ran the risk of being hit by falling shell fragments. But the compensation was that people got relief from the yet worse problem of feeling helpless, of being sitting targets without the means to hit back. The Ministry of

Information's Home Intelligence Division reported that the night of 11 September was a great stimulus to civilian morale.[13] Mass-Observation recorded some reactions a week after the new barrage started, confirming the Government's judgement that the barrage, if militarily ineffectual, was worth its weight in gold as a booster of morale: 'I love the sound of the guns!'; 'I must say that though the noise was awful last night, we were all relieved to hear it. The louder it was, the greater confidence we had'; 'You can't sleep with the guns, but it's a good sound.'[14] The effect was purely local, of course, and could not be repeated on anything like the same scale in every place where there was serial bombing. But this was, after all, the time when London was 'taking it' and the morale of the capital's large population was a matter of some importance.

The use of nightfighters did not stop entirely. In time, it was possible, through phasing and zoning, to have the AA barrage and nightfighters operating more or less simultaneously. Methods of interception were developed and radar was introduced for the AA guns and by March both planes and guns were getting more 'hits'. This expertise, coming towards the end of the Big Blitz, was not wasted. When the V-weapons began, the combined AA barrage and nightfighter operation was reactivated, AA units being brought in from all over the country; for by this time, the Government was worried that after five years of war the civilian population was more vulnerable to the strain of living with bombing than in 1940–41.[15] Once more, then, visible and audible retaliation was called in for what was believed, by then, to be its proved value for morale.

Whether the desired effect of all this effort was achieved is difficult to say. The best indication that the upgrading of ARP helped civilian morale is that the bitter accusations of official negligence that were heard in London in the first weeks of the Big Blitz and elsewhere as the bombing campaign widened to the provinces, were never repeated in the remaining four years of the war; people seemed satisfied that what could be done was done and they felt better for it.

Food

Only a small minority of the population was actually bombed; and of these a smaller number still was rendered homeless by bombing. Food, however, involved everybody. Here, the spectre of 1914–18

was never far from the minds of ministers. It was held to be impera-
tive for the morale of the nation that its will to work for victory
was not undermined by having too little to eat, whether through
shortage of food supplies or their high cost. Feeding the nation – a
nation mobilized for total war – was deemed as important as supplying the armed forces with the weapons of war. At the most basic
level, then, the problem was to ensure that there was enough food
available at affordable prices for the normal calorific needs of the
average person to be maintained. Maintaining the supply was to be
achieved by rationalizing total imports, increasing home food production and controlling food distribution.[16]

Getting right the arithmetic of total food available divided by
the number of mouths to be fed was just the start of the task, however. Just as important was to make sure that, when margins were
tight, some did not – through wealth or influence – get more than
they needed. For if normal market forces were allowed to operate,
this was inevitably what would happen. Attached though they mostly
were to the virtues of the free market, ministers and officials understood that the exigencies of total war would require compromises.
From this basic assumption the scheme for food rationing and the
control of food prices was devised. There would be enough of most
sorts of food, but not enough for everyone to have as much as they
might like of any one sort.[17] The scheme would be calculated ex-
pressly to prevent anyone from feeling that others were getting more
because they were richer and could simply pay for it. In short, the
scheme's watchword was fairness, or 'fair shares for all', as the
official slogan had it.

Chapter 2 demonstrated how the Government was reluctant to
depart from 'natural' economic laws even though the inflationary
and inequitable consequences of clinging to them soon became apparent, and how this, by November 1939, had been needlessly allowed to become a source of public discontent. But once the
principles of food control, food rationing and food subsidy had
been conceded, there was no going back. Government management
of the nation's food became a significant way of exerting influence
on the public state of mind, and the man at the heart of food policy,
the Minister of Food, Lord Woolton, became a key figure in maintaining the people's morale. It should be stressed that, sympathetic
and well-liked though he was, Woolton, like most of his colleagues,

did not act from considerations of social justice when he promoted the idea of 'fair shares for all'. His own philosophy tended more towards the virtues of self-help and the nightwatchman state. But his political instinct told him that in total war these principles would spell disaster for the government that insisted on them. The simple facts were that in working-class families about three-fifths of income was spent on food and that rapid, uncontrolled increases in food prices would give rise to distress, quickly followed by political trouble in the form of demonstrations, strikes, and trade union demands for wage increases to match the price rises. A spiral of inflation would be created that could derail the entire war economy. Food, in short, was political dynamite; Woolton's task was to so manage the consumption of food that its explosive potential was never released.[18]

An early indication of official recognition of the political importance of food was discernible even before Woolton's arrival at the Ministry after Chamberlain's reshuffle of early April 1940. The Ministry could not control world prices, of course, and food items in the Ministry of Labour cost-of-living index had risen by sixteen points in the two months to the end of October 1939. This was alarming enough in its political implications; but the rise would have been bigger still had not the Ministry of Food absorbed heavy losses on its trading account – running at the rate of £1m a week by mid-December.[19] Without this hidden subsidy the retail price of a standard loaf of bread, for example, would have risen another 12 per cent. For want of a better alternative, the Government allowed the Ministry to continue to absorb the inflation in the prices of imported foods. By January 1940, it had decided to carry on fixing food prices and was coming round to the view that the practice should be extended to all imported commodities included in the index. Its rationale was that it was in the long term cheaper to subsidize staple items of consumption than to allow price rises that would stimulate demands from organized labour for wage increases and which, moreover, would produce an atmosphere of conflict that was damaging to the war effort in general.

The case of milk, however, showed that there were some voices within government that did not share this purely instrumental attitude to food policy. When in December 1939 it looked as though the Ministry of Food was about to announce a flat increase in the price of milk, officials in the Ministry of Health lobbied for special measures to be taken to ensure that the beneficiaries of the pre-war cheap milk schemes, especially mothers, and children under five, should not suffer as a result. Their worry was that the price would be a deterrent and that consumption would fall, with consequent loss of benefit to the health of the poor. They argued for a national scheme that would provide milk at twopence a pint to all 'priority classes', without a means test. This was opposed by the Treasury, but the matter was still unresolved by the time the coalition government was formed. Woolton, the new Minister of Food, was persuaded that some sort of national scheme was necessary to offset the imminent price rises. In the meantime he obtained a temporary continuation of the subsidy on all milk prices until July. The next step was a momentous one: Woolton got the Food Policy Committee to approve the inclusion in the scheme of the right to free milk for very poor mothers and children. This was more than a mere food regulation; whatever its intention, in effect it was a piece of social reform, one that became a precedent for the Welfare Foods Scheme (which began in December 1941) whereby free or cheap cod liver oil, orange juice and National Milk-Cocoa were made available to vulnerable groups such as expectant and nursing mothers, children, adolescents and invalids.

But on the general question of food subsidies, the Government was still strictly instrumental in its attitude. The Cabinet resolution of August 1940 set out the basis for the policy that was to be adhered to, with little adjustment, for the remainder of the war: 'the prices of essential foods should be kept down by subsidy in order to secure cheap food, to restrain a rise in the cost-of-living index figure, and to prevent wages rising ... luxury foods shall be allowed to find their own price level'.[20] This did not mean no price rises at all – the cost-of-living increased about 30 per cent during the war – but most of the rise occurred in the first two years, prices remaining stable thereafter. Subsidies on food prevented the retail price of basic foods from rising further. Without the subsidy, bread would have cost 45 per cent more, meat 33 per cent more, milk 11 per cent more.[21]

The adjustments that were made to the food rationing scheme after its introduction on 8 January 1940 reflected the basic thinking that underlay it from the start. Items of basic foods were added to the list only when the supply situation worsened to the point where an unacceptably large increase in price threatened. Thus meat was rationed from 11 March 1940 and tea from 9 July. Some adjustments looked like concessions to humanity – the extra cheese ration allowed to certain manual workers, like miners and farm labourers, who had no access to canteens, for instance – but in reality, behind every such adjustment was the principle that where neglect of grievance could lower morale in key sectors of the war economy, then the prudential course was to remedy the grievance.

Two adjustments, however, responded to grievances that were more generally felt: those relating to unrationed foods and to restaurant meals. Until November 1941, a wide range of food – mostly tinned or dried – was unrationed. In theory, when prices were subject to controls, everyone had an equal chance, subject to availability, of obtaining these items. In practice, the better-off had an advantage because they could use their greater disposable income to stock up on these storable foods whenever they appeared in the shops, if necessary going from shop to shop to do so. Some shopkeepers limited the amounts each customer might buy at once but others were willing to sell in bulk, or even to put the sought-for items 'under the counter', for sale at inflated prices. Naturally, in this situation there was much potential for social discord. To prevent this, a points rationing system was devised which gave unrationed foods a points rating and allowed every person sixteen non-specific points every four weeks, to be used only for these items, according to preference. An attraction of the system for the Government was that it was flexible: the points rating of items could be increased or reduced according to their fluctuating availability. The system was introduced piecemeal, beginning with certain tinned foods – meat, fish and vegetables in November and then by stages over the year to December 1942, to rice, sago, tapioca; dried pulses and fruit; tinned tomatoes, peas and fruit; cereals, condensed milk, treacle, syrup, biscuits, and oats. Since the sixteen points were valid for four weeks only, there could be no question of accumulation. This went a long way towards solving the problem of the customer with the bottomless purse hogging the supplies of tinned pilchards, or whatever unrationed item happened to become available. It also gave people some choice – to indulge in a 'luxury' or get more of an item whose supply fluctuated.

The rich could continue to eat well, however, by taking coupon-free meals in restaurants. Although the scale of this scarcely mattered in terms of the national food strategy, luxury feeding at a time of general austerity was difficult to defend and it was certainly disproportionately damaging to the idea of equal shares and everyone pulling together. Home Intelligence reported in March 1942 that there was growing evidence of a perception among certain sections of the public of 'inequality of sacrifice', a perception created in the first instance by the resort of the rich to expensive restaurants.[22]

After considering and rejecting as administratively too complex or expensive various ideas for bringing restaurant meals within the framework of rationing, the Government settled for the simple, if flawed, device of a maximum charge. From mid–1942 a restaurant meal might cost no more than five shillings (the equivalent of 25p).[23] In theory this made it unprofitable for restaurateurs to buy on the black market knowing they could recoup their costs in the cover price. However, while most probably accepted the new regime, some luxury establishments were able to get round the intention of the regulation by adding to the five shillings an artificially high charge for the 'extras' – the orchestra, the dancing, the cabaret, and the like. The Government had done its best in what was admittedly an administratively difficult matter. Complaints about people eating out to dodge rationing did disappear from the soundings of opinion, at least, so it might reasonably be inferred that the matter's morale-eroding potential was checked.

A contributory factor in this was undoubtedly the appearance of one of Woolton's most inspired innovations: British Restaurants. Canteen-like food in canteen-like conditions at canteen-like prices was what these establishments offered. This was off-ration eating out, too, but at a price ordinary people could afford. They were an immense success, catering to capacity wherever they opened. It would certainly have been an unpopular move to include *these* meals in some sort of points or tokens scheme, which in fairness they would have to have been were this imposed on restaurants catering to the well-off.[24] As it was, British Restaurants, by giving some relief from the constraints imposed by the basic rations, were a powerful force for public contentment.

Other initiatives by Woolton showed an equally sure touch in winning popular confidence and approval: the setting up of the

Queen's Messengers – volunteers using 144 vehicles to take in food relief after air raids; the 'Food Trains', which ran in the Underground from 7.00–9.00 a.m. and 5.00–7.00 p.m. to feed shelterers; the 'Pies Scheme', whereby WVS teams took pies out to farm workers on certain days of the week; the extra cheese ration for agricultural workers; the creation of local Food Officers in every village, with stocks to supply local people in the event of a serious interruption of supply; the placing of soldiers on administrative duties in Britain onto the same rations as civilians; the programme of vitamins and extra foods for babies, children and pregnant women. Even the US Army was persuaded to cooperate. The relatively higher standard of food American servicemen enjoyed on their bases was naturally a cause of some envy among native inhabitants when the – often exaggerated – details got out. It was therefore a shrewd move to get the European Theater of Operations, US Army to agree that the troops' bread would be made not with specially imported North American wheat but with the basic ingredient of the unloved British National Loaf – National Wheatmeal Flour.[25] All even, then – at least as far as the staff of life was concerned.

When Mass-Observation reported on 'Food Tensions' in March 1942, it concluded that the Government's food policy was working. Among women questioned, there was less tension than there had been over the inconveniences and restriction of choice. A figure of 77 per cent felt the situation was better than they had expected and felt they were managing well in the circumstances.[26] In his analysis of the food situation a month later, Tom Harrisson thought people were more satisfied because they were more convinced that food was being fairly distributed; the system of points rationing seemed fair; many of the causes of friction, such as queuing, had been removed or eased; and Woolton was thought to be sympathetic and doing a good job – a verdict confirmed in a Gallup poll in May, in which 79 per cent thought he was doing a good job as opposed to only 12 per cent who thought not.[27]

They were not alone in thinking well of Woolton. When the extra foods and vitamins scheme was established, the Ministry of Food received many grateful letters from recipients and from serving soldiers, thanking the Ministry for taking care of their dependants.[28] On the occasion of his appointment in November 1943 to the new post of Minister of Reconstruction, the *Montreal Gazette* wrote:

'the famous British morale can be credited as much to Lord Woolton as to any individual'.[29] For the Government, the Food brief was crucial in the maintenance of civilian morale and Woolton more than fulfilled his mission. It has to be admitted that he was also a skilful self-publicist; but it was all for the cause and no one disputes that his reputation was deserved. His 'Fair Shares for All' slogan had just the right populist appeal in a 'people's war'. It was never literally achieved, but then, no one realistically imagined that it could be. The grosser disparities were removed and for most people this was enough. A significant minority of the population actually fed better – in terms of both quantity and variety – than before the war. Full employment and increased average real income were the real basis for this, but Woolton's wartime food regime was also seen as part of it. Above all, like the good businessman he was, Woolton turned a situation of deficit into one of healthy profit: instead of being a threat to morale, the food issue became – for a sizeable proportion of the nation, at least – a significant factor of good morale.

The cost of living

Food policy was part of a wider policy to hold down inflation. Inflation was recognized as an inevitable concomitant of war, but the Government took the view that a determined and imaginative policy could prevent it from getting out of control. Rampant inflation would have spelt economic trouble for an economy that was in any case having to adjust to extraordinary circumstances, and it was also guaranteed to stimulate social, and possibly political, unrest. Rejecting a policy of wage controls as likely to create conflict between it and the workers, the Government instead adopted measures designed to control the cost of living and thereby to check the demand for inflationary wage increases.[30]

One of the biggest problems was unfortunately one that the Government was powerless to resolve: the price of imported goods. These increased sharply – those, at least, from sources other than the Dominions. The Government gave subsidies to shipping and transport and it rationalized imports to eliminate inessential items; this helped to limit the inflationary effect of the increasing cost of imports, but it nonetheless remained something that simply had to be lived with.

The demand side of inflation could be tackled more easily. The inflationary gap between supply and demand that opened up as war production expanded and consumer goods production fell was addressed by fiscal measures: income tax went up from 9 to 50 per cent, personal allowances were reduced, and purchase tax was increased from 60 to 100 per cent. Any remaining excess demand was absorbed by forced savings, war bonds at attractive rates and control of bank lending.[31] Rationing, too, by controlling demand, played its part in the war against inflation. Finally, prices were held down by subsidies on key items in the cost-of-living index and by the imposition of price controls.

Through this battery of interventions the cost of living was stabilized. Although retail prices generally continued to rise – by 42 per cent from the start of the war to the end of 1943, according to one estimate – the cost-of-living index scarcely fluctuated at all after April 1941 and the overall increase at the war's end, largely the result of the inflation of 1939–41, was about 30 per cent.[32] At that point about 95 per cent of all household expenditure was on price-controlled goods.

Since average wage rates rose 30 per cent by 1942 and 50 per cent by 1945, the real income of the average family was actually higher during most of the war than before it.[33] If average earnings rather than average wages are considered, the improvement was greater still: the average weekly male earnings in industry (the best case) increased by 76 per cent, giving a rise in real income of 46 per cent.[34] Average figures, of course, conceal individual situations. But the Government was ready to respond to these when unacceptable inequality was demonstrated, as in the 1940 Old Age and Widows' Pension Act, which greatly increased the value of pensions and empowered the Assistance Board to pay supplementary pensions when need was shown (this immediately tripled the number of pensioners receiving supplementary allowances, bringing the total to over one million); or when in 1942 and again in 1944 the allowances for private soldiers' wives were increased.[35] Accepting that there were individual cases of hardship, the effect of the changes in prices and wages during the war was not damaging to the living standards of the average family. There were naturally certain frustrations built into a situation in which enhanced purchasing power coincided with reduced choice of things to be purchased, but this was for many families more than compensated by the possession of a margin of financial manoeuvre. The disappearance of the hidden undernourishment of the 1930s was just one manifestation of this. Insofar as discontent fuelled by perceptions of falling living standards was potentially a threat to civilian morale, Government action achieved its purpose. The soundings of public opinion do show continuing grumbles about consumption-related matters, such as shortages and queuing, but the real complaints about prices and the difficulty of making ends meet that marked such surveys in the first eighteen months of the war, fall out of the picture thereafter. All rationing – of food, clothes and fuel – restricted choice; but when asked, the majority approved because in a free-for-all, only the rich could do well, at the expense of others. Most of the informal record of the war years – letters, diaries, memoirs – was made by people who belonged to the middle classes, people, that is, whose lifestyle was usually adversely affected by the rather basic consumption standards the war imposed. But for the majority, these standards did not constitute a worsening, and for a significant section among that majority, they were actually an improvement on what they were accustomed to before the war. In the battle for civilian morale, the Government knew it was the majority that mattered. If the better-off felt the pinch more, this was judged a small and acceptable price to pay to win the battle.[36] One member of the middle classes, the journalist J. L. Hodson, recorded with approval the remarks of 'a young Radical friend' on the spin-off benefits of the war:

> We've given coalminers a minimum of five pounds a week; we've opened up shipyards that had been derelict; we've made wastelands fruitful, and cultivated millions of acres that lay idle ... Our heavy taxation and our rationing of foods has, willy-nilly, achieved some levelling up of the nation; fewer folk have gone hungry and fewer have gorged themselves; the poor have been a trifle better off and the rich a little less rich.[37]

Allusion has already been made to the role of wages in the state of civilian morale. The fact that wages kept ahead of prices was not entirely the product of the increase of the demand for labour over the supply; it was also a result of a deliberate policy by the Ministry of Labour and National Service. When Ernest Bevin accepted the post of Minister in Churchill's coalition government, he did so on condition that he be allowed to take measures to improve the wages and conditions of the workers from whom he was going to demand extraordinary productive effort. A rise in the working-class standard of living seemed to him both morally justified and a practical proposition, even in the midst of a war for survival. The practical side of the argument won the day, for who could doubt the logic of the productive payoff of a well-motivated workforce? Bevin was therefore permitted to ride the unsaddled horse of wage inflation, which he proceeded to do with great skill, allowing wages to catch up and overtake the price rises he inherited and then, by carrot and stick, holding them at a level that did not damage the overall financial strategy. In return for controls over prices and profits, and comprehensive regulations for industry as a whole, Bevin was able to get the trade unions to accept a policy that gave higher rewards for workers but within a framework of wage restraint. His special skill lay in getting employers to support this, too.[38] All the troubles of wartime labour pale into insignificance besides this achievement. Like Woolton, by his actions rather than his words, Bevin had far more friends than enemies among the mass of the people; and like Woolton, he succeeded in winning their cooperation.

Working conditions

Bevin was the prime mover in another area of government action that had morale implications: industrial welfare. This was a neglected aspect of the industrial scene; in fact after the start of the war, because of problems like transport, lodging and feeding, the welfare of workers was deteriorating. The arrival of Bevin at the Ministry of Labour turned the tide. He raised the profile of welfare as soon as he was in post, insisting first that the Factory Inspectorate be detached from the Home Office and incorporated into the Ministry of Labour; and then in July 1940 issuing an order that empowered factory inspectors to compel businesses employing more than 250 people to appoint welfare officers, backing this up with subsidized training courses for welfare officers. In 1941 the Ministry guided employers to match the increase in the proportion of women workers by appointing more women welfare and personnel officers.

Under Bevin's proactive policies the working environment of factories was improved in all sorts of practical ways. Factory medical services, which varied greatly between firms, were generally improved by Ministry persuasion, but it was made clear to employers that the inspectors had power to direct them to appoint such a number of full- or part-time doctors as seemed needed, given the number of employees. Factory doctors were given the role of consultants and examiners on the matter of an individual's fitness to carry out a specific job. At the time of the order, July 1940, there were only thirty full-time factory doctors in the country; by 1944 there had been a six-fold increase, with the number of part-time doctors going up from 50 to 890. Factory nurses, meanwhile, increased from 1,500 in 1939 to 4,000 by 1942, and to 8,000 by 1943.[39] Bevin made it clear that these changes were more than a wartime expedient: he intended them to become permanent. In November 1940 the Factories (Canteens) Order was made, under which factory inspectors could direct employers on munitions or other government contracts, who employed more than 250 workers, to provide canteens for them. The pill was sweetened by an accompanying provision for up to 60 per cent of the cost to be met by the Government. At the end of 1941 the same help was offered to smaller enterprises outside the scope of the Order. By 1944 there were 5,000 canteens operating in the larger firms – an increase of 300 per cent. Canteens in smaller enterprises increased from 1,400 in 1941 to 6,800 in 1945. Quality trailed behind quantity for a while; then, after complaints about poor canteen food, an Order of October 1943 imposed tighter control of catering licences and gave factory inspectors the power to force employers to remedy any defects revealed by inspections.[40] The problems of long, crowded and expensive journeys to work were tackled in various ways. A massive hostel-building programme was undertaken – enough for 65,000 workers – but they were never as attractive as living at home, despite the journey problems. So the Government worked with the grain of popular preference and produced the Assisted Travel Scheme, which subsidized travel costs of over three shillings (15p) a week and modified the detailed working of transport systems to reduce the frustrations of travelling for workers.[41] Meanwhile, in the special conditions of the Royal Ordnance Factories, the Government set an example by putting its own house, as it were, in order. Reports by the Welfare Advisory Panel highlighted persistent problems to be remedied: bad ventilation and lighting; inadequate facilities for drying clothes in wet weather; unsupervised restrooms; a shortage of seats for women workers; dirty and slippery shopfloors; unhygienic canteens; fumes from explosives. Within a year, all ROFs had shown improvement in these areas, including effective measures to reduce the incidence of dermatitis and toxic jaundice.[42]

By the end of the war, the welfare of workers had taken a sizeable leap forward. In other ways, wartime work remained a stressful affair; but the long hours, the shiftwork and the difficult journeys to and from work were to some degree compensated by the tangible effects of the new resources that were introduced and of the official pressure on employers to look after their workers better.

Health

It has often been remarked that the health of the nation was in general better in the war years than it had ever been – a paradox, given the facts of bombing, shortages, rationing and mental and physical strain. While to some degree this was an unanticipated development, there is no doubt that it was also the product of measures calculated to achieve this outcome. More accurately, the measures were designed to prevent anticipated *deterioration* of health; the fact that – from 1942, at least – the usual indices of health showed an improvement, was a welcome bonus. Already in September 1941, Lord Woolton was triumphantly proclaiming that the nation had 'never been in better health for years'. Woolton, of course, had reason to think he himself had had a hand in this; 'it is my responsibility', he said, 'to secure that so far as food is concerned, the nation is kept fit and well'.[43] Nutrition was at the heart of his rationing system. It did not matter much that the massive campaign to persuade people to eat more healthily largely fell on deaf ears; the basic facts of rationing and food management automatically ensured this outcome. The National Wheatmeal Loaf, for instance, was nutritionally far superior to the white bread that most people ate before the war; and if people had less meat and filled up on vegetables and grain products, this incidentally gave a better nutritional balance to their diet.[44] As far as the improvements in child health are concerned, among the factors involved – though no direct cause and effect relationship can be demonstrated – few doubt that the welfare foods programme was significant. But the fact that death rates among the elderly declined in the war years reminds us that the more general improvement in health did not depend on such targeted provision. Insofar as this is explained by government interventions, the afore-mentioned policies of price control, food subsidies and 'fair shares for all' were the likely agents.

Mass-Observation tried in December 1940 to discover what the main influences were on people's state of mind, that is, what things kept up their spirits and what things depressed them. It did this by asking its national panel of voluntary observers to observe themselves, keeping a daily chart on the things that affected how they felt. The initial findings were equivocal. But when the factors were rated according to the number of references made to each without regard to its supposed effect, the resulting table put 'Health' first, well clear of 'Work', 'Weather', 'War News' and 'Friends', which followed.[45] Tom Harrisson later conceded that this was a rather rough measure.[46] But it showed that a 'non-war-related' factor was important to how people felt, even at this very bleak and dangerous time in the war. In aiming to prevent health standards from deteriorating under the impact of war, then, the Government had stumbled on what appeared, in the event, to be a significant factor in civilian morale. People may not have made any connection between their health and the policies of the Government (although the more thoughtful might well have done so); but the important thing – if the statistics mean anything – was that people must have felt their general health was at least not worsened by the war, which was undoubtedly more than they had expected. An inquiry into public attitudes to health in July and August 1942, based on a sample of 1,795 people, found that 53 per cent thought their health was the same as before the war, 10 per cent thought their health had improved, 37 per cent that it was worse or slightly worse.[47] Insofar as this was about what people felt rather than how they actually were, it was some comfort to the Government to know that despite the adverse circumstances of war most people had positive feelings about their health. And to the extent that such feelings translated into good morale, official policies were helping to produce it. The state of the nation's health, like the standard of its food, was not allowed needlessly to impair the effectiveness of the home front; it may even have been a force for improving that effectiveness.

Recreation and leisure

So far, the review of the Government's attempts to 'ease the strain' of war on the home front has concentrated on the necessities of life. While this remained the priority, it came to be accompanied, after a while, by a parallel strategy of promoting popular well-being through recreation and leisure. We have seen how in the early months of the war the official attitude was characterized by an almost puritanical attitude to such things.[48] The positive steps subsequently made to relax the restrictions on sport and entertainment and even to expand provision in certain areas, testifies to the strengthening recognition in Government circles of the therapeutic value of such activities for a hard-worked, overstrained and war-weary civilian population. Nothing is more indicative of this than the licence given to the BBC and the cinema industry to provide virtual escape routes from the war and to make the people laugh.

At the BBC the main means of fulfilling this brief was the Forces Programme, set up initially to cater for the taste of the thousands of conscripted young men in barracks and training camps across the country and overseas, but quickly becoming the whole nation's favourite listening. The FP broadcast mainly dance and popular music and variety shows, presented in a relaxed and informal manner. It ran some news, talks and discussions, but in the main it left these areas to the National Programme. The original aim of providing diversion and entertainment for the armed forces never disappeared; but as time went on the value of the service for the nation as a whole came increasingly to be appreciated in official quarters. Entertainment, while appearing merely to entertain, could actually help to make workers more efficient. This was context of the introduction of *Music While You Work* (*MWYW*) in mid-1940. Half an hour of seamless dance band music was put out on the Forces Programme three times a day – at mid-morning, mid-afternoon and 10.30 pm. Its target audience was factory workers, the theory being that the tedium of repetitive tasks on long shifts could be relieved by a background of cheerful and familiar music. Experiments in the 1930s, mostly in the USA, suggested that the technique could improve productivity, too. Background music was a long way from BBC traditions; it liked to think of all its programmes in terms of the 'attentive listener' even when, as in the case of *MWYW*, the

Variety Department was the organizer. However, if it made workers more contented and more productive, as was claimed, it was
not to be denied, especially since the BBC was at the time still anxious about its future and therefore looking for ways to please its
political masters. The experiment was hugely successful on every
count. By 1944, four and a half million workers in over 8,000 factories were hearing *MWYW*. This was spectacular enough, but the
unexpected bonus was that the broadcasts were equally popular
with listeners at home and in the Forces. While the BBC never seriously claimed that *MWYW* measurably increased factory production – after all, it went out for only ninety minutes in every
twenty-four hours – it could feel sure the programme positively
served the cause of popular morale. Workers, service personnel and
listeners at home were united, metaphorically speaking, as they tuned
in, knowing that at the same time their family members in distant
places were doing likewise. For the managers of the BBC there was
also the clear and comforting evidence that the Government was
interested and impressed.[49] Beyond the specific function of *Music
While You Work* the barriers to the idea of 'background music'
more generally were removed. The resistance to indiscriminate 'on
tap' listening that was strong in the Music Department, was in effect bypassed by the creation of the Forces Programme, whose *raison
d'être* it was to supply it. As a result, serious music did not have to
make way for the burgeoning upstart, since it was able to continue
as before on the Home Service; and the proportion of total output
devoted to dance music, which had been at 5 per cent in 1938,
increased to 10 per cent by 1942.[50]

On the variety side, the war years saw a substantial blossoming
of diversion and laughter production over the airwaves. Some managers in the BBC were in fact itching to expand this aspect of broadcasting even before the Ministry of Information's injunction to cheer
the nation up. In August 1940 the Listener Research Department
produced a policy statement based on its soundings of the audience, in which it stressed the importance for audience morale of
programmes that provided colour, stimulation and laughter. 'It is
not too much to claim', it said, 'that such programmes are a valuable part of the cement which binds the nation together as a community.'[51] This document followed a survey conducted by
Mass-Observation in May 1940, which showed that even at this

time of worrying developments in the war in France, listeners wanted lighthearted, cheerful programmes. A majority thought the BBC was 'too serious' and there was a desire, especially among respondents in social classes C and D, for a greater proportion of variety programmes in the output. Typical responses: 'Well, you don't want to be too serious in wartime', 'we want something cheerful in this crisis', ''Oh I like them [variety shows]. I think they cheer us up quite a bit .... You get so low and depressed these days and then that comes along, and we feel better afterwards, for a little while.'[52] The signs were clear: if the BBC wanted to fulfil its entertainment brief, it had to make changes. It did so by shifting somewhat from its tradition of top-down programming. The demand was met with an increase in the air time for variety programmes, mostly on the Forces Programme, making it a working principle that there should be at least one substantial variety programme every night.

The FP in effect quickly became the preferred service of 60 per cent of the listeners as a whole and no less than 90 per cent of the sixteen to twenty age group.[53] On the BBC's programmes more generally, a listener survey made in April and May 1944 revealed the popularity of its dance music and variety shows. On the FP the top ten programmes were either of dance music or comedy. Even on the Home Service, three of the top ten fell into these categories and the most popular programme of all was a comedy show, Tommy Handley's zany and irreverent *ITMA*.[54] If it did not know it already, the BBC discovered that its previous programming had not given the audience what it really wanted and that it was now more in tune with this newly-desirable idea of what a national broadcasting service ought to be offering in time of war. And the 'wireless' thereby became more truly a means of escape from the stresses of the war. The policy even had a payoff in terms of external propaganda. As recalled by a former monitor of German broadcasts, working at the listening station at Caversham, there was utter perplexity in the Axis countries about what they were hearing when they tuned in to the BBC's domestic programmes; for more often than not, what they got was the sound of upbeat dance music or, even more puzzling at a time when they presumed everyone in Britain was in a state of fright about the prospect of invasion, gales of wild audience laughter at the crazy comedy of *ITMA* or *Hi Gang!*[55] What they were in fact hearing was the sound of the BBC, working at the Government's behest, successfully doing its bit to sustain the morale of the people. As the war developed, it became increasingly clear just how important this particular means of escape was. Chapter 2 discussed how the war was a manufactory of human loneliness. For the millions of people affected, radio was simply able to ease the burden. How significant it was in this therapeutic role depended on individual circumstances. That it was helping people to laugh at their fears and difficulties seems borne out by the hilarious welcome given weekly to ITMA's Jack Train announcing himself as 'Funf, your favourite spy', (to which Tommy Handley would respond: 'It may be Funf for you, but it's not much funf for me'), and to Mona Lott's lugubriously delivered catch-phrase, 'It's being so cheerful as keeps me going'. Radio's very ubiquity, its presence – if only as mere background – to people's lives at home and at work, suggests that what it offered was needed and that in meeting the need the BBC was helping people to 'carry on'.

The cinema was, of course, no stranger to the business of providing escape routes: thrillers, costume dramas, romances and comedies were its stock in trade. While there is no evidence that the Government took an active interest in this aspect of film making, it had an interest in keeping down the huge cost of making propaganda films by allowing the commercial enterprises, whose skills they used, to remain economically viable – and for this they needed to continue making films that were 'good box office'. And the very fact that it allowed some of the scarce resources needed by film makers to be used to make such apparently frivolous products in these serious times, suggests that it knew well enough what it was doing. A delegate of the Bristol and West England branch of the Cinematograph Exhibitors' Association, H. F. Wren, a man with his ear close to the ground, wrote as early as January 1940: 'People want something that will take them out of themselves and help them overcome the depression of the blackout … They do not want heavy drama – they have all the drama they need in the news these days.'[56] Just so: common sense dictated, quite as much as objective calculation, that entertainment was good for people, good for morale. In time, the Ministry of Information followed where Mr Wren led – at least, once Brendan Bracken had become Minister – and the official climate for films of pure escapism became more helpful.

Given the green light to continue to do what they did best, producers set to make the 'dream palace' live up to its sobriquet, in the somewhat unfamiliar service of war. Alongside the films dutifully produced in fulfilment of the propaganda brief handed to them by the Ministry of Information, therefore, came a stream of pure escapism. This stream, moreover, was a golden one as far as the box office was concerned. The most popular British film of 1943 was Gainsborough Films' costume melodrama, *The Man in Grey*, and another of the genre, *The Wicked Lady* (1945), was one of the British industry's biggest box office successes in the whole of the 1940s. Meanwhile, The Crazy Gang, George Formby, Gracie Fields, Will Hay, Tommy Trinder, Frank Randle and other stars of comedy filled the cinemas with audiences only too content to forget the war for an hour or so and drink the medicine of laughter. And if proof were needed that escapist cinema was fulfilling a vital human need, the most popular of all films shown in the war (which happened to be from Hollywood) was *Gone With the Wind* – a war film of sorts, of course, but an exercise in escapism, none the less. It should be added that some films, such as Korda's *Lady Hamilton* (1940), Carol Reed's *The Young Mr Pitt* (1941), and Thorold Dickinson's *The Prime Minister* (1941), contrived both to meet the demand for escapist costume drama and at the same time drive home the message that through heroic figures like Nelson, Pitt, and Disraeli, Britain had long been the upholder of liberty and democracy against European tyrants.

The practicalities of getting to the cinema were naturally made more difficult by bombing alerts, the blackout and curtailed bus services; and the domestic circumstances that forced many people – especially service wives with young children – to settle for the radio, remained little-changed throughout the war. Despite this, the figures for cinema attendance show no decline. In the 1943 Wartime Social Survey it was revealed that 32 per cent of the population went at least once a week. The cinema industry, then, like the radio – although without radio's advantage of a half-captive audience – was succeeding in reaching a significant proportion of the people. And like the radio, it willingly shouldered a large part of the burden of entertaining the nation. Its financial reward was high, but this takes nothing away from the value this role had for the important objective of easing the strain of war.

As if putting its money where its mouth was, the Government itself went indirectly into the entertainment business. It did this by funding two organizations, the Council for the Encouragement of Music and the Arts (CEMA), and the Entertainments National Services Association (ENSA). CEMA aimed to help fill the spaces in the cultural landscape caused by the dislocation and disruption of war: the breakup of orchestras, choirs, repertory companies, and the like under the impact of evacuation, bombing and conscription. ENSA concentrated – though not exclusively – on light entertainment for service personnel and factory workers. Together these two organizations took entertainment and diversion to the people all over the country, often in their places of work or training. In 1944, its peak year, CEMA put on 6,140 recitals and concerts; and over the course of the war ENSA staged over two million concerts, more than five hundred of them full-scale symphony concerts.[57] It did not stop at concerts, however. The cultural range was in fact very wide: George Formby and Gracie Fields as well as Sadler's Wells Ballet, the London Philharmonic Orchestra, the Royal Opera, the sculpture of Henry Moore, the paintings of Graham Sutherland and John Piper, to mention only some of the better-known of the hundreds of musicians, dancers, actors, variety performers and artists whose work was sponsored by CEMA and ENSA. There were undoubtedly occasions when there was a serious mismatch between the promoters' offerings and the tastes of the half-captive audiences in canteens and hostels; and some of the variety acts, especially, compared badly with what people were used to from the cinema and radio. However, the effect, such as it is possible to gauge it, was generally positive for its intended purposes. Overall, there was an acknowledged deficit of entertainment and cultural diversion, compared with the years before the war – as for most aspects of life, this was a time of austerity. Anything, therefore, that reduced the deficit and mitigated the austerity – easing the strain – was a contribution to the wider aim of sustaining the morale of the people.

Partly in response to the Government's promptings, publicly assisted entertainment also became the concern of local authorities. The 'Holidays at Home' initiative was aimed to provide some compensation to war-weary citizens, deprived by the necessities of war of the annual battery-recharge of a stay abroad or, more typically, of a week or two at a British seaside resort – by the summer of 1940 mostly given over to barbed wire, tanktraps and pillboxes. Summer entertainments in parks were, of course, a long-established institution in most cities; what the scheme did was simply to expand and extend the idea. The London County Council, for instance, spent £25,000 on summer entertainments in 1943, twice the budget for the previous year. This funded not only the usual bandstand concerts, but in addition a circus, which moved from venue to venue during the summer, a regatta on the Thames at Hackney, numerous evening dances – a choice of thirteen every evening – and stagings of musical comedy, opera and even ballet.[58]

None of this quite made up for the change of scene and pleasures of the seaside. But since these were in effect unavailable – in their pre-war form, at least – it was a case of making the best of it. The efforts of local councils were generally well-supported by the public, so one might reasonably infer that their effect was positive, that they helped in a small way to lessen the stress and boredom of war, particularly in the summers of 1941 to 1944.

Some essential inessentials

The apparatus of controls, as has been shown, established a rather low threshold for the classification of consumer goods as 'inessential'. By any rational process, tobacco, alcohol, cosmetics and flowers would have little chance of avoiding such a classification. Yet all escaped it – and the explanation is not really so irrational, after all.

Distilling was effectively stopped, except for a small amount of whisky produced entirely for export. But beer production was allowed to continue as before – at reduced strength, to be sure – but enough to allow an increase in consumption of 25 per cent during the war. It was never rationed, moreover, except by price, for it didn't benefit from price control and was subjected to several increases in excise duty. There were occasional supply problems related to bombing and the more urgent transport needs of the military, but on whole it was everywhere freely available throughout the war. With increased consumption came a rise in drunkenness. For a government anxious to ensure the maximum efficiency of the workforce, this should have been cause for concern. But magistrates, presumably acting on their own initiative, invariably treated cases brought before them with considerable leniency, as if recognizing that in such stressful times the resort to the amnesiac properties of alcohol was perfectly understandable and scarcely to be penalized. In any case, the toleration of high levels of alcohol consumption came from the top, by example, if not by writ. Churchill himself consumed prodigious quantities of wine and spirits and was virtually a stranger to tea and coffee. 'To Mr Churchill a meal without wine is not a meal at all', his Private Secretary recalled.[59] And round the corner in Whitehall, as civil servant Robert Bruce Lockhart recorded in his diary, things were much the same: 'I am drinking far too much – like most people in Whitehall these days ... The ministers are no better; Dalton has a strong head, drinks hard and has a particular liking for brandy. Brendan [Bracken] is rarely completely sober after 11 pm, and even Eden takes a man's full share in the evening. War's effect on nerves, I suppose.'[60]

Tobacco, likewise, had the favoured treatment of never being rationed. The price rose, too, and there were interruptions to supplies – for civilians, if not for the forces. But cigarettes were generally to be had everywhere, at all times, for the Government decided that supplies should be maintained at the level of demand. And just as people drank more, they smoked more, too. Nerves again? For many people a strong cup of tea would do the trick, but for millions, smoking was what enabled them to carry on. One of the striking incidental features of photographs and documentary and newsreel films of the time is the ever-present cigarette in the hands of workers and office staff, off-duty service personnel, diplomats and politicians – male and female alike.

For both alcohol and tobacco, official indulgence of popular demand was not brought about simply by the needs of the Treasury – although the Chancellor was doubtless well-pleased with the receipts. The logic lay in the familiar connection between good cheer and good morale – something manufacturers of 'inessential' products like alcoholic drinks and cigarettes understood well and relentlessly promoted in their advertisements. If civilians were cheered by being able to drink and smoke more or less at will, they would be more efficient and committed participants on the home front. So sure was the Government of this presumption, it never seriously considered departing from it. Exactly the same psychological logic lay behind the decision to ease the application of the Limitation of Supplies Order to the music industry: a small supply of gramophone records and needles was made available to the ordinary civilian, and the mental sustenance of favourites heard at will was thereby retained.

In the case of cosmetics the arguments for keeping production going were stronger still. For not only was the appearance of wives and sweethearts judged important to the morale of their service-men partners; it was equally essential to the morale of women in their various home front roles. If servicemen coming home on leave found their loved ones' appearance as attractive as before, they would return to their own duties in good heart. If women doing their patriotic duty in, say, the inherently unfeminine world of mu-nitions could continue to be able to obtain their favourite aids to beauty, then their morale, too, would be more likely to survive the change. Since both groups were self-evidently crucial to winning the war, it was equally obvious that the small cost in the resources entailed was more than justified. Official acknowledgement of this is discernible in the special allowances of high-grade make-up given to women munitions workers from August 1942, Bevin's exemp-tion of the most highly skilled hairdressers from conscription into war work, also in 1942, and the decision late in 1943 to allow a small increase in the supply of cosmetics for sale. And so, although supplies were never enough and the range of what was available was much reduced, the 'beauty industry' kept going and its morale-boosting products had no shortage of customers. Many testified to the therapeutic effect of a hair-styling or of 'putting on a face'. Even the down to earth Nella Last cheered herself up on the day before her younger son Clifford went to join his regiment in Sep-tember 1939: 'Tonight I looked a bit washed out, so after tea I changed into my gayest frock and made up rather heavily.'[61]

In a move to save transport, the special trains that traditionally took cut flowers from the Isles of Scilly and the West Country to London, were taken off in the autumn of 1942. Desperate traders tried to get round this by using passenger trains instead. Churchill got to hear of it and immediately ordered the restoration of the flower trains.[62] Once again, an apparently indefensible indulgence; and once again, a shrewd appreciation of how small things can have large effects. The Prime Minister made sure that the weary citizens of the battered capital got their flowers; and who knows how much the true value of this outweighed the cost of letting it happen?

Notes

1 T. H. O'Brien, *Civil Defence* (HMSO, 1955), p. 526.

2 M-O, File Reports 501 (22 November 1940) and 508 (29 November 1940).

3 M-O, File Report 811, 4 August 1941.

4 O'Brien, *Civil Defence*, p. 392.

5 West Ham Council had refused to build street shelters when instructed to do so by the Government in 1937–39, insisting that since there would be no war, it was a waste of money. Pressed by the Government, it finally agreed to build the shelters but on condition that the Government pay the full cost. The matter was still unresolved when the Blitz began. See L. Mosley, *Backs to the Wall: London Under Fire 1939-45* (Weidenfeld & Nicholson, 1971), p. 128.

6 O'Brien, *Civil Defence*, p. 547.

7 R. Titmuss, *Problems of Social Policy* (HMSO, 1950), p. 245.

8 *Ibid.*, p. 259.

9 *Ibid.*, p. 286.

10 *Ibid.*, p. 348.

11 O'Brien, *Civil Defence*, p. 384.

12 J. Leutze (ed.), *The London Observer: the Journal of General Raymond E. Lee 1940–41* (Hutchinson, 1972), p. 78.

13 Home Intelligence Weekly Report, 12 September 1940, INF/292.

14 M-O, File Report 408, 'Human Adjustments to Air Raids'. The Government tackled the matter of sleep disturbance by issuing earplugs. The public response was apathetic, however. According to Tom Harrisson, 90 per cent of people wanted 'to listen to possible death'. Listening seemed to be an important part of peace of mind: 'With them things in, you'd never know if you was copping it or you wasn't.' T. Harrisson, *Living Through the Blitz* (Collins, 1976), pp. 108–9.

15 O'Brien, *Civil Defence*, pp. 654–5.

16 See W. Hancock and M. Gowing, *British War Economy* (HMSO, 1949), pp. 47–52.

17 See CAB 16/157, Sub Committee on Food Supply in Time of War, Reports, F.S. 13; Report of Sub-Committee on Rationing, 5 October 1936; MAF 72/5998 Rationing, 4 January 1937; Board of Trade, Report of the Food (Defence Plans) Department for 1937 (HMSO, 1938), pp. 10, 25–6.

18 For further discussion of food policy, see E. F. Nash, 'Wartime Control of Food and Agricultural Prices', in D. N. Chester (ed.), *Lessons of the War Economy* (Cambridge University Press, 1951).

19 R. J. Hammond, *Food, vol. 1: The Growth of Policy* (HMSO, 1951), pp. 99–100.

20 *Ibid.*, p. 104.

21 *Ibid.*, p. 400.

22 H. I. Report, 'Inequality of sacrifice', 25 March 1942, INF 1/292.

23 The average weekly earnings of men aged 21 and over in July 1942 was £5 11s, HMSO, *Facts and Figures*, p. 233.

24 When a meal-tokens scheme was shown to the Trades Union Congress Advisory Committee early in 1943, the response was uncooperative. Hammond, *Food*, vol. 1, p. 292.

25 D. Reynolds, *Rich Relations: the American Occupation of Britain, 1942–1945* (Harper Collins, 1995), p. 149.

26 M-O, File Report 1155.

27 M-O, File Report 1224; G. H. Gallup, *The Gallup International Public Opinion Polls: Great Britain, 1937–1964*, vol. 1 (Random House, 1976), p. 87.

28 Lord Woolton, *Memoirs* (Cassell, 1959), p. 263.

29 *Ibid.*, p. 228.

30 See A. Milward, *War, Economy and Society* (Allen Lane, 1977), pp. 105–6.

31 Forced savings were compulsory deductions from pay, to be invested at the employee's choice in a Post Office savings account, a trade union or a Friendly Society and repayable after the war.

32 HMSO, *Fighting with Figures* (HMSO, 1995), p. 234.

33 *Ibid.*, p. 233. Between 1938 and 1945 the increase in wage rates in all industries over the increase in the cost-of-living was 17.5 per cent.

34 *Ibid.*, p. 236.

35 (Pensioners) Titmuss, *Problems of Social Policy*, p. 516; (soldiers' wives) S. Ferguson and H. Fitzgerald, *Studies in the Social Services* (HMSO, 1954), p. 22.

36 Petrol rationing, for example, was a great deprivation for the better-off but had practically no effect on the working and lower middle classes.

37 J. L. Hodson, *The Land and the Sea* (Gollancz, 1945), p. 238.

38 H. M. D. Parker, *Manpower* (HMSO, 1957), p. 425.

39 *Ibid.*, pp. 412–15.

40 *Ibid.*, pp. 417–19.

41 P. Inman, *Labour in the Munitions Industries* (HMSO, 1957), p. 252.

42 *Ibid.*, p. 239.

43 Speech at a food production exhibition at Watford. Reported in *The Times*, 15 September 1941.

44 In 1988 the historian Peter Hennessy tried living for a week on the rations allowed at the end of the war. He found the diet very monotonous and lost two pounds in weight, but admitted that he rarely felt hungry during the experiment. See P. Hennessy, *Never Again: Britain 1945–1951* (Jonathan Cape, 1992), pp. 49–50.

45 M-O, File Report 532.

46 Harrisson, *Living Through the Blitz*, p. 282.

47 Summary report of the Ministry of Health for the year ended 31 March 1943, *Parliamentary Papers 1942–43*, vol. 4, Cmd. 6468, 1943, pp. 7–8.

48 See Chapter 3.

49 See, for example, Letter from R. Lloyd Roberts, Ministry of Labour, 18 November 1943, cited in A. Briggs, *The War of Words* (Oxford University Press, 1970), p. 576.

50 D. Cardiff and P. Scannell, 'Radio in World War II', *U203 Popular Culture*, Block 2, Unit 8 (Open University Press, 1981), p. 35.

51 Listener Research, 'Broadcasting Policy', 27 August 1940, BBC WAC R9/15/1.

52 M-O, File Report 149, 28 May 1940.

53 LR/433, 2 December 1941, BBC WAC R/9/5; LR/556, 13 January 1942, R9/9/6.

54 (Full title *It's That Man Again*). See A. Briggs, *The War of Words* , vol. 3 of his *History of Broadcasting in the United Kingdom* (Oxford University Press, 1970), p. 595.

55 'What Did You Do in the War Auntie?' Produced for BBC 1 by Jeremy Bennett, May 1995.

56 'Open Forum', *Daily Film Renter*, 1 January 1940. Cited in J. Chapman, 'British Cinema and "the People's War"', in N. Hayes and J. Hill (eds), *Millions Like Us? British Culture and the Second World War* (Liverpool University Press, 1999), p. 41.

57 See N. Hayes, 'More Than Music While You Eat? Factory and Hostel Concerts, "Good Culture" and the Workers', in Hayes and Hill (eds), *Millions Like Us?* (Liverpool University Press, 1999), p. 223.

58 P. Ziegler, *London at War: 1939–1945* (Alfred A. Knopf, 1995), pp. 246–7; N. Longmate, *How We Lived Then* (Hutchinson, 1971), p. 254.

59 Cited in P. Fussell, *Wartime* (Oxford University Press, 1989), p. 98.

60 K. Young (ed.), *The Diaries of Sir Robert Bruce Lockhart* (Macmillan, 2 vols, 1973–80, vol. 2) p. 130.

61 R. Broad and S. Fleming (eds), *Nella Last's War*, p. 15.

62 See A. J. P. Taylor, *English History 1914–45* (Oxford University Press, 1965), p. 669.

6

Beveridge and all that

RECONSTRUCTION AND SOCIAL REFORM plans, it might be thought, were an obvious means of sustaining the morale of the nation: a vision of a more benign future during the necessarily arduous and stressful struggle that occupied the immediate present. Richard Titmuss suggested that in the summer of 1940 the nation's leaders consciously or unconsciously recognized that assurances of social reconstruction were, indeed, an essential ingredient in the strategy to keep morale high and keep the nation united.[1] Until 1943, however, the Government did not make any formal initiatives in this direction, and did not make peace aims – as distinct from war aims – an element in its propaganda. Judged by what the Government had to say on the subject, reconstruction appeared not to be on its agenda at all. The people had instead to be content with little more than the mitigation of the war's discomforts, backed by reminders of their glorious past. Stephen Taylor at the Ministry of Information, in an analysis that jars with Titmuss's view, clearly thought anything more was unnecessary. 'The public is unimaginative', he wrote, 'It is unable – and has, apparently, no great wish – to picture the details of the postwar world. It speculates relatively little about the end of the war.'[2] But official inertia did not prevent reconstruction from becoming an issue of debate, none the less. Beginning as a low profile discourse, mainly in intellectual and academic circles, reconstruction dramatically took centre stage with the publication of the Beveridge Report in December 1942, thereafter becoming the leading issue in domestic politics and potentially a significant influence on popular commitment to the war effort. To the extent, moreover, that the concrete reality of many ordinary citizens' lives actually improved during the war in some important respects, the cautious optimism generated by the Beveridge Report and the subsequent debate on reconstruction was complemented by a modest expectation that the trend would continue beyond the war.

Thinking about the future

Social reconstruction was, of course, on some people's agenda well before the war. There were dozens of organizations – of all political persuasions and none – actively thinking about ways and means to make society more rational and prosperous for all its citizens. The most prominent were the Fabian Society, Political and Economic Planning, The Next Five Years Group and, of course, the Labour Party. Much of the sense of urgency in this was naturally a result of the hugely dislocating consequences for society of the malfunctioning of the world economic system, following the Wall Street stock market crash of 1929.

Far from displacing this debate, the war itself seemed to provide a further stimulus. By 1943 there were more than one hundred unofficial organizations studying and putting out ideas and proposals on different aspects of post-war reconstruction: land and town planning, industry and economics, agriculture, housing and public amenities, education, medicine and health. Each imparted to its offerings its own particular perspective. When the Church of England joined the throng, for instance, it held a conference at Malvern in January 1941 'to consider from the Anglican point of view what are the fundamental facts which are directly relevant to the ordering of the new society that is quite evidently emerging, and how Christian thought can be shaped to play a leading part in the reconstruction after the war is over'.[3] The following year the initiator of the conference, William Temple (who had meanwhile become Archbishop of Canterbury), wrote a Penguin Special, in which he set out 'a Christian social programme' for a comprehensive reshaping of society, touching on public control of land and money, the role of organized labour in the management of industry and a national housing programme, as well as on the more traditional Church concerns of education and the family. However, what the Church had to say on reconstruction, while it certainly had a geographically wide currency, could hardly be said to be on everybody's lips; the Church, for all its formal national standing, spoke for a small and declining minority. Regular church attendance (all sects) was 25 per cent, according to a pre-war Gallup poll, but in 1943 Mass-Observation found that only 10 per cent of the population had close links with organized religion.[4]

In terms of the awareness of the ordinary citizen, much the same reservation that one would make about the views of religious bodies could be made about the contributions to the reconstruction debate made by the other groups and organizations. An exception to this, perhaps, was the Labour Party, for in addition to being a national body with established ways – notably at election times – of getting national coverage for its views, it was from May 1940 a participant in the Coalition Government, with the automatic salience this gave to its public profile. There can be no doubt that alongside the sense that the national situation in May 1940 required an all-party government, the Labour Party leadership's decision to accept Churchill's invitation was influenced by a belief that power-sharing would give the party the opportunity to realize some of its social policy aims and thereby to improve the lives of ordinary people. As the leader, Clement Attlee put it to the assembled delegates at the spring conference in Bournemouth: 'I am quite certain that the world that must emerge from this war must be a world attuned to our ideals ... There will be heavy sacrifices and we have to see to it that those sacrifices shall not be in vain.'[5] At about the same time, 'Labour's Home Policy' was published, presenting the war as an opportunity for socialism. The efficient prosecution of the war, it argued, would necessarily entail central planning and control of the economy along lines that the Party had always advocated as more efficient for peacetime, too. At the same time, there would be opportunities for significant steps to be taken to 'lay the foundations of a juster and more generous life'.[6]

When the perilous twelve months or so that followed had been survived, the party turned its energies to active thinking and planning. A Committee on Problems of Post-War Reconstruction was set up and began work in July 1941. Various working parties were quickly created to investigate and report on a wide range of issues, including social insurance, health, housing and education. The regional councils of the party were also invited to submit their own reports on the major areas of reconstruction. A distillation of all this activity eventually appeared in a general statement drafted by Harold Laski under the title *The Old World and the New* and approved by the national executive in February 1942. To the extent that the Labour Party had a national presence and an influence on the outlook of a significant section of the population, its work on reconstruction in the pre-Beveridge period might be presumed to have made a national impact. But it could equally well be argued that the detail of political parties' thinking and policies, outside election periods, was known only to the activists, it remaining more or less a closed book to the great majority of the people; and that the Labour Party was no exception to this basic political truth.[7]

A much more likely source of facts and ideas was the mass media. It so happened that the editors of national newspapers and magazines and the makers of films for mass consumption were very interested in the whole question of 'Whither Britain?' and were using their respective media to air the issues of reconstruction long before the Government – and even William Beveridge – joined the debate. Unexpectedly, it was the paper of the political elite, *The Times*, that fired the starting pistol. In a famous editorial on 1 July 1940 readers found themselves confronted with a call for a new social order that was almost revolutionary in its implications. Taking as its starting point the Prime Minister's depiction of the struggle with fascism as a defence of the values of European civilization, it warned:

> We must indeed beware of defining these values in purely 19th century terms. If we speak of democracy we do not mean a democracy which maintains the right to vote but forgets the right to work and the right to live. If we speak of freedom we do not mean a rugged individualism which excludes social organisation and economic planning. If we speak of equality we do not mean a political equality nullified by social and economic privilege. If we speak of economic reconstruction we think less of maximum (though this job too will be required) than of equitable distribution ... The European house cannot be put in order unless we put our own house in order first. The new order cannot be based on the preservation of privilege whether the privileged be that of a country, of a class or of an individual.

Was this merely a sinew-stiffening exercise, a sop to the urgent need for national unity at all costs, or was it rather a heartfelt recognition that much was wrong with British society – defender of European values or no – and that nothing less than a root and branch refashioning was the necessary moral complement of the 'blood, sweat and tears' that Churchill promised? Whichever it was, it is certain that the message remained unread by the masses who stood to benefit from such a refashioning. After all, *The Times* –

influential though it was in the corridors of power – was not a mass circulation newspaper.

Picture Post, however, could claim to have a hotline to the masses. This weekly tabloid magazine, launched in 1938, had quickly become established as essential reading in millions of homes, apparently appealing to an unusually wide social range. During the war it gained a reputation as a keen supporter of the war effort yet at the same time a persistent critic of the Government's conduct of the war – as its editor Tom Hopkinson put it: 'to criticise when there is need for it, to applaud when it is deserved'.[8] In November 1939 it had criticized the official failure to tell the people enough about the war; in June 1940 it campaigned for the arming of the people and the upgrading of the Home Guard; in November 1940 it featured the scandal of inadequate shelter provision in London and in the same month, the scandal of empty country houses when the bombed-out were in crowded, makeshift billets; in September 1941 it questioned the vigour of the programme of arms build-up. This gadfly role fitted it well to make the case for action on the matter of reconstruction.

It began, with impressive thoroughness, in its first number for 1941, to which it gave the title 'A Plan For Britain'. With 'expert' contributions from the scientist (and regular member of the BBC's weekly *Brains Trust*), Julian Huxley; the Secretary of Political and Economic Planning, A. D. K. Owen; the academic economist, Thomas Balogh; the Master of Balliol College, Oxford, A. D. Lindsay; the poplar novelist and broadcaster, J. B. Priestley, and others, a comprehensive programme of social reform was presented – for employment, housing, health, education, leisure and recreation. On employment, for example, labelled 'the first necessity in the new Britain', the plan was for: 'a job for every able-bodied man; State control of the banks and individual investment; a State-managed company to make community investment; lower income tax, but a tax on property; the national plan related to an international plan'. On the question of social security, in a remarkable anticipation of Beveridge, the plan envisaged: a minimum wage for all able-bodied adults, to cover the minimum standard needs of a married man and his wife; the introduction of children's allowances, financed by taxation, to cover their minimum standard needs; an all-in contributory scheme of social insurance, covering unemployment, sickness, invalidity, workmen's compensation, widows', orphans' and old age pensions, and a burial grant; extra help and special forms of help from public assistance for people such as the self-employed who could not easily participate in the contributory scheme. And so on, for each of the main areas of reform, a pungently argued programme of far-reaching change.

It is difficult to be sure of the effect of the plan on popular attitudes in the country as a whole; but its effect on the readers was enormous. The magazine always made a point of trying to elicit its readers' opinions and to create a dialogue sequel to its features. For this special issue the response was unprecedentedly large and continued well into February. Some of the letters were critical, complaining of 'socialistic' propaganda in the articles and announcing the cancellation of subscriptions. But the great weight of the mail was enthusiastic. Some of it was from the great names in the land, including the distinguished playwright, Sean O'Casey and the former leader of the Liberal Party, Lord Samuel, who wrote: 'I hold this issue of *Picture Post* is the best short statement of social needs and remedial methods I have seen'.[9] But there were lots of letters, too, from ordinary people in routine occupations. Even the young joined in: a fifteen-year-old pupil at Winchester College, Michael Dunnett, wrote to say, 'it is the best thing done here since "Rights of Man"'. At the very least, one might reasonably surmise that in the millions of households that took *Picture Post*, *some* discussion followed this *coup de theatre*.

Two months after 'A Plan For Britain' *Picture Post* ran a feature in support of J. B. Priestley, the second series of whose popular weekly talks on the radio, entitled *Postscripts*, had come to an end with the announcement that there would be no further series. Towards the end of his first series in July 1940, Priestley had begun to inject an element of social comment into the talks that listeners of Conservative leanings found uncomfortably 'leftish'. On 21 July, for example, he made an attack on property, 'an old-fashioned idea', he said, which sees Britain as 'a thing' and which ought to be replaced by 'community', which sees it as 'the home of a living society'. The war was making us all realize 'we're all in the same boat', a boat that 'can serve not only as our defence against Nazi aggression, but as an ark in which we can all finally land in a better world'. On 22 September, after deploring the owners of large houses in the reception areas who refused the shelter of their empty rooms to mothers and infants fleeing the bombs being rained on London, he spoke of bringing 'into existence an order of society in which nobody will have far too many rooms in a house and nobody have far too few'. And in his final talk, on 20 October, he defended himself against the charge of 'bringing party politics into my talks', and recalling 'the high mood of the summer', he warned that 'if the privileges of a few are seen to be regarded as more important than the happiness of many ... then the great opportunity will pass us by, and soon the light will be going out again'. Since the leading complainers about the talks were Conservative MPs, there was no preventing the popular conviction from gaining ground that Priestley was taken off the air as a result of Government pressure on the BBC. The aftermath was a spate of newspaper articles and letters to editors, most of which were opposed to what they saw as the muzzling of a popular speaker who was asking questions that needed to be asked. *Picture Post*, of course, having already used Priestley as one its contributors to 'A Plan For Britain', took his part, and gave him space to amplify his views in print, generating a lively debate among readers about the rights and wrongs of the affair. The combined effect of the *Postscript* broadcasts, *Picture Post*'s reform proposals and 'the Priestley affair' was to sustain the momentum of the debate about peace aims and reconstruction, and to ensure that it was carried on among a much wider constituency than before. Together, two mass media outlets – *Picture Post*, deliberately, and the BBC, inadvertently – got ordinary people talking about the future of British society and in so doing laid the groundwork for getting it onto the popular agenda.

This groundwork was being simultaneously complemented by the film industry. It does not seem to have been part of the understanding between the MoI and the film industry that film makers be permitted freedom to introduce into their work material in the potentially contentious area of peace aims. Yet this is what some film makers proceeded to do, as early as 1941, and sometimes while actually working under contract to the Government. The Boulting Brothers' documentary *The Dawn Guard* is an audacious example. The 'guard' of the title is the Home Guard, and the screenplay includes a dialogue between two of its members, on duty on a rural hillside. They talk about the real meaning of the war. One sees it as basically a defence of the British way of life, threatened by the Nazis; for him, everything will have been achieved when the old life can be resumed. The other, the younger of the two, looks at it differently. For lots of people the 'old life' meant poverty and unemployment. He thinks the war has shown people capable of making a better society than they had before it: 'We've made a fine big war effort. Well, when it's all over, we've got to see to it we make a fine big peace effort. There must be no more chaps hanging around for work that doesn't come – no more slums neither – no more filthy dirty back streets – no more half-starved kids with no room to play in. We got to pack all of that up and get moving into the brightness of the sun.' Coming before the public so soon afterwards, this film, in its rather vague and homespun way, served to underscore the spirit of *Picture Post*'s 'A Plan For Britain'.

Three films made by John Baxter in 1941–42 were entirely focused on the question of the impossibility of a return to the conditions of the 1930s. If wartime full employment was causing some people to begin to forget the years of idleness, Baxter kept the image clear. In *Love on the Dole* (1941), closely based on Walter Greenwood's 1933 novel about the Depression years, he reminded everyone of the wretchedness of that time for so many families. The film's implied message was underlined by a postscript caption at the end, signed by a Labour member of the Coalition Government, Albert Alexander: 'Our working men and women have responded magnificently to any and every call made upon them. Their reward must be a new Britain. Never again must the unemployed become the forgotten men [sic] of peace.'[10] *The Common Touch*, which came out the same year, and *Let the People Sing,* which followed in 1942, reiterated the themes of the need for change and of the way the war was itself bringing about changes – in attitudes, especially – that could lead to a better society. *The Common Touch* ended with a dialogue between two inmates of the dosshouse that provided its main location:

> *Tich*: All this talk about better things, homes and all that – do you
>   s'pose they really mean it? Or will they forget?
>
> *Ben*: No, I really think they mean it this time, Tich.
>
> *Tich*: Blimey, it'll be like heaven on earth.
>
> *Ben*: And why not?

Humphrey Jennings's *Fires Were Started* (1941), made, like *The Dawn Guard*, for the MoI, seems to be simply about the present – the story of one firefighting crew's experience on one night in the Blitz. But there was a subtext. In its depiction of the social dynamics of this group of men, brought together from a variety of backgrounds for a common purpose, the film, as Angus Calder observed, is 'replete with intimations of a classless new order'.[11]

The film industry, then, despite the real constraints under which it was working, was somehow managing to get away with making films that, wholly or in part, failed either to keep within their official propaganda remit or to offer the audience simply light relief and mental escape. As film historian Nicholas Pronay concluded: 'by the close of World War Two, significant sections of the British people had been treated to visions of a grandiose postwar Utopia which exceeded anything promised during World War One'.[12] Because of the cinema's salience in the leisure time of the population, films contributed to the 'Never Again' climate of opinion that was forming in 1940–42 and helped to keep the debate about the future going.

The Government, however, had so far done nothing at all to encourage this debate. Certainly, there was support for the idea among some officials at the Ministry of Information – Harold Nicolson, in particular, believed it to be a necessity to sustain the people through the trial of war. Indeed, *Picture Post*'s 'A Plan For Britain' originated as a response to a suggestion of the director of the Ministry's Films Division, Sir Kenneth Clark, in November 1940, that it might do a special number devoted to 'the Britain we hope to build when war is over'.[13] But the work of the War Aims Committee came to nothing when, at the very time that everyone was talking about the *Picture Post* special issue, Churchill vetoed the idea of a Government statement on war aims. As Nicolson recorded it in his diary: 'The reason given in Cabinet is that precise aims would be compromising, whereas vague principles would disappoint.'[14] Thereafter, in view of the Prime Minister's attitude, the MoI was unable, even if it wished, openly to encourage discussion of postwar aims. After Bracken became Minister in July 1941, this did become a matter of some tension in Cabinet, for he shared Nicolson's view that deliberate official silence about post-war aims was throwing away a potentially valuable means of sustaining morale. Soon afterwards an unexpected event took place that greatly cheered the 'reconstructionists'. The Prime Minister went to Placentia Bay in Newfoundland to meet President Roosevelt, in the hope of advancing the aim of a US declaration of war. Roosevelt was not ready yet for a declaration and the outcome was instead a declaration of general war aims, 'a working paper setting out the basis on which a new and fairer world would be constructed'.[15] Included, at Ernest Bevin's suggestion, was a clause recognizing the wish of the partners to collaborate to secure 'for all, improved labour standards, economic advancement and social security'. It was rather vague, but it was believed by the campaigners for reform to be important because Britain's leader, on an international stage, had made a commitment to the principle of social security.

The MoI's Home Intelligence Division, meanwhile, was recording a significant increase in public interest in post-war aims during 1941. In April 1942 it summarized its findings. Most people, it thought, felt that there would be no return to the society of the 1930s, although many feared that the politicians might fail to ensure this. The things most people wanted to see were: an end to unemployment; an end to 'dismissal without notice or without reason'; proper provision for sickness and old age; income redistribution, 'with higher minima and lower maxima'; reform of education to give 'an equal chance for all children'.[16] On the whole, the findings suggested more optimism than pessimism about what would eventually happen. Mass-Observation's surveys confirmed this. In August 1942 it reported a growing interest in reconstruction and higher public awareness of the necessity for change. It also noted a lessening of the overwhelming pessimism about post-war conditions that it had recorded fifteen months earlier.[17]

During 1942 the calls for a public statement on post-war aims became more insistent. Although these came from predictable quarters – the largely middle-class organizations referred to above – there is no doubt that there was, as Home Intelligence, had noted, widespread interest in the issue among all classes throughout the country. This was the background, then, for Beveridge's bombshell.

The impact of Beveridge

Like the former journalist he was, Beveridge made sure that his report would be a bombshell, preparing the ground in the six weeks that preceded its publication on 1 December, by getting his friends and contacts in the press to allow him space to give broad hints about its contents and to trail the Report in special articles.[18] By the time it came out, therefore, it was already everywhere a topic of conversation.

Simply stated, the Beveridge Report proposed subsistence benefits for all within a unified system of compulsory social insurance. In return for a flat-rate weekly contribution, flat-rate benefits would be made for sickness, unemployment, old age, maternity, industrial injury, orphanhood and widowhood. Through this, a 'national minimum' of income was guaranteed to every person and every family when need arose. In addition, special payments were proposed in relation to the costs of birth, marriage and death. This system, Beveridge emphasized, depended for its operation on concurrent action by government to maintain full employment, introduce family allowances and establish a comprehensive national health service.

The public reaction was massive: never had an official report been the focus of such widespread interest. Every newspaper carried detailed analysis and comment – almost entirely favourable – and the Report itself was a best-seller, some 635,000 copies being bought.[19] *The Times* described it as 'a plainly realizable project of national endeavour' and declared that 'The central proposals must surely be accepted as the basis of Governmental action.'[20] Reaching a much wider audience, Beveridge himself gave a radio talk, outlining the proposals in plain language. But most ordinary citizens would have acquainted themselves with the details via the mass circulation dailies and weeklies. Here great efforts were made by editors to translate 'this heavy two-shilling slab of involved economics' into language that anyone could understand.[21] The *Daily Herald* and *Daily Mirror* concentrated on the cash implications for individuals and families, devising charts headed 'What a Family Gets' (*Herald*) and 'What the Plan does for Everyone' or 'How to be Born, Bred and Buried by Beveridge' (*Mirror*). In subsequent days the *Herald* followed up the subject with a feature entitled 'Life Under Beveridge', an imagined journey into the future in which the fortunes of a working-class family were followed from marriage, through the birth of their four children, to old age, helped at every stage by the social security system, set up, it was assumed, in 1944. The *Herald* also published its own guide to Beveridge, sold though newsagents, and started a lively discussion of the Report on its readers' letters page.

Similar analyses and follow-up features were to be found in the other popular dailies and even in the large-circulation Sunday papers, where news normally took second place to entertainment and gossip. But of all the words read by the people on the Beveridge Report, those that probably had most impact were those of *Picture Post*, not simply because the magazine was taken in millions of homes, but because its coverage was particularly thorough and strikingly well-devised to get and sustain popular attention.

To follow up its initial coverage, it brought out a special issue on 2 January 1943, entitled 'Changing Britain'. Repeating the approach it had used exactly two years previously, it invited well-known people to write features on different aspects of Britain and how the Beveridge proposals could change them. One of the 'experts', Frank Pakenham, writing on 'Social Security', spoke from the inside, so to speak, for he had been Beveridge's assistant during the preparation of the Report. In the following three months the magazine kept the subject on the boil. A broadcast feature about the 2 January issue was arranged with the BBC, and subsequent issues featured the opposition to Beveridge in the Society of Individualists, a discussion on the pros and cons of state planning, and the struggle to get the Plan (as everyone was now calling the Report) onto the Government's agenda. In addition, the subject dominated the readers' letters page – sometimes in fact becoming two pages – under headlines such as 'Beveridge: Readers Write'.

Picture Post liked to think of itself as the voice of the people.[22] But neither it nor any of the popular daily papers really managed to get more than a small contribution from ordinary working-class people to the dialogue conducted in their readers' letters pages. These pages were dominated, as they seem to have been throughout the history of the press, by letters from the 'well-qualified, well-placed and well-heeled'.[23] Impressive though the total volume of correspondence received by the popular press on Beveridge was, therefore, it discloses little about the opinions of the great mass of the people. However, one can reasonably infer that, to the extent that the opinions of the masses were influenced at all by what they read in newspapers and magazines, then the sheer amount of space those outlets gave to Beveridge must have made some impression; and that since the coverage was almost entirely favourable, then this, too, is how ordinary people felt about what was proposed. If nothing else, the press, in rooting for Beveridge, made it difficult for an objective critique to be heard, still less that of outright opposition.

Whether influenced or not by press coverage, when public opinion was tested by the survey organizations, there was overwhelming confirmation of popular support for the Beveridge Plan. A Gallup survey showed that no less than 86 per cent thought it should be adopted, against a mere 6 per cent who thought it should be dropped. Support came from all social groups but, remarkably, it was as strong among those higher income groups that did not especially stand to gain from it – support ranging from 73 to 91 per cent.[24] Mass-Observation's survey of first reactions also confirmed a very favourable reception for the Plan, along with a widespread assumption that the Government was committed to it.[25] Organizations everywhere felt moved to register their feelings. The Women's Institute, for instance, received many resolutions for the annual conference from its regional branches along the lines of that proposed by Toft WI in Cheshire and accepted nationally: 'This meeting records its appreciation of Sir William Beveridge's great work for social security and particularly of his recognition that health insurance for housewives and children's allowances are essential if family life is to be free from want.'[26]

But alongside this enthusiastic support for the Plan, there was also a great deal of scepticism about the likelihood of it being implemented. Home Intelligence, while confirming the findings of Gallup and Mass-Observation, noted reports from eleven Regions suggesting 'real anxiety that the plan would not materialize'. The reasons given reveal that at this stage the hope of a better post-war society was yet to become a source of commitment to the war effort. In ten Regions, 'vested interests' were mentioned as a major impediment to implementation – 'big business', the insurance companies, the British Medical Association. These were seen as likely to 'hotly contest every inch of the ground ... the final plan will therefore be so mutilated that the benefits ultimately received by working people will be small'. In six Regions the Government was thought to be a significant obstacle. Its attitude was seen as ambivalent, and a minority thought the Report was no more than an official propaganda exercise, designed 'to keep us at it till the war is over'. Other reasons included the discouragingly high cost of the scheme and party political wrangling, both of which could lead, it was thought, to a watering down of its proposals.[27] Some of the scepticism derived, Home Intelligence found, from bitter experience. A former soldier caustically put it: 'This new plan for social security makes me laugh; I don't forget the Land Fit for Heroes of the last war.'[28] Mass-Observation, too, noted that among all the enthusiasm there was a minority who saw it as a carrot, the people being the donkey.[29]

Public enthusiasm, then, seems to have been touched by doubt. In this the perceived attitude of the politicians – and more particularly the Government – was critical. Initially, it almost seemed that the Government had accepted the Plan; for Bracken authorized maximum publicity, including a press conference and a radio broadcast, and asked the Army Bureau of Current Affairs to make the Report required reading for servicemen's organized discussion groups. According to Paul Addison, he did this because he realized that 'the report would serve as a brilliant propaganda weapon against his opposite number, Goebbels' – for which, as Ian McLaine observed, Churchill's permission would have been needed.[30] Beveridge got his big official launch, then, but soon afterwards the Government seemed to pour cold water on the impression that it fully supported the Plan by ordering the withdrawal of the ABCA leaflet for servicemen only two days after it was published on 21 December. And as the weeks went by without any Government statement, a counter-impression of its attitude inevitably developed in the public mind, such as was suggested by the reports referred to above.

The scepticism was justified. For in the weeks before the debate on the Report in the House of Commons in mid-February, the Cabinet decided that while reconstruction planning should begin at once, there could be no actual legislation on the Beveridge proposals until the war was over. The debate itself, as Government spokesmen – both Conservative and Labour – tried to put a favourable gloss on their 'yes, but not yet' decision, was nevertheless a huge disappointment, even to those who were not insisting on 'Beveridge in full now!' (the new slogan of the Common Wealth Party). Commitment in principle, but with no action plan, was a stance that came over as at best lukewarm and cautious, at worst a confirmation that the Plan would be shelved.

There was naturally a lot of public noise about this from pro-Beveridge groups, not least in Parliament itself. A group of forty-five members of the Tory Reform Committee, led by Quintin Hogg and Lord Hinchingbrooke, put down an amendment calling for the creation of a Ministry of Social Security. Labour backbenchers were so angry with their leaders that ninety-seven of them (out of ninety-nine) voted against the Government in the division. The popular newspapers and magazines, who had done so much to raise people's expectations, shared the disappointment and were unsparing in their comment about the Government's stance. Even the staider papers joined in the general disapproval. *The Times* wrote of this week's 'disappointment' and of 'a crisis which need never have arisen', while the *Economist* spoke of 'a crisis of free government and democracy' and declared that 'The question: "Has the Government accepted the Beveridge Report?" remains unanswered.'[31]

After the debate, Mass-Observation in a survey of popular opinion asked people if they thought the Beveridge Plan would be implemented. While 37 per cent thought it would; 24 per cent thought some of it would; 15 per cent thought it would not; and 24 per cent offered no opinion. As the summarizers of the survey commented, just over half expected compromise or non-implementation (although they might just as easily have said that 61 per cent expected implementation or part-implementation). Men were in fact markedly more sceptical than women – 55 per cent as opposed to 25 per cent. A typical 'compromise' comment, from a 35-year-old working-class woman: 'It won't be accepted absolutely, but I think they'll pass it with modifications, to keep the people quiet. I'm sure there'd be a minor revolution if they threw it out altogether'. The tail end of that comment was also characteristic of another interesting development disclosed by the survey: the apparently widespread belief in the power of public opinion. Seemingly as a consequence of the changed relationship between leaders and led in the 'people's war', there was, Mass-Observation inferred, a new confidence that future governments would have to take more heed of what the people wanted. Thus, a 25-year-old male worker: 'They daren't throw it over now. They might keep it hanging in mid air till the war turns one way or the other, but at the present time we wouldn't stand for it'; and a 55-year-old working-class woman: 'They'll talk and talk, but have to pass it in the end. People won't stand for it if they drop it.'[32] Home Intelligence also sought popular reactions to the Commons debate; an analysis of its Regional Reports found that the disappointment of the press and of committed lobbyists for the Plan was largely shared by the public. It ruefully concluded that the Government did not realise how attached the ordinary people were to the Beveridge Plan: 'It has become a religion to some people ... like the Ark of the Covenant, quite apart from the actual benefits it promises.' The reports said that the majority were cynical, disappointed or angry, and they included in this majority 'the working classes, Liberals, Labour and the Left, a proportion of the middle classes and, according to three reports, a number of the rank and file of the Conservative Party'. People apparently thought the Government was trying to kill or shelve the Report and had 'promised little or nothing'. Home Intelligence gave a sample of other comments in the same vein: 'a forecast of what we may expect when the war is over', 'augurs ill for the future of social security', 'crystallized people's worst fears of the postwar period', 'vested interests have won again', and 'vested interests are at work to ensure that things will remain as they did after the last war'.[33]

If half of what these soundings suggested was correct, then the Government had clearly presided over a public relations disaster. For it had certainly not been its intention to signal a 'thumbs down' to Beveridge. In fact, the position set out in February indicated a remarkable shift of ground for what, after all, was a largely Conservative Government in a parliament numerically dominated by the Conservative Party. Who would have thought that the Tories would come so quickly to accept not only the basic elements of Beveridge's rather un-Conservative proposals, but would also endorse, as they did, the introduction of a comprehensive state medical service and family allowances? But the truth was that the ground shared between the partners in the Coalition Government was not all-inclusive. They knew that the implementation of Beveridge in full would run into difficulties in the detail, because at certain points it touched on incompatible elements in their respective ideologies. In the interest of unity for the winning of the war, it seemed wiser to defer business that would inevitably prove contentious and divisive – not least *within* the Conservative wing of the Coalition, for it became clear during the course of 1943 that the enthusiasm for the Report among the forty-odd members of the progressive Tory Reform Group (TRG), founded partly to promote the Party's adherence to Beveridge, was matched by the equally enthusiastic opposition to all it stood for among the members of the ultra-conservative Progress Trust, set up specifically to counter the influence of the TRG on Party policy.[34] There was in the stance of the Coalition partners, then, a tacit understanding, perhaps, that the Coalition would not long survive the end of the war, at which point there would be a resumption of normal party politics and the people could make their choice between parties that were not constrained by the special circumstances of war. The position adopted in February, then, reflected the political realities of coalition government. What made sense as political tactic, however, was in conflict with other facts about the real world, notably the almost palpable desire of the people to see the Beveridge Plan implemented. The debacle of February was the predictable consequence; an obvious opportunity for the Government to boost the nation's flagging energy had been thrown away.

Or so it seemed: for all was not lost for the Government. In the next eighteen months both parties worked to undo the impression they had given that they were lukewarm towards the Beveridge Plan. As coalition partners, too, they sought to give reassurance of the certainty of reconstruction. This began with a damage-limiting broadcast by Churchill in which, echoing Beveridge, he outlined his own 'Four Year Plan' for economic and social recovery, including 'national compulsory insurance for all classes, for all purposes, from the cradle to the grave'. Under the slogan 'Food, Work and Homes For All' he authorized schemes to be prepared for the transition period between war and peace. This does not seem to have impressed or convinced many people, however. Mass-Observation, aggregating the views of its National Panel, concluded at the end of May that 'The signs are now that postwar expectations are, if anything, rather more gloomy than they were before the report was published', adding that 'the greatest need at present is for some tangible and incontrovertible sign that postwar promises are in earnest. Without some sign of goodwill, people are likely to remain impatient of words.'[35] Advised of this, in November Churchill created a Ministry of Reconstruction and, with his usual gift for appointments, invited as its first Minister, Lord Woolton, then at the height of his success and popularity at the Ministry of Food.

In 1944 came a series of White Papers, several of which concerned Beveridge's 'five giants' of 'Want, Disease, Ignorance, Squalor and Idleness'. That on social insurance contained proposals that were so close to those in Beveridge's report that Beveridge himself gave them his general approval. Those on a national health service and full employment were rather more vague and general, for the reality was that on both these issues bipartisanship did not go far enough to permit legislation under the Coalition. The Education White Paper, however, was translated into concrete reality in the 1944 Education Act, which, for all its faults and limitations was regarded, not least within the Labour Party, as a significant step towards a more egalitarian society.

All this activity at Westminster naturally received the media coverage normally due to such activity, except that its relationship to reconstruction made it more newsworthy and therefore earned it more column inches. Film makers continued to keep the issue before people's eyes. John Baxter, for instance, made *The Shipbuilders* in 1943, about the then frantically busy shipyards of Clydeside, raising the question of whether they would return to dereliction once the war was over. The same year, Michael Hankinson did a similar treatment for the North East, in *Tyneside Story*. This documentary, made for the MoI, was intended by its sponsor to be an upbeat celebration of the heroic patriotism of the shipyard workers, as the epic final words of the commentary showed: 'As long as Britain calls for ships, the call will be answered by the ringing of steel on steel in the shipyards of the Tyne'. But then a cloth-capped worker walks into view and directly addresses the audience:

> Ah! But wait a minute. Tyneside's busy enough today. Old ones and young ones hard at work making good ships. But just remember what the yards looked like five years ago. Idle. Empty. Some of them derelict. The skilled men that worked in them scattered and forgotten. Will it be the same again, five years from now? That's what we on Tyneside want to know.

The following year Ealing Studios made an adaptation for cinema of Priestley's *They Came to a City*, which Richards and Aldgate linked with the films of Baxter, Gunn and the Boulting brothers, as 'imbued with the same vision of a "brave new world" arising from the ruins of the old and of the war as the "midwife of social progress."'[36] At the same time, thousands of people saw films shown by the Workers' Film Association, mainly to labour movement organizations, such as co-operative education committees, Labour Party branches and local trades councils, but also to the 'uncommitted' in workers' hostels and deep shelters (during the Little Blitz and the V-weapon raids). Among those specifically focused on reconstruction were: *When We Build Again*, sponsored by the Bournville Trust (1944), *Life Begins Again*, made with the cooperation of the TUC, *Home of the People*, sponsored by the *Daily Herald*, and two directed by Paul Rotha: *World of Plenty* (1943) and *Land of Promise* (1945), the latter made for the Gas Council.[37]

Even the BBC, which had cautiously steered clear of Beveridge altogether for a year after the Commons debate, finally began to join in and allow on the air discussions of the main issues of post-war reconstruction – employment, housing, health, education – in series like *The World We Want* (from October 1943), *Homes for All* (March–April 1944) and *The Friday Discussions* (from October 1944).[38] For editors, readers and audiences alike, reconstruction remained the dominant subject of domestic politics and domestic news during the rest of the war.

How much the millions who were exposed to these media forays into the future were influenced in their views by what they saw and heard is difficult to say. But what is certain is that the reconstruction of Britain was never allowed to drop from their horizons. Whatever else it did, the media succeeded in making it difficult for the politicians to sideline the big reconstruction issues until the war was over.

In May 1944 the Government, conscious of the uncertainty of the prospects of an early end to the war and anxious about the stamina of the home front's civilian warriors, tried to ascertain if its reconstruction activity was having any effect on the public's expectations of post-war society, that is, whether people were convinced of the Government's sincerity in its acceptance of the principles underlying the Beveridge Report. The Ministry of Reconstruction asked Home Intelligence and Gallup to conduct parallel investigations into public attitudes. Home Intelligence concluded that the public remained unconvinced: 'There is widespread suspicion of the Government's attitude to the Beveridge Plan. A great many, perhaps the majority, are convinced that it will either be shelved, mutilated, or whittled away, or else an inferior substitute put forward instead.'[39] But Gallup, asking people how satisfied they were with the progress reported on the Government's steps to deal with reconstruction, found that 43 per cent were satisfied, 35 per cent dissatisfied.[40] While this approval rating did not match the 75 to 80 per cent on the Government's conduct of the war, in polls conducted about the same time, it does suggest, perhaps, that some modest progress had been made in the year following the morale-sapping parliamentary debate on Beveridge. And the rather gloomier conclusions of Home Intelligence might be attributed to the general regret among officials in the Ministry of Information that the Government had not allowed them fully to exploit reconstruction for civilian morale, condemning them, rather, to damage-limitation activity, after the disaster of the debate. Mass-Observation, in a study of attitudes towards demobilization, predictably found some anxiety about employment, noting that one man in ten, and one woman in five, expected to have difficulty finding a job.[41] (These figures, of course, could be read much more positively, that is that 90 per cent of men and 75 per cent of women did *not* expect to have difficulty finding a job.) Meanwhile, summarizing its own findings on popular expectations about postwar society, Mass-Observation tended to confirm Gallup's more optimistic picture: 'Post-war expectations were increasingly based on compromise within the present framework, the continuation of some measure of state control, better social services based on war-time experiences.'[42]

Another sign of things to come?

In terms of popular perceptions of the likely nature of post-war society, the effect of all the official planning and preparation in the reconstruction field could, on its own, scarcely have been negligible. But in reality, it was not on its own: there was also the concrete reality of social reform, taking place in a piecemeal, ad hoc fashion during the course of the war, subtly changing pre-war arrangements and implying further changes in the future.

In the final chapter of his history of wartime social policy, Richard Titmuss, reviewing developments in the social services, believed it to have been a period of momentous change: 'the Government had, through the agency of newly established or existing services, assumed and developed a measure of direct concern for the health and well-being of the population which, by contrast with the role of Government in the nineteen-thirties was little short of remarkable'.[43] Titmuss's special interest here was in the evidence of a shift in the policy assumptions of the political elites and their advisers. But the effect of the changes he described on the attitudes of the ordinary citizen – the 'client', as he was now to be called – of the social services, is, for present purposes, of equal interest.

Depending on one's age, sex or circumstances, the war years brought the citizen into a deeper and more extensive relationship with the dispensers of state organized benefits. Mention has already been made, in relation to the rise in prices, of the 750,000 more old age pensioners receiving supplementary allowances after 1940. But much of the expansion and innovation was targeted at the welfare of children.

Meals at school were well-established before the war, usually operating at low nutritional levels, depending on the local authority, and always seen by beneficiaries as an admission of social failure because of their explicit association with malnutrition and poverty. From July 1940, however, the scope of the service was widened, to the point five years later where one child in three – a ten-fold increase – was taking a midday meal at school; and its quality was improved through the redesigning of the meals in the light of nutritional knowledge. The 'charity' stigma had gone, too, for the conditions of wartime – bombing, evacuation, greater employment of women – meant that those taking the meals were not exclusively the children of the poor but came from all classes. Thus, the 14 per cent who continued to get the meal free were effectively assimilated into the remaining 86 per cent who paid four or five pence (2p).[44]

In the same way, under the impact of official policy, the milk-at-school scheme drew in a much greater proportion of all children during the course of the war. By February 1945 it had increased from 50 to 75 per cent, 10 per cent of the children receiving the milk free, the rest paying one halfpenny (1.25p) for one-third of a pint per day.[45]

The interventions of the Ministry of Food and the Board of Education in the matter of school meals and milk was complemented by the National Milk Scheme, which was conceived and developed by the Ministry of Health and administered by the Ministry of Food. Here the main target groups were expectant and nursing mothers and pre-school infants. From July 1940 all individuals in these categories were eligible for a pint of milk daily at the price of two pence, instead of the normal price of four and a half pence. Poor families, those whose income came below two pounds a week (plus six shillings a week for each non-earning dependant) received the milk without charge. The scheme was as successful as those for school meals and milk: already by September 1940 70 per cent of the 3,500,000 mothers and children eligible were participating, and during the course of the war it became a national institution, valued by all classes.[46]

In December 1941 the vitamin welfare scheme was introduced, building on pre-war schemes at some welfare centres to supply 'vitamin foods' at cost price and conceived as a complement to the national milk scheme. It made available free blackcurrant juice and cod liver oil for all children under two, extending the latter to children under five in February 1942. By the end of the year, through the Lend-Lease arrangement with the USA, concentrated orange juice replaced blackcurrant juice and the supply of this, too, was extended to all children under five. In April 1943 vitamin A and D tablets were offered to expectant mothers as an alternative to cod liver oil.[47] The vitamin foods scheme was never as popular as the national milk scheme, but even so, the proportion taking up the offer rose from 35 per cent of those eligible in 1943 to a maximum of 54 per cent in 1944.

Another benign intervention in the lives of many families was the Ministry of Health's campaign launched in 1940 for the immunisation of children against diphtheria. This disease of childhood had infected about 50,000 children under fifteen every year before the war, killing 3,000 of them in an average year. As a direct result of the initiative, by which immunisation was funded by the State and administered by the local authorities, the figures were reduced by 1945 to 24,275 cases and 720 deaths. In some especially proactive local authorities, over 90 per cent of under-fifteens were inoculated.[48] The scheme might have been invented to demonstrate the potential benefit to the health of the nation of preventive medicine organized by a state medical service.

Finally, in this review of significant social service interventions by the Government in response to the contingencies of war, mention should be made of the great expansion from mid-1941 of day and residential nursery provision for children under five. At its peak in the autumn of 1944, this development was accommodating 112,338 children in the various types of day nurseries in Britain and 16,402 children in state-funded residential nurseries (England and Wales only).[49] The increase in provision was naturally linked to the drive to exploit female labour by releasing mothers of young children from daytime care. But it was at the same time a sort of liberation for those who took up the opportunity and thereby brought more variety to their lives. It was also one more unexpected way in which the quality of life was improved – and perceived to have improved – for many families during the course of the war. 'It's the best thing that has happened', said one mother, 'I couldn't buy the little luxuries I wanted for Ann out of an Army Allowance. Why, before I started work I had to count the coppers 'ere buying a bag of apples; now everything runs smoothly.'[50]

When at any time people are asked what they expect life will be like for them a few years ahead, many give responses that are, characteristically, on the side of caution; and the older – and therefore more life-experienced – they are, the more likely they are to desist from extravagant optimism. As we have seen, when the question was put to civilians at any time during the war, the note of anxiety, doubt or even pessimism is always to be discerned in the replies. Most interestingly, as an official at the MoI remarked, the view that 'things will never be the same again' was often, illogically, held by the same people who worried that they 'may be as bad as they were last time'.[51] The sources of anxiety, apart from the individual's own constitutional disposition, naturally derived from experience – of life before the war – but also from a projection of the circumstances of the present into the imagined future. And recent times did not encourage an optimistic outlook. George Orwell wrote in 1940: 'It is an age in which every *positive* attitude has turned out a failure. Creeds, parties, programmes of every description have all flopped, one after another. The only "ism" that has justified itself is pessimism.'[52] For the poorer and less privileged of the 1930s the mental legacy of that time was naturally largely negative. And to those who could remember the previous war and its aftermath, the thought must inevitably have occurred that something similar might happen after this war.

Present circumstances, however, must surely have argued for a different scenario? Simply by reason of reconstruction's position as the big issue of domestic politics during the last four and a half years of the war, a general expectation of *some* change for the better after the war, *some* belief in 'Never Again' became entrenched. How could it not be so, when on all sides, with increasing insistence, assurances were being made that the quality of everyone's life really would be improved? 'I'll expect it when I see it' may well have been the smart thing to say even as the party manifestos appeared in the weeks before the 1945 general election. But only the absolute, out-and-out cynic really thought nothing would change, that the old interests would combine to prevent the making of a fairer society. And as it has been suggested in this chapter, the averagely-distrustful citizen did not have to rely on mere promises for his estimate of how things would be. The evidence of beneficial change presented itself concretely for him and his family through the reforms being undertaken during the war itself. Was he, in the face of this, to take the wholly negative view that these improvements were mere bribes that would be withdrawn or otherwise rendered nugatory when the state had no further use for him as a home front warrior? Every indication denied this, especially the special measures to protect and nurture the welfare of the elderly and the very young. This time, the signs were that life really would be better for all, and very much better for those who before the war had been most deprived.

In March 1941 Mass-Observation took soundings of morale in many cities around Britain. It found, at this (pre-Beveridge) stage of the war, great lack of optimism about the economic future, it being widely assumed that a big post-war slump would follow the wartime boom.[53] By the spring of 1945, although anxiety about housing, jobs and social security still appeared in social surveys, the outlook seemed much brighter to most people. The visions of Britain to come that had for five years occupied so large a place in public discourse, together with the piecemeal betterments experienced during this time, seem to have undermined the pessimism born of hard experience that prevailed four years later.

In his taxonomy of the factors of morale the director of Home Intelligence was correct to include the 'mental factors'. But his list was incomplete. For it accorded no place to the factor that has been the subject of this chapter. Here it has been suggested that how people actually behaved was, in part, a consequence of their perceptions of the future – more precisely of their own personal future. And to the extent that this was a relatively more appealing future than might have been in prospect before the war, it helped to sustain the people's commitment to the task of winning the war.

Notes

1 R. Titmuss, *Essays on the Welfare State* (Unwin, 2nd edn, 1963), p. 77.

2 S. Taylor, 'Home Morale and Public Opinion', September 1941, INF 1/292.

3 *Malvern 1941: The Proceedings of the Archbishop of York's Conference* (Longmans Green, 1941), pp. vii–viii.

4 M-O, File Report 1566, 13 January 1943.

5 Report of the 39th Annual Conference (Labour Party, 1940), pp. 123–5.

6 *Ibid.*, pp. 191–5.

7 A full discussion of Labour's pre-Beveridge reconstruction planning may be found in S. Brooke, *Labour's War: the Labour Party and the Second World War* (Oxford University Press, 1992), pp. 104–60.

8 'Should we stop criticising?', *Picture Post*, 31 January 1942.

9 *Picture Post*, 25 January 1941.

10 An indication, perhaps, of his unconscious exclusion of the 'forgotten women'?

11 A. Calder, *The Myth of the Blitz* (Jonathan Cape, 1991), p. 244.

12 N. Pronay, 'The Land of Promise: the Projection of Peace Aims in Britain', in K. R. M. Short (ed.), *Film and Radio Propaganda in World War II* (Croom Helm, 1983), pp. 53–4

13 Letter from *Picture Post* to K. Clark, 19 November 1940, INF 1/234.

14 H. Nicolson, *Diaries and Letters 1939–45* (Collins, 1967), diary entry for 22 January 1941, p. 139.

15 P. Calvocoressi and G. Wint, *Total War* (Penguin Books, 1972), p. 333.

16 Memorandum by S. Gates, 21 April 1941, INF 1/864.

17 M-O, File Report 1414, 'Reconstruction: hopes, fears and expectations for the post-war world', September 1942; File Report 688, 5 May 1941.

18 Assistance was given by Cecil King at the *Daily Mirror*, Tom Hopkinson and Edward Hulton at *Picture Post*, Gerald Barry at the *News Chronicle*, David Astor at the *Observer*, E. H. Carr at *The Times,* and by journalists Francis Williams and J. B. Priestley. See M. Bromley, 'Was it the Mirror Wot Won it? The Development of the Tabloid Press During the Second World War', in N.

Hayes and J. Hill (eds), *Millions Like Us? British Culture and the Second World War* (Liverpool University Press, 1999), p. 109.

19 *Report of the Committee on Social Insurance and Allied Services* (HMSO, 1942).

20 2 December 1942.

21 The description is by Mollie Panter-Downes in *London War Notes 1939–1945* (Longman, 1972), p. 252.

22 For a discussion of this and a detailed comparative analysis of how tabloid papers and magazines developed during the war, see Bromley, 'Was it the Mirror Wot Won it?' in Hayes and Hill (eds), *Millions Like Us?*, pp. 93–124.

23 *Ibid.*, p. 116.

24 The British Institute of Public Opinion, *The Beveridge Report and the Public*, 1943.

25 M-O, File Report 1538.

26 *Speaking Out: a Public Affairs Handbook* (Women's Institute, 1994), p. 52.

27 H. I. Weekly Report, 1–8 December 1942, INF 1/292.

28 H. I. Weekly Report, 8–15 December 1942, INF 1/292.

29 M-O, File Report 1538.

30 P. Addison, *The Road to 1945: British Politics and the Second World War* (Pimlico, 1994), p. 217; I. McLaine, *Ministry of Morale: Home Front Morale and Ministry of Information in World War II* (Allen & Unwin, 1979), p. 181.

31 *The Times*, 19 February 1943; *The Economist*, 20 and 27 February 1943.

32 M-O, File Report 1634.

33 H. I. Weekly Report 16–23 February 1943, INF 1/292.

34 See discussion in J. Ramsden, *The Age of Churchill and Eden 1940–1957*, vol. 5 of *A History of the Conservative Party* (Longman, 1995), pp. 42–5.

35 M-O, File Report 1786, 25 May 1943.

36 A. Aldgate and J. Richards, *Britain Can Take It: British Cinema in the Second World War* (Edinburgh University Press, 1986), p. 15.

37 For a discussion of the work of the WFA, see A. Burton, 'Projecting the New Jerusalem: the Workers Film Association, 1938–1946', in P. Kirkham and D. Thoms (eds), *War Culture: Social Change and Changing Experience in World War Two* (Lawrence & Wishart, 1995), pp. 73–84.

38 S. Nicholas, *The Echo of War: Home Front Propaganda and the Wartime BBC* (Manchester University Press, 1996), pp. 253–5.

39 H. I. Special Report, 31 May 1944, INF 1/293.

40 R. J. Wybrow, *Britain speaks Out: 1937–1987* (Macmillan, 1989), p. 16.

41 M-O, *The Journey Home* (John Murray, 1944), p. 116.

42 M-O, 'Social Security and Parliament', *Political Quarterly*, vol. 14, 1943.

43 R. Titmuss, *Problems of Social Policy* (HMSO, 1950), p. 506.

44 *Ibid.*, p. 509.

45 *Ibid.*, p. 510.

46 S. Ferguson and H. Fitzgerald, *Studies in the Social Services* (HMSO, 1954), p. 157.

47 *Ibid.*, pp. 160–2.

48 *Ibid.*, pp. 163–6.

49 *Ibid.*, pp. 190, 231.

50 'Christine Reporting on War Nurseries', *Walton Times,* 21 October 1943. Cited in P. Ayers, *Women at War* (Liver Press, 1988), p. 27.
51 Memorandum by S. Gates, 21 April 1942, INF 1/864.
52 G. Orwell, 'The Limit to Pessimism', *New English Weekly,* 25 April 1940.
53 M-O, File Report 600.

CONCLUSION

The invisible chain

I N THE FIRST PART of this study an attempt was made to consider afresh the familiar civilian experience of the Second World War in Britain with a view to assessing how well the morale of the ordinary people came through that time of trial. That it did not break was not the point at issue – no one has ever suggested it did. The issue was, simply, where on the continuum from 'low' to 'high', from 'poor' to 'good' would one, in retrospect, place the spirit and behaviour of the people during those six years.

This investigation arrived at an unequivocal conclusion: the 'negative' features emphasized by revisionist historians, although indisputably present, were not on such a scale as to invalidate the orthodox picture of a people who became actively committed to the project their leaders put before them, who cooperated with the drastic re-ordering of daily life that this entailed and who, on the whole, did so in a spirit of stoical endurance that did not exclude good humour. Undoubtedly, as contemporary observers recorded, there were times when spirits appeared generally low and when commitment and active effort seems to have slackened. But so, too, there were times when the reverse was true: it is not possible to argue that there was consistency of mood and behaviour – although one doubts the value of attempts to find significance in this. In any case, the 'lows' did not last for long and were more than outweighed by the 'highs', the mean coming, perhaps, between 'middling' and 'good'. It is clear, moreover that the great majority of the civilian population were for rather than against the war effort: those who were apathetic or obstructive were so few as to be tolerated without official resort to repression. It was possible in 1941 for people opposing the war or critical of the Government to address their views to their fellow citizens every weekend in Hyde Park without any more harassment than the largely good-humoured heckling of the onlookers.

How does war-weariness fit into this picture? That it existed and that the Government saw it as something to be countered is undeniable. But in retrospect, it seems unimportant. What could be more natural than to long for the war to be over – as everybody surely did? Few among even the most committed would look back on the war years as 'the time of their lives' – though having taken part would be something about which many more remained intensely proud – like Ethel Singleton, who hadn't wanted to leave her job as shop assistant, but who later looked back proudly on her five years welding aircraft fuel tanks in an engineering factory: 'I think afterwards it made us feel good, you know, that we'd actually done a job that was worthwhile.'[1] For most people, the war was at the time rather something to be got through, something they did not expect to enjoy but knew they had to take part in. War-weariness, in short, was an inseparable part of war itself. Potentially, it was dysfunctional for the war effort, but at a certain level, it was not incompatible with it. People could hate the war and resent its massive intrusion into their lives and yet carry on performing their allocated roles on the home front. For the logic of the situation was that only by such effort would come the longed-for end to the war.

The situation, however, required more than just going through the motions. In assessing *how well* civilians performed, one needs to bear in mind that the subjects under scrutiny here were ordinary, fallible human beings, caught up in a situation not of their choosing that at the very least turned their lives upside down and at worst threatened them and their families with violent, premature death. In these stressful circumstances, on the evidence, most people behaved well, and it is on this fact that generalization about the nation must rest, rather than on the behaviour of the minority who behaved badly. Even at critical periods in a nation's history – and this was one – when people feel that the things that bind them to one another are strengthened rather than weakened, there will always be some who think and act in anti-social ways. It should come as no surprise that prejudice, selfishness and criminality continued to exist in wartime Britain, despite the obvious damage to the communal project these defects could – and did – inflict. The firing of the starting-gun in September 1939 did not – could not – transform everybody into model citizens, all equally anxious

to demonstrate their civic and patriotic virtue. To presume, therefore, that any behaviour that deviated from the stereotype of 'the
spirit of Dunkirk' is evidence of the absolute emptiness of that
stereotype would be as absurd as an insistence on its absolute
veracity. And more seriously, it would be a libel on the majority –
the great mass of ordinary people whose attitude and behaviour
was more consistent with that phrase than not. A more reasonable presumption to make would be that among a nation of forty-
five million there would be a proportion to whom the very concept
of 'nation' meant little or nothing, who had no respect for law or
for the constituted authorities, who could not understand – let
alone become part of – the notion of communal effort in a 'people's
war'. The wonder is that so many of them chose to become part
of that effort or at the very least did nothing to impede it.

Before the war and during its first eighteen months the ruling
elites, and many others besides, had had serious doubts about the
capacity of British society to hold together under the intense pressures of another total war. In the event, their pessimism proved
ill-founded. The bogeys of pacifism, class antagonism, regional
separatism and political dissidence receded to the point where they
could effectively be disregarded. And in the meantime the Government organized the people for total war to a degree only sur-
passed by the Soviet Union.[2] It is quite probable that many among
them were largely unmoved by lofty appeals to their patriotism or
were perfectly aware that the public image of how others were
already behaving contained some imaginative embellishment. But
they did not in consequence refuse the cooperation on which the
winning of the war depended. Rather they went along with it to a
degree that permitted the national project to succeed. If the traditional picture of the British people during the war is misleading, it
is only in this – its assumption that most people did much more
than put up with things, that selfless and enthusiastic cooperation
was virtually the norm, that people like the unusually proactive
Richard Brown and Nella Last were typical. This is not tenable. It
seems, therefore, that there are grounds for reviewing the traditional picture, to acknowledge that it is in need of some modifica-
tion – as, perhaps, unduly influenced by the propaganda myth
constructed at the time. The evidence however, does not support
its total rejection as merely the product of myth-making. In its

broad contours it remains a largely truthful representation of how things were in the home front war.

To re-assert the basic veracity of the received picture of the British people in the war is not difficult: the evidence is clear enough. But to *explain* it, the historian is obliged to move onto altogether less certain terrain – the inside of people's minds. The picture here is constructed – ultimately, can *only* be constructed – from the glimpses afforded into why people felt and acted as they did that survives in the incomplete patchwork record of contemporary voices, some specifically attempting to set down the motivation of others, others speaking only for themselves. What emerges is a predictably complex picture in which, for every individual, morale was created out of an interplay between the public and the private, the sense of being part of a community and the private need to meet the war on one's own terms.

Much official effort went into trying to win and retain the people's hearts and minds for the task in hand, to get them to think and behave 'correctly'. The Government did not take for granted that in war the people would acquire a heightened sense of national identity and would have confidence in victory, even when these characteristics manifested themselves at quite an early stage. How much, if any, of the official effort was actually necessary is difficult, probably impossible, to determine. On the other hand, people appreciated the steps taken by the Government to protect them and to improve the material conditions of their lives, albeit without having any illusions as to why it did so. None of these steps was a waste of effort. The real value of these measures lay in making a potentially unbearable situation bearable, in providing, as it were, a culture medium in which good behaviour would flourish. While they may not, therefore, have been absolutely essential to the mental buoyancy of the civilian body nor to its generally supportive attitude and cooperative behaviour, they nevertheless form part of the wider framework of explanation. Given the generally low regard in which parties and politicians were traditionally held – the war did not overnight lead people to abandon the mildly cynical attitude towards politicians that was the cultural norm in mid-twentieth century Britain – it is notable that during the war years, when politicians meddled in people's lives as never before, there was no sense that the country was badly governed by men who did not deserve the backing of the citizens. Most people felt that the war-time regime, for all its flaws, was basically fair and that the Government was as responsive to welfare needs as the constraining economic situation allowed. This was the context in which auster-ity – and its creator, the Lord Privy Seal, Sir Stafford Cripps – was actually popular and in which rationing and even the conscription of women were welcomed.[3]

Since things did not fall apart, since the more optimistic scenario of civilian 'performance' was in fact realized, one is tempted to wonder whether it would have happened thus, anyway, regardless of the carefully calculated policies of the authorities. Seen from the official standpoint, however, the depth of the well of popular good-will was unknowable. One can only speculate upon the consequences had the leaders relied only on appeals to national sentiment and neglected the welfare of the people. For its part, the Government could with reason feel quietly gratified when intelligence was re-ceived in March 1943 that the failure of the Italian authorities ad-equately to protect and care for civilian workers in the northern cities, who at that time were being subjected to heavy RAF bomb-ing raids, had seriously undermined morale and stoked the fires of anti-war and anti-Mussolini sentiment. It was the avoidance of just such negative consequences of total war that provided the ratio-nale for its own policies of care and protection on the home front.

Mostly, when asked, people did not see themselves as much per-suaded – nor needing to be persuaded – by propaganda or other inducements to cooperate. There is quite strong evidence that the people knew very well their performance was being watched and worried over, and that they rather resented the implication that they were poor-spirited or could not be trusted to know just what was happening in the war – nor do the proper thing when they did know. They cooperated because they understood it was necessary. Churchill was right, therefore, when he instinctively felt that his resolute and defiant stance in 1940 was what most people wanted him to adopt, because that was how they felt, too; and he was right in believing, during the long haul that followed, that they might grumble continuously, but underneath they were as determined as he to see the war through to a victorious conclusion. By all ac-counts he paid little attention to his standing in opinion polls, but if he had, he would surely have been confirmed in his conviction that his instincts about the collective will were correct. He offered them a single, uncompromising course of action, and they rallied behind him and continued to have confidence in him through the long wait for the turn of the military tide. When Churchill spoke of Britain standing between civilization and barbarism, the average citizen took this to mean that the British way of life was threatened by an alien force; and, for all its faults, that way of life was preferable to Nazism and worth fighting to retain. At its most basic this is what patriotic feeling consisted of – an attachment to familiar ways of doing things, rooted in a familiar place. In the autumn of 1941 Mass-Observation asked its observers to set down 'What Britain Means to You'. The replies, though hardly constituting a representative sample of the population, nevertheless provide a revealing insight into some of the national attributes with which people identified at this point in the war. In contrast to the high-flown stuff of leaders' speeches and heroic films, the content was altogether more prosaic, banal even. Above all things came the countryside – the variety of the orderly farms and picturesque villages, the rocky coves, the gentle hills and rugged uplands. Then, in order, came politics, people and home, and again the emphasis was on how things worked, looked and felt, rather than on abstract ideas about constitutional rights and freedoms. Thus we read of the 'easy tolerance and good humour' of the British, and 'the feeling that in Britain you need not feel afraid'.[4] Flag-waving patriotism was notable by its absence. As Tom Harrisson observed in an article based on the survey that he wrote for the *World Review*, when British people think about their country they bring to mind 'tangible and visible things they know and individual people whose characteristics they have known and can trust and feel affection for ... this is the land [they] were brought up on, that is the beginning and end of it'.[5]

This 'gut patriotism' was already aroused a year or more before Mass-Observation's survey. 'In those weeks in May and June', wrote Margery Allingham in the autumn of 1940, 'I think ninety-nine percent of English folk, country and town, found their souls ... They'd rather die when it came to it than be bossed about by a Nazi ... If we are not free tomorrow, we shall not be happy tomorrow.'[6] The delusion that the British way of life could survive without a fight – without victory over Nazism – was evident to most by the time of the fall of France in June 1940 and quite dispelled by the deadly dual of the Battle of Britain and the murderous experience of the Blitz in the months that followed. 'We are carrying on because we have got to', wrote a 20-year-old Mass-Observation diarist during the bombing in Manchester in December 1940 – a plain-spoken recognition that everyone was in the same boat and there were no real alternatives to the course that Churchill had set.[7] But to interpret this as evidence that cooperation resulted merely from a sense of the futility of resistance would be to underestimate the strength of the visceral emotions the threatening situation aroused. The support was unconditional, requiring no promises, no prior deal. And significantly, it was given *before* leaders and led went together through the unifying cauldron of the Blitz.

At the start of that experience it seemed to the inhabitants of the East End that they alone were to be the victims. This apprehension was short-lived, however, fading away as the bombing extended to other parts of the capital and then to other cities, and the same sense of being 'all in it together' was reinforced: suffering shared was suffering endured. There is even some evidence that the bombing actually strengthened morale and the determination to survive and rebuild – evidence matched, incidentally, by the German experience under Allied bombing.[8] This was how the young diarist Colin Perry saw it after viewing the spirited way the people of bomb-hit Morden 'carried on': 'There will never be any breaking of the British morale; we do not get jittery, only harder, grimmer and determined the more.'[9] Angus Calder believed that the decline in the suicide rate during the war derived from the heightened sense it brought of being part of a community, of having a common experience and a common goal, which gave 'a proud and even gay motive for existence'.[10] Contemporary observers often acknowledged the existence of disharmonies in the war effort. But they invariably discounted their significance alongside the broad picture. As Margery Allingham, in her small rural community, put it: 'It was all talk, and we are fighting to say what we like.'[11]

No one was more surprised by this than George Orwell, who believed that the bitterly class-ridden society that Britain was in the 1930s could hardly pull itself together to fight a war, let alone win one. To his credit he admitted his error when he was proved wrong. In December 1940 he wrote: 'England is the most class-ridden country under the sun ... But in any calculation about it one has got to take into account its emotional unity, the tendency of nearly all its inhabitants to feel alike and act together in moments of supreme crisis ... The nation is bound together by an invisible chain ... Patriotism is finally stronger than class-hatred.'[12] In this the Coalition Government that Churchill formed was itself powerfully symbolic: when erstwhile political adversaries had sunk their differences and became part of a single team, their call for the people to do likewise was bound to succeed. But it did not matter that in standing together the British people had various, even opposing, notions of what they were fighting for – as various as the things about Britain that were important to them.[13] The point was that, for whatever reason, they had common ground in the belief that compromise with the enemy was unthinkable, that there was no alternative to seeing the struggle through and that this was best achieved by acting together. As the war proceeded, the accumulated shared experience of life on the home front, together with the public discourse about what it meant to be British, served to reinforce people's sense of being part of a national community.

The instinctive closing of ranks that Orwell witnessed helps to explain the remarkable upsurge of morale in June 1940 and the almost enthusiastic acceptance by the people of the extraordinary measures and demands the Government announced. Mollie Panter-Downes was already anticipating this at the end of May: 'They are ready emotionally for the most drastic measures Mr Churchill may choose to take', she wrote.[14] When the official historians came to reflect on this time they confirmed those contemporary impressions: [The British people] 'now passionately attached themselves to the war. This was the great transforming fact, the motive power of all subsequent achievement.'[15] Of great symbolic importance in all this was Churchill's decision to reject 'Black Move' – the plan made before the war to shift the Government itself out of London when the bombing began. By deciding to stay, Churchill – like the King, who also stayed, to the lasting esteem of the House of Windsor – made yet more solid the support of the ordinary citizen for his stand and for his programme of action.

While it is true that the Government gave itself enforcement powers that in theory could have enabled it to get its way at any point in the war, in practice it was not the fear of compulsion that led the mass of the people to cooperate. In fact, when a matter of principle was involved, particular groups were prepared to depart from their cooperative stance and stand firm against the Government, as in the Betteshanger miners' strike in 1941–42. In this instance the Government ultimately retreated from compulsion and the miners achieved their objective.[16] The argument which is sometimes heard, that the people did as they were told in the Second World War because they were cowed into acquiescence by the threat of vigorous official action against resisters, is not easily sustained in the face of such evidence. In practice the Government normally judged strong-arm tactics to be counter-productive, literally – striking miners produced no coal. In any case, the reality was that most workers never contemplated striking. More typical was Doris Scott, who was twice evacuated from London's dockland with her two young children and who worked part-time at an engineering firm in Henley, making aeroplane parts: 'Oh well, Churchill was exhorting everyone to do their bit. Oh! I was thrilled! I thought, my God, I'm helping in the war effort, and I was so thrilled to be taken on and given my own lathe to work on – oh! I felt so important and happy about it!' Or Molly Weir, who also volunteered for war work: 'I was directed into this factory making what they called fragmentation bombs. I was proud to be there for I was very patriotic and never had any doubt that we'd win.'[17] Or, more mildly, Denise Aylmer-Moore, who went to train army horses: 'Did I feel patriotic at eighteen and a half? I don't know. I was glad I was doing war work, and I certainly would have gone on to the land if I hadn't been at the Remount Depot.'[18]

The positive response to the Government's call for an increase in the national effort on all fronts owed much to a mental context in which the possibility of defeat was denied. Constantine Fitzgibbon believed spirits were so high in Britain in May–June 1940 because the British people 'had no first-hand knowledge of defeat and, being a remarkably unimaginative people, have never been able to conceive of it as more than a theoretical possibility'.[19] Looking back from the comparative safety – in Ipswich, at least – of September 1944, Richard Brown reflected on the range of mental qualities the war had put to the test and concluded: 'Patience, I think, has been most exercised but I can't say that fear, fear of the outcome, I mean, was ever experienced except for a few days in the Dunkirk period perhaps.'[20] And in the long retrospect of 2000, some women recalled for a radio programme that even at the height of the Emergency, they were certain of ultimate victory: 'Everyone knew that we'd got our backs to the wall, but we had this confidence that somewhere, something would happen. It would take a long time. But it was all going to be all right in the end'; 'Nobody said: "Oh, let's give in", or anything like that. It just made us all the more determined to carry on'; 'It never occurred to me – it never occurred to any of my family – that we were going to lose that war. And that sort of kept us going, you know?'[21]

This conviction was buttressed by the knowledge, assiduously supplied by the press and radio, that offensive operations were being conducted against the enemy. In the early years this meant exclusively the bombing of Germany. There is no doubt that merely knowing that this was happening was important to many people's whole outlook. In the dreadful first week of the Blitz, the US military attaché, Raymond E. Lee visited Whitechapel and recorded in his diary: 'People were evacuating, others were grubbing about in the wreckage to salvage what they could. But no one was complaining. One workman said, "All we want to know is whether we are bombing Berlin. If they are getting all or more than we are, we can stick it".'[22] A month later, Churchill, also visiting the East End, heard the same refrain on every side: 'We can take it', but also 'Give it 'em back.'[23] Vere Hodgson, who stayed in London throughout the Blitz, recorded seeing the bombers going off to bomb the enemy in August 1943: 'It is a fine sight, and gives us a feeling of strength', and later, 'As I lay in bed ... I heard the deep purr of our bombers winging their way to Hamburg ... This is a comfortable feeling.'[24] Such an effect on morale was undoubtedly in the Government's mind when it began the strategic bombing campaign against Germany. In the 1940–42 period, for most of which Britain stood alone, bombing was arguably less a strategy for winning the war than a device to sustain morale at home. The 1000-bomber raid on Cologne on 30 May 1942, for instance, while undoubtedly successful in purely military terms, also helped to offset the morale-sapping effect of the 'Baedeker' raids, which were being made at this time on some of England's historic towns.[25]

It was perhaps fortunate that confidence in ultimate victory was subjected to its most testing time so early in the war. For after 1940–41, when nothing could seem worse than what was then experienced, the home front was able to be sustained, increasingly, by good news on the military fronts, balancing the war-weariness that was the inevitable effect of the sheer length of the war. And crucially, the long haul, dreary and burdensome though it was, was free of the undertow of fear that, for all the brave words, lurked in the minds of many in 1940–41 – that the war might be lost. A glimpse of the working of this factor can be seen in an entry from Mollie Panter-Downes's journal during the euphoria over the victory at El Alamein and the success of Operation Torch in Tunisia: 'The British success effectually knocked on the head the dangerous notion that German arms and leadership are infallible … Today, though sensible Britons think there's certain to be plenty of grimness ahead, for the first time they believe that sober reasons for hope are at last in sight.'[26] The stimulus of good news upon the war effort is widely attested to – when J. B. Priestley wrote his novel *Daylight on Saturday*, set in an aircraft factory, there was authenticity in his representation of the workers increasing their efforts and improving the factory's production figures on hearing the news of El Alamein.[27]

At several points in this study allusion has been made to the widely-shared sense that the war was a time of trial not just for the state and its institutions but for individuals in their own setting of family, workplace and local community. At the level of the local community it is evident – once the Phoney War gave way to the real war, at least – that the test became a matter of local pride, especially in relation to how the community bore up when the bombing came. How the people of London endured the Blitz with bravery and good humour was quickly established – doubtless in part through instant myth-making by propagandists – as a sort of yardstick against which every town that was subsequently bombed felt it was being measured or, indeed, measured itself. Mass-Observation judged that the stoicism it saw in the people of Coventry, ten days after the terrible raid of November 1940, came as much as anything from a shared feeling of pride – no community had suffered as badly as they and yet they were 'up and doing' in no time at all.[28] This ingredient of 'carrying on' was to be found practically everywhere, as if each city, as its turn to be bombed came, had a mental picture of how to behave, constructed from the newsreels and documentary films about previously raided cities. The sense of being on trial, of being under a national spot-light, typically extended through the entire community, from the councillors and paid officials who insisted on retaining local con-trol of operations, to the numberless individuals who acted self-lessly and sometimes heroically. This is only partly explained by the attempt to live up to the officially inspired media myths that were being created about the sturdy stoicism of the British. More impor-tant was society's moral pressure on the citizen to conform to the special norms of war, the norms that banished the very idea of de-featism. As Harrisson put it: 'In war ... the sanctions on staying steady are stronger in terms of respectability, good citizenship, the due observance of familiar and wider obligations.'[29] Thus were the primitive instincts of self-preservation and self-interest – themselves heightened in times of danger and disorder – frequently overridden by the group norms of the tribe at war.

The enhanced sense of being part of a group can also be attrib-uted, in part, to the special institutional structures of communal action that the war situation itself created. During these years positions of responsibility – in the ARP, the AFS, the Home Guard, the WVS, and the like – were held by many millions of adults who in the normal course of events would never have expected, or been expected, to have such roles. These positions usually entailed the absorption of knowledge and procedures and the acquisition of skills, during the course of which the individual became more fully a part of the structure of the local community. Citizenship, in short, had for a significant proportion of the civilian body a concrete referent in the performance of these roles. It ought also to be re-membered that the years of war, when everyone had a job to do, followed a long period of mass unemployment, when millions experienced demoralization and loss of self-respect. The war of-fered opportunities for relieving these feelings. Such a development was intrinsically favourable to the steadiness of the community first under fire and then through the long years of regimentation and restriction. It also, naturally, had a *political* dimension, cre-ating sources of potential conflict between and within the new groupings and between them and existing institutions. But far outweighing the pulling and hauling that inevitably accompa-nied the operation of the new arrangements was the strong sense of mutual dependence that stemmed from the basic reality of the situation: at this time the whole community, national and local, was threatened – everyone was equally a potential victim. This time, war was not something that only happened far away. The fact that it was brought literally into everyone's path made it impossible to put it out of mind for long and impossible not to feel more intensely part of a larger community than oneself and one's intimates. The contrast between the relatively weak sense of community that characterized the period of the Phoney War and the transformed mentality that emerged after the trauma of the bombs is indicative: war imagined was replaced by war experienced. Mass-Observation recorded this process in microcosm when it looked at the situation in Bristol in March 1941 and discovered a new social sub-stratum in the institution of fire-watching. In some districts the fire-watchers got together in one another's houses in turns to play cards; some met as a group in particular pubs. Since the members were typically drawn from all classes, Mass-Observation thought the functional activity that had brought them together was probably serving to break down class barriers. This was Richard Brown's own experience in the Home Guard. Writing at a much later point in the war – May 1944 – he reflected on one of the unexpected outcomes of taking part: 'There is a camaraderie in the [HG] platoon which one doesn't get anywhere in peace life. It's a sort of mass friendship I would never have experienced in peacetime.'[30] For him and his colleagues, at least, the spirit of the Blitz seemed as strong after nearly five years of war as it had been in 1940.

Perhaps it was the existence of such feelings that encouraged people to hope the war experience would foster the construction of a better society after victory was won and to reject the jibe of 'wishful thinking'. Illusion or not, the salience of reconstruction talk from 1941, the laying of some of its building blocks in 1943–44 and the ubiquity of the 'Never Again' mentality were powerful counters to the inherent tendency of extended war to depress the human spirit. Since without hope there is no energy and no commitment, the performance of the British in this regard for several years beyond the point where defeat threatened, suggests a nation that looked to a better future. In the several years it took to defeat the Axis powers, the promise of that future gave added purpose to the task.

Heightened sense of national identity, participation, shared dangers, the hope of a better future – all these created a favourable context for the maintenance of civilian morale. But no scrutiny of the contemporary social record and the retrospective recall of those who lived through the war years can fail to notice that, strong though the communitarian spirit was, for many people – probably most people – an absolutely essential ingredient of personal morale was having some entirely self-centred means of mental escape from the war. The precondition of being able to do this was to have become accustomed to the nature of war – including the risk of being hit by bombs. It is evident that the ability to do this was so common as to be counted normal, even allowing for the fact that the really fearful had mostly left the danger areas at an early stage, leaving behind only the mentally more resilient majority.[31] Thereafter, people increasingly appear to have simply adjusted to the changed 'normality', and settled into its special routines. Vere Hodgson gave several instances of this remarkable adaptation. She recorded a tale told her by a woman with whom she had got into conversation in a café: 'She was having luncheon in Oxford St. Suddenly a terrific wonk shook the place; all the cups and saucers danced and rattled about the table. The man opposite her said calmly: "That was a bomb, wasn't it?" She replied: "I'm sure it was". And they all continued to eat their meal.' Taking a lunchtime walk in Kensington Gardens, Vere Hodgson found that despite the fact that part of the park was roped off because of an unexploded bomb, people still sat in seats alongside. 'People were peacefully sitting in those seats, and some had even penetrated the barrier, and were happily basking on the grass in the sunshine. Shows how indifferent we have got.'[32] Reading her journal one also notices that she herself unconsciously slipped into referring to the raids as if reporting on the weather: 'Very blitzy tonight'. The nonchalance of individuals was not exceptional. It was encountered by Mass-Observation whenever it studied a community that was experiencing air raids. In Southampton, for instance, one month after the raids that gutted the town centre, it noticed that people were taking little or no notice of sirens unless they were accompanied by the noise of bombs or guns.[33]

Getting away from the war for most people meant defying the constraints of dark streets, fewer buses and trams and engaging in social activity of some kind. In Sheffield, J. L. Hodson came across 'fellowship groups' – informal gatherings in people's homes to play music, read plays, discuss art and religion or work at some handicraft.[34] For young people a much more typical getaway was dancing. The war years witnessed a great increase in dancing; regular dance halls extended the dancing week and in every place where the war threw young people together – hostels, army camps, air bases – dances were organized for the growing throng of enthusiasts for the craze. It was again in bomb-shattered Southampton – although in this it was not unusual – that Mass-Observation found the otherwise dead and desolate centre enlivened by youthful crowds flocking to dances at the Guildhall and Banister Hall.[35] The dancing craze was given an extra stimulus when bases were set up to house the thousands of US forces that arrived in Britain for the strategic bombing offensive against Germany and for the build-up to Operation Overlord. May Reeves recalled their enormous impact on her and her friends in Wigton: 'For teenagers it was heaven. We just didn't realise there was a war on. All we were doing was having a good time. I had brothers away fighting; naturally, I worried about them, but we were having such a good time that you didn't realise that they were away actually fighting in the war. We were too busy enjoying ourselves all round the place. Dances all round.'[36] Was this ability to banish troublesome thoughts about the war simply the callousness of youth? More probably it reflected a psychological need – one that everyone shared – to do precisely this. And it is clear that, in one way or another, everyone did. For many it came in the form of a visit to the cinema or theatre; Vere Hodgson braved the bombs to do so: 'Went to the theatre ... *Dear Brutus* ... Most enjoyable – felt we had just been let out of prison.'[37] For others it was the less structured mental escape of reading or music. The increase in the sales of poetry books and the appearance of several new poetry magazines was one of the more remarkable aspects of a general upsurge in reading. As for music, Mollie Panter-Downes was unequivocal: 'we need the rectifying influence of music, which can stand for an immutable order of being, unshaken by the shocks of politics'.[38] And *The Times* recorded people satisfying that need in the National Gallery's lunchtime concerts: 'People hurry out into Trafalgar Square, shouldering their gas masks and looking all the better for having been lifted for an hour to a plane where boredom and fear seem irrelevant.'[39] That was for the few; most people relied for musical (and other) escape on the BBC, that taken for granted but comforting background to millions of lives through the long years of war.

But what is striking about the 'escaping' phenomenon is that it could take a great variety of forms – there was no formula that served everyone equally well. It might consist of no more than finding space for a long-established pastime. For the little group of men with whom the writer H. E. Bates spent many hours on a Kentish riverbank it was plain what worked for them. As one of them put it: 'If it wasn't for the fishing, we should all go bloody crazy!'[40] Retaining one's sanity was, indeed, the whole *raison d'être* of such apparently profligate use of time, when victory supposedly depended on maximizing the nation's labour potential. Human beings caught up in the whirlwind of that mobilization and its side-effects instinctively found their own special ways of coping with it: ultimately, in this time of community, one had to make the personal adjustment that enabled one as a unique individual to carry on. This surely comes close to what Tom Harrisson meant when he spoke of morale 'going on at another level'.[41]

Everyone who lived through this time would readily have understood this idea that there was more to morale than what the Government and its agents said or did. And yet there was always an awareness that the process of individual adjustment was not wholly divorced from – indeed, needed as its complement – what others in the wider community were feeling and doing. And most felt to some degree assisted in it by the measures the leaders of that community – the Government – took to create an environment helpful to adjustment and commitment, one that afforded protection and reassurance and which eased the burdens of war, even down to releasing the resources that enabled new poems to be read and new feature films to be seen. As it was perceived so it was in reality. In the end it was this combination of 'public' and 'private' factors, operating within a mental framework of common identity and shared destiny – the 'invisible chain' – that determined civilian morale. Uncoordinated and lacking comprehensiveness or even consistency, it was nevertheless a combination that worked well enough for that contradictory and perplexing entity, the British nation, to survive with honours its most threatening and taxing challenge.

Notes

1 P. Summerfield, *Reconstructing Women's Wartime Lives* (Manchester University Press, 1998), p. 96.

2 In a comparison of resource mobilization in Britain, Germany, the USA and the USSR, M. Harrison concluded that Britain had 45.3 per cent of its working population in war-related work, alongside the USA's 35.4 per cent and Germany's 37.6 per cent and the USSR's 54 per cent. See M. Harrison, 'Resource Mobilization for World War II: the USA, UK. USSR, and Germany', *The Economic History Review*, vol. 41, no. 2, 1988, p. 185.

3 A. Calder, *The People's War: Britain 1939–45* (Jonathan Cape, 1969), pp. 275–82.

4 M-O, File Reports 878 September 1941, and 904, October 1941.

5 T. Harrisson, 'What Britain Means to Me', M-O, File Report 904.

6 M. Allingham, *The Oaken Heart: the Story of an English Village at War* (Sarsen Publishing, [1941], 1987), p. 220.

7 T. Harrisson, *Living Through the Blitz* (Collins, 1976), p. 249.

8 See, for example, C. Bielenberg, *The Past is Myself* (Corgi, 1984), p. 127.

9 C. Perry, *Boy in the Blitz*, (Colin A. Perry, 1972), p. 69.

10 Calder, *The People's War*, p. 357.

11 Allingham, *The Oaken Heart*, pp. 369–71.

12 S. Orwell and I. Angus (eds), *The Collected Essays, Journalism and Letters of George Orwell*, vol. 2, (Penguin,1970), pp. 87, 118.

13 John Baxendale has made a compelling case for the heterogeneous nature of feelings of national identity in the war years. See J. Baxendale, '"You and I – All of Us Ordinary People": Renegotiating "Britishness" in Wartime', in N. Hayes and J. Hill (eds), *Millions Like Us? British Culture and the Second World War* (Liverpool University Press, 1999), pp. 295–322.

14 M. Panter-Downes, *London War Notes 1939–1945* (Longman, 1972), p. 61.

15 W. Hancock and M. Gowing, *The British War Economy* (HMSO, 1949), p. 209.

16 The miners at Betteshanger had gone on strike over pay. Although the three leaders of their local trade union branch were jailed and all the men were fined, the strike continued until settled in the miners' favour nineteen days later. Their victory was reinforced by the release of the imprisoned officials soon after.

17 Doris Scott, recorded interview, Imperial War Museum audiotape, *The Home Front 1939–1945*; Molly Weir, in M. Nicholson (ed.), *What Did You Do in the War, Mummy?* (Chatto & Windus, 1995), p. 139.

18 *Ibid.*, p. 101.

19 C. Fitzgibbon, *The Blitz* (Macdonald, 1957), p. 37.

20 H. Millgate (ed.), *Mr Brown's War: a Diary of the Second World War* (Sutton, 1998), p. 228.

21 'The Summer of 1940', BBC Radio 2 programme, August 2000.

22 J. Leutze (ed.), *The London Observer: The Journal of General Raymond E. Lee 1940–41* (Hutchinson, 1972), p. 51.

23 T. H. O'Brien, *Civil Defence* (HMSO, 1955), p. 398.

24 V. Hodgson, *Few Eggs and No Oranges* (Denis Dobson, 1976), pp. 329, 331.
25 See N. Frankland, *Bomber Offensive: the Devastation of Europe* (Purnell, 1969), p. 49.
26 Panter-Downes, *London War Notes*, pp. 249–50.
27 J. B. Priestley, *Daylight on Saturday* (Heinemann, 1943), p. 286.
28 Harrisson, *Living Through the Blitz*, p. 137; M-O, File Report 495.
29 Harrisson, *Living Through the Blitz*, p. 94.
30 Millgate (ed.), *Mr Brown's War*, p. 218.
31 Tom Harrisson calculated that by October 1940 something like a quarter of London's population was gone from the capital. See Harrisson, *Living Through the Blitz*, p. 96.
32 Hodgson, *Few Eggs and No Oranges*, pp. 112, 153.
33 M-O, File Report 603.
34 J. L. Hodson, *The Land and the Sea* (Gollancz, 1945), p. 254.
35 M-O, File Report 603.
36 May Reeves (née Charters). Cited in M. Bragg, *Speak for England* (Secker & Warburg, 1976), pp. 265–6.
37 Hodgson, *Few Eggs and No Oranges*, p. 152.
38 Panter-Downes, *London War Notes*, 24 November 1939, p. 27.
39 *The Times*, 24 November 1939.
40 H. E. Bates, *In the Heart of the Country* (Robinson, 1985), p. 123. First published in *Country Life*, 1942.
41 See the final paragraph of Chapter 4.

BIBLIOGRAPHY

Primary sources

Manuscript sources

BBC Written Archives, Reading

Mass-Observation Archive, University of Sussex

Public Record Office, London:

CAB 16/157 Reports of the CID Sub-Committee on Food Supply in Time of War

CAB 65 War Cabinet Minutes

CAB 66 War Cabinet Memoranda

CAB 67 Other memoranda

CAB 68 Reports by government departments to the Cabinet

CAB 71 Lord President's committees

CAB 72 Board of Trade (Defence Plans) Department (1936–39)

HO 199 Ministry of Home Security intelligence reports, reports on air raids and civilian morale

HO 262 Ministry of Home Security correspondence with Ministry of Information

INF 1 Ministry of Information minutes, memoranda and correspondence, Home Intelligence reports and related propaganda material

MAF 72 Ministry of Food

RG 23 Wartime Social Survey: reports and papers

Printed sources

Hansard, House of Commons Debates, Fifth Series.

The Gallup International Opinion Polls: Great Britain, 1937–1964, vol. I, Random House, 1976.

Fighting with Figures, HMSO, 1995.

Report of the Food (Defence Plans) Department of the Board of Trade, HMSO, 1937.

Report of the Committee on Social Insurance and Allied Services, HMSO, 1942.

Report of the Committee on Evacuation, HMSO, 1940.

Council of Social Services (Liverpool) Bulletin No. 51, 'Rest Breaks for Women Workers', 1941.

Report of the 39th Annual Conference, Labour Party, 1940.

Labour's Aims in War and Peace, Labour Party, 1940.

The Old World and the New Society, Labour Party, 1942.

The Beveridge Report and the Public, British Institute of Public Opinion, 1943.

Malvern 1941: The Proceedings of the Archbishop of York's Conference (Longmans Green, 1941).

Diaries, letters and other contemporary writing

Allingham, M., *The Oaken Heart: the Story of an English Village at War*, Sarsen Publishing, 1987 (first published 1941).

Bates, H. E., *In the Heart of the Country*, Robinson, 1985 (first published in *Country Life*, 1942).

Beardmore, G., *Civilians at War: Journals 1938–46*, Oxford University Press, 1986.

Berlin, I., *Mr. Churchill in 1940*, John Murray, 1949.

Broad, R., and S. Fleming (eds), *Nella Last's War,* Falling Wall Press, 1981.

Crompton, M., Diary, Imperial War Museum.

Hodgson, V., *Few Eggs and No Oranges*, Denis Dobson, 1976.

Hodson, J. L., *The Land and the Sea*, Gollancz, 1945.

Hodson, J. L., *Towards the Morning*, Gollancz, 1941.

Jameson, S. (ed.), *London Calling*, Harper, 1942.

Katin, Z., *'Clippie': the Autobiography of a War Time Conductress*, John Gifford, 1944.

Leutze, J. (ed.), *The London Observer: the Journal of General Raymond E. Lee 1940–41*, Hutchinson, 1972.

MacCurdy, J. T., *The Structure of Morale*, Cambridge University Press, 1943.

Mass-Observation, *The Journey Home*, John Murray, 1944.

Mass-Observation, *People in Production: an Enquiry into British War Production*, Part I, John Murray, 1942.

Mass-Observation, 'Social Security and Parliament', *Political Quarterly*, vol. 14, 1943.

Milburn, C., *Mrs Milburn's Diaries*, Fontana/Collins, 1980.

Millgate, H. (ed.), *Mr Brown's War: a Diary of the Second World War*, Sutton, 1998.

Minney, R. J. (ed.), *The Private Papers of Hore-Belisha*, Collins, 1960.

Morton, W. A., *British Finance 1930–1940*, University of Wisconsin Press, WI, 1943.

Nicolson, H., *Diaries and Letters 1939–45*, Collins, 1967.

Orwell, G., Review of Crozier's *The Men I Have Killed*, *New Statesman and Nation*, 28 August 1937.

Orwell, S., and I. Angus (eds), *The Collected Essays, Journalism and Letters of George Orwell*, 4 vols, Penguin, 1970.

Padley, R., and M. Cole, *Evacuation Survey*, Routledge, 1940.

Panter-Downes, M., *Good Evening Mrs Craven*, Persephone Press, 1999.

Panter-Downes, M., *London War Notes 1939–1945*, Longman, 1972.

Parker, D., 'Goodbye, My Love', in *The Portable Dorothy Parker*, New York, Viking Penguin, 1973 (first published 1944).

Partridge, F., *A Pacifist's War*, Phoenix, 1996.

Perry, C., *Boy in the Blitz*, Colin A. Perry Ltd., 1972.

Priestley, J. B., *Daylight on Saturday*, Heinemann, 1943.

Priestley, J. B., *Postscripts*, Heinemann, 1940.

Richards, J., and D. Sheridan (eds), *Mass-Observation at the Movies*, Routledge & Kegan Paul, 1987.

Sanford, R. N., and H. S. Conrad, 'Some Personality Correlates of Morale', *Journal of Abnormal and Social Psychology*, vol. 38, 1943.

Sheridan, D. (ed.), *Among You Taking Notes: the Wartime Diary of Naomi Mitchison 1939–1945*, Oxford University Press, 1986.

Sheridan, D. (ed.), *Wartime Women*, Heinemann, 1990.

Smith, H., *Britain in the Second World War: a Social History*, Manchester University Press, 1996.

Waugh, E., *Put Out More Flags*, Weidenfeld and Nicholson, 1997 (first published 1943).

Women's Institute, *Speaking Out: a Public Affairs Handbook*, Women's Institute, 1994.

Wyatt, W. (ed.), *English Story, 6th Series*, Collins, 1945.

Young, K. (ed.), *The Diaries of Sir Robert Bruce Lockhart*, Macmillan, 2 vols, 1973–80.

Newspapers and journals

Daily Express
Daily Herald
Daily Mail
Daily Mirror
Daily Telegraph
The Economist
New English Weekly
News Chronicle
Picture Post
The Spectator
The Sunday Times
The Times
Time and Tide

Memoirs and biography

Bielenberg, C., *The Past is Myself*, Corgi, 1984.

Blishen, E., *A Cackhanded War*, Thames & Hudson, 1972.

Bragg, M., *Speak for England*, Secker & Warburg, 1976.

Cudlipp, H., *Publish and be Damned!*, Andrew Dakers, 1953.

Dalton, H., *The Fateful Years*, Frederick Muller, 1957.

Fairbrother, N., *Children in the House*, The Hogarth Press, 1954.

Longmate, N., *How We Lived Then*, Hutchinson, 1971.

Macmillan, H., *Winds of Change*, Macmillan, 1956.

Morrison, H., *An Autobiography*, Odhams, 1960.

Nicholson, M., *What Did You Do in the War Mummy?* Chatto & Windus, 1995.

Ritchie, C., *The Siren Years*, Macmillan, 1974.

Townsend, C. and E., *War Wives: a Second World War Anthology*, Grafton Books, 1989.

Winant, J. G., *Letter from Grosvenor Square,* Hodder & Stoughton, 1947.

Woolton, Lord, *Memoirs*, Cassell, 1959.

Secondary sources

Addison, P., 'Introduction', *The British People and World War II: Home Intelligence Reports on Opinion and Morale, 1940–1944*, University of Sussex, 1983.

Addison, P., *The Road to 1945: British Politics and the Second World War*, Pimlico, 1994.

Aldgate, A., and J. Richards, *Britain Can Take It: British Cinema in the Second World War*, Edinburgh University Press, 1986.

Ayers, P., *Women at War*, Liver Press, 1988.

Bardon, J., *A History of Ulster*, The Blackstaff Press, 1992.

Barnett, C., *The Audit of War*, Macmillan, 1986.

Baxendale, J., '"You and I – All of Us Ordinary People": Renegotiating Britishness in Wartime', in N. Hayes and J. Hill (eds), *Millions Like Us? British Culture and the Second World War*, Liverpool University Press, 1999.

Beaven, B., and D. Thoms, 'The Blitz and Civilian Morale in Three Northern Cities, 1940–1942', *Northern History,* vol. 32, 1996, pp. 195–203.

Bowen, E., *The Heat of the Day*, Jonathan Cape, 1949.

Briggs, A., *War of Words*, vol. 3 of *The History of Broadcasting in the United Kingdom,* Oxford University Press, 1970.

Bromley, M., 'Was it the Mirror Wot Won It? The Development of the Tabloid Press During the Second World War', in N. Hayes and J. Hill (eds), *Millions Like Us?*

Brooke, S., *Labour's War: the Labour Party and the Second World War*, Oxford University Press, 1992.

Burton, A., 'Projecting the New Jerusalem: the Workers' Film Association, 1938–1946', in P. Kirkham and D. Thoms (eds), *War Culture: Social Change and Changing Experience in World War Two*, Lawrence & Wishart, 1995.

Calder, A., *The Myth of the Blitz*, Jonathan Cape, 1991.

Calder, A., *The People's War: Britain 1939–45*, Jonathan Cape, 1969.

Calvocoressi, P., and G. Wint, *Total War*, Penguin, 1972.

Cardiff, D., and P. Scannell, 'Radio in World War II', *U203 Popular Culture*, Block 2, Unit 8, Open University Press, 1981.

Chapman, J., 'British Cinema and 'the People's War'', in N. Hayes and J. Hill (eds), *Millions Like Us?*

Chapman, J., *The British at War: Cinema, State and Propaganda, 1939–1945*, I. B. Tauris, 1998.

Clarke, F., *Voices Prophesying War: Future Wars 1763–3749*, Oxford University Press, 1992.

Cook, T., 'Perception of Gas Warfare, 1915–1939', *War and Society*, vol. 18, 1, 2000.

Court, W. H. B., *Coal*, HMSO, 1951.

Crosby, T., *The Impact of Civilian Evacuation in the Second World War*, Croom Helm, 1986.

Curran, J., 'Broadcasting and the Blitz', in J. Curran and J. Seaton, *Power Without Responsibility: the Press and Broadcasting in Britain*, Routledge, 1985.

Deighton, L., and M. Hastings, *Battle of Britain*, Michael Joseph, 1990.

Douglas, R., *The World War 1939–1945: the Cartoonists' Vision*, Routledge, 1990.

Ferguson, S., and H. Fitzgerald, *Studies in the Social Services*, HMSO, 1954.

Fielding, S., 'The Good War, 1939–1945', in N. Tiratsoo (ed.), *From Blitz to Blair*, Weidenfeld and Nicholson, 1997.

Fielding, S., P. Thompson and N. Tiratsoo, *'England Arise': the Labour Party and Popular Politics in the 1940s*, Manchester University Press, 1995.

Fitzgibbon, C., *The Blitz*, Macdonald, 1957.

Fleming, P., *Invasion 1940*, Hart-Davis, 1957.

Fussell, P., *Wartime*, Oxford University Press, 1989.

Hammond, R. J., *Food, vol. 1: The Growth of Policy*, HMSO, 1951.

Hancock, W., and M. Gowing, *The British War Economy*, HMSO, 1949.

Harman, N., *Dunkirk: the Necessary Myth*, Hodder and Stoughton, 1980.

Harrison, M., 'Resource Mobilization for World War II: the USA, UK, USSR, and Germany, 1938–1945', *Economic History Review*, vol. 41, no. 2, 1988.

Harrisson, T., *Living Through the Blitz*, Collins, 1976.

Hayes, N., and J. Hill (eds), *'Millions Like Us'? British Culture and the Second World War,* Liverpool University Press, 1999.

Hayes, N., 'More Than Music While You Eat? Factory and Hostel Concerts, "Good Culture" and the Workers', in N. Hayes and J. Hill (eds), *Millions Like Us?*

Hennessy, P., *Never Again: Britain 1945–1951*, Jonathan Cape, 1992.

Hitchens, C., *Letters to a Young Contrarian*, Perseus Press, 2001.

HMSO, *Persuading the People: Government Publicity in the Second World War*, HMSO, 1995.

Inman, P., *Labour in the Munitions Industries*, HMSO, 1957.

Klein, Y., *Beyond the Home Front*, Macmillan, 1997.

Mackay, R., 'Being Beastly to the Germans: Music, Censorship and the BBC in the Second World War', *The Historical Journal of Film, Radio and Television,* vol. 20, no. 4, 2000.

Mackenzie, S. P., *British War Films 1939–1945,* Hambledon and London, 2001.

Macnicol, J., 'The evacuation of schoolchildren', in H. Smith (ed.), *War and Social Change: British Society in the Second World War*, Manchester University Press, 1986.

Macnicol, J., *The Movement for Family Allowances 1918–45*, Heinemann, 1980. Marwick, A., 'People's War and Top People's Peace? British Society and the Second World War', in A. Sked and C. Cook (eds), *Crisis and Controversy: Essays in Honour of A. J. P. Taylor*, Macmillan, 1976.

Marwick, A., *Britain in the Century of Total War*, Penguin, 1970.

Marwick, A., *The Home Front*, Thames & Hudson, 1976.

Mass Observation, *People in Production*, John Murray, 1942.

McLaine, I., *Ministry of Morale: Home Front Morale and the Ministry of Information in World War II*, Allen & Unwin, 1979.

Mosley, L., *Backs to the Wall: London Under Fire 1939–45*, Weidenfeld & Nicholson, 1971.

Nash, E. F., 'Wartime Control of Food and Agricultural Prices' in D. N. Chester (ed.), *Lessons of the War Economy* (Cambridge University Press, 1951).

Nicholas, S., *The Echo of War. Home Front Propaganda and the Wartime BBC*, Manchester University Press, 1996.

O'Brien, T. H., *Civil Defence*, HMSO, 1955.

Parker, H. M. D., *Manpower*, HMSO, 1957.

Pearton, M., *The Knowledgeable State: Diplomacy, War and Technology Since 1830*, Burnett Books, 1982.

Pelling, H., *Britain and the Second World War*, Fontana, 1970.

Pelling, H., *A History of British Trade Unionism*, Penguin, 1976.

Ponting, C., *1940: Myth and Reality*, Hamish Hamilton, 1990.

Pronay, N., 'The Land of Promise: the Projection of Peace Aims in Britain', in K. R. M. Short (ed.), *Film and Radio Propaganda in World War II*, Croom Helm, 1983.

Pronay, N., and D. Spring (eds), *Propaganda, Politics and Film 1918–45*, Macmillan, 1982.

Ramsden, J., *The Age of Churchill and Eden 1940–1957*, vol. 5 of *A History of the Conservative Party*, Longman, 1995.

Ray, J., *The Night Blitz 1940–41*, Arms and Armour, 1996.

Reynolds, D., *Rich Relations: the American Occupation of Britain, 1942–1945*, HarperCollins, 1995.

Richards, D., *The Hardest Victory: RAF Bomber Command in the Second World War*, Hodder & Stoughton, 1994.

Richards, J., *Films and British National Identity*, Manchester University Press, 1997.

Richards, J., *The Age of the Dream Palace*, Routledge, 1984.

Richards, J., and D. Sheridan (eds), *Mass-Observation at the Movies*, Routledge & Kegan Paul, 1987.

Smith, H., *Britain in the Second World War: a Social History*, Manchester University Press, 1996.

Smith, M., *Britain and 1940: History, Myth and Poplar Memory*, Routledge, 2000.

Smithies, E., *Crime in Wartime: a Social History of Crime in World War Two*, Allen & Unwin, 1982.

Summerfield, P., *Reconstructing Women's Wartime Lives*, Manchester University Press, 1998.

Summerfield, P., *Women Workers of the Second World War*, Croom Helm, 1984.

Taylor, A. J. P., *English History 1914–1945*, Oxford University Press, 1965.

Taylor, A. J. P., *A Personal History*, Hamish Hamilton, 1983.

Thames Television, *World at War*, 1970.

Thomson, D., *England in the Twentieth Century*, Penguin, 1965.

Thorpe, A., 'Britain', in J. Noakes (ed.), *The Civilian in War: the Home Front in Europe, Japan, and the USA in World War II*, Exeter University Press, 1992.

Titmuss, R., *Essays on the Welfare State*, 2nd edn, Unwin, 1963.

Titmuss, R., *Problems of Social Policy*, HMSO, 1950.

Townsend, C. and E., *War Wives: a Second World War Anthology*, Grafton Books, 1989.

Watt, D. C., *Too Serious a Business*, Temple Smith, 1975.

Wheeler, H., *Huddersfield at War*, Sutton, 1992.

Wybrow, R., *Britain Speaks Out:1935–1987*, Macmillan, 1989.

Ziegler, P., *London at War 1939–1945*, Alfred A. Knopf, 1995.

Zukermann, S., *From Apes to Warlords*, Hamish Hamilton, 1978.

Zweiniger-Bargielowska, I., *Austerity in Britain: Rationing, Controls and Consumption, 1939–1955*, Oxford University Press, 2000.

INDEX